# TREATING THE ABUSIVE PARTNER

# Treating the Abusive Partner
## *An Individualized Cognitive-Behavioral Approach*

CHRISTOPHER M. MURPHY
CHRISTOPHER I. ECKHARDT

THE GUILFORD PRESS
New York    London

©2005 The Guilford Press
A Division of Guilford Publications, Inc.
72 Spring Street, New York, NY 10012
www.guilford.com

Printed in the United States of America

This book is printed on acid-free paper.

Last digit is print number: 9 8 7 6 5 4 3 2 1

Murphy, Christopher M. (Christopher Mark)
    Treating the abusive partner: an individualized cognitive-behavioral approach /
Christopher M. Murphy, Christopher I. Eckhardt.
        p. cm.
    Includes bibliographical references and index.
    ISBN 1-59385-207-X (cloth: alk. paper)
    1. Abusive men—Rehabilitation.   2. Abusive men—Counseling of.   3. Wife
abuse—Treatment.   4. Cognitive therapy.   I. Eckhardt, Christopher I.   II. Title.
    RC569.5.F3M87 2005
    362.82′92—dc22

                                                                2005009026

# About the Authors

**Christopher M. Murphy, PhD,** is Associate Professor of Psychology and director of the doctoral program in clinical psychology at the University of Maryland, Baltimore County. Dr. Murphy also directs the New Behaviors Program at the Domestic Violence Center of Howard County, Maryland, a comprehensive clinical training, service, and research program focused on perpetrators of intimate partner violence. His research focuses on cognitive-behavioral and motivational treatments for abusive behavior in intimate adult relationships, emotional abuse in relationships, and the links between intimate partner violence and use of alcohol and drugs. This work has been supported by the National Institute of Mental Health and the National Institute on Alcohol Abuse and Alcoholism. Dr. Murphy has authored more than 40 scientific articles and book chapters on the topic of intimate partner violence.

**Christopher I. Eckhardt, PhD,** is Associate Professor of Psychological Sciences at Purdue University in West Lafayette, Indiana. His research focuses on the cognitive, emotional, and behavioral characteristics of partner-abusive individuals, with a particular emphasis on anger and hostility in this population. This work has been supported by the National Institute of Mental Health, the National Institute on Alcohol Abuse and Alcoholism, the National Institute of Justice, and the Harry Frank Guggenheim Foundation. Dr. Eckhardt has authored more than 30 scientific articles and book chapters on the topic of intimate partner violence.

# Preface

Intimate partner abuse is one of the most vexing social and public health problems in contemporary society. The obvious social costs include criminal justice and legal interventions in abusive situations, shelter and advocacy services for victims, and medical care for injured parties. Even more important are the often hidden effects on emotional, relationship, and family functioning. For example, partner abuse victimization is a significant factor in traumatic stress reactions, depression, and substance abuse. In addition, many child witnesses develop anxiety and stress reactions, conduct problems, academic difficulties, and a repetitive cycle of coercive behavior in their own relationships. Partner abuse is a common contributing factor to family instability, including relationship separation, divorce, family displacement, and homelessness.

One logical approach to social intervention in partner abuse is to provide counseling services for perpetrators. Over the last quarter century, over a thousand such programs have been developed in the United States. A wide variety of program models and practices have emerged, ranging from didactic presentations about gender and power to group psychodynamic therapy. Yet, to date, no specific program model or intervention practice for partner-abusive individuals has strong research support for its efficacy. Indeed, given the limited empirical support for abuser intervention, some scholars have questioned whether such programs should be offered at all.

Our goal in this book is to propose and describe a new intervention approach for partner-abusive clients, an approach informed by current research on the causes and correlates of abusive behavior. Our approach begins with the observation that partner-abusive individuals vary widely in their presenting problems, readiness to change, and motivations for engaging in abuse. Rather than providing a standard, one-size-fits-all group intervention, as is the typical practice in the field, we have spelled out a multiphase, individual treatment for abusive individuals.

The treatment described here has a number of important innovations relative to the standard practice in the field. First, an individualized case formulation guides the selection and delivery of interventions. The clinician is encouraged to carefully evaluate the nature and forms of abusive behavior, the conditions under which it occurs, its consequences, underlying beliefs and thinking styles that promote abusive behavior, and other associated life complications and problems. Second, our approach is infused with techniques designed to motivate change in resistant clients, promote a collaborative working alliance, and apply directive interventions in a fashion designed to support a self-directed change process. Third, we provide a detailed presentation of cognitive and behavioral treatment strategies designed to undermine abuse-maintaining beliefs and hostile thinking patterns and to promote relationship skills that can supplant the need for coercive control. Finally, long-term change is addressed through a focus on trauma recovery and relapse prevention. As far as we can gather, this is the first comprehensive, individualized manual for the treatment of partner-abusive clients.

It is important to acknowledge right from the outset that scientific research and clinical practice, as yet, have not provided sufficient answers to the key questions of why partner abuse occurs and what are the most effective means to change abusive behavior. In this book, we are equally interested in providing an impetus for future research on individualized intervention services for abusive clients as well as creating a guidebook for practitioners that is useful, comprehensive, up to date, and informed by available research and clinical experience.

A book such as this, and the clinical and research efforts it represents, could not have been completed without the help of many important colleagues and supporters. We would like to acknowledge support from the National Institute of Mental Health in the form of a psychosocial treatment development grant (MH064562) to facilitate the specification and preliminary investigation of the treatment outlined here, and to the National Institute on Alcohol Abuse and Alcoholism, the National Institute of Justice, the Centers for Disease Control and Prevention, and the Maryland Governor's Office of Crime Control and Prevention, which have provided research support to one or both of us in our efforts to understand partner abuse and develop effective treatments for abusive clients. We would also like to acknowledge the consistent involvement of the agency staff at the Domestic Violence Center of Howard County, Maryland, including Judith Clancy, Jodi Finkelstein, Linda Meade, and Tori Shequine, who have provided Dr. Murphy with a remarkable context in which to conduct clinical research and training for over a decade. Finally, this work would not have been possible without the extensive involvement of current and former graduate students who have served as research collaborators and treatment providers, including Laura Lynch, Judy DeDeyn, Christina Watlington, Danielle Black, Fabio Van der Merwe, Casey Taft, Peter Musser, Tara Neavins, Jeff Elliott, Nancy Remington, Tanya Morrel, Jamie Winters, Theresa Schmitz, Marie Cugini, Stella Mantakos, Ashley Sibley, Bradley Norlander, and Angie Utschig. Special thanks are due to research therapists who have helped to refine and test out the clinical procedures outlined here, including Drs. Cindy Eaves, Andy Goode, Manu Singh, and Sharon Stephen. Finally, we would like to thank our mentors, K. Daniel O'Leary (C. M. M.) and Howard Kassinove (C. I. E.), who helped to instill in us the motivation and confidence to tackle this project.

# Contents

# TREATING THE ABUSIVE PARTNER

# / 1 /

# *Introduction*

Since they were first developed in the late 1970s, counseling programs for partner-abusive individuals have proliferated rapidly. Well over 1,000 such programs are currently in operation in the United States (Adams & Cayouette, 2002). Most programs serve predominantly court-mandated populations, and many work exclusively with men who have assaulted women. Although a range of program philosophies and practices exists, the overwhelming trend is to counsel abusive men in groups that focus primarily on gender socialization and its effects on power and control in relationships (Adams & Cayouette, 2002; Gondolf, 1985; Pence & Paymar, 1993; Stordeur & Stille, 1989). Many such programs also employ techniques from cognitive and behavioral therapies to address anger, self-control, and alternatives to aggression (e.g., Saunders, 1996; Sonkin & Durphy, 1997; Wexler, 2000).

Psychosocial counseling[1] for abusive individuals holds great promise as a response to the pernicious and pervasive public health problem of intimate partner violence. Counseling is a lower-cost alternative to incarceration and can be used in some cases to defer prosecution and related court costs. Many abused spouses want the abuse to end but are not interested in seeking punishment for the abuser. In fact, abused women often refuse to press charges or testify against their abusive partners for a variety of reasons. Many are financially dependent on the abusive spouse and may face social and economic disruption if he is incarcerated. Even after a woman manages to extricate herself from an abusive relationship and establish safety, the abuser remains at high risk of harming subsequent relationship partners. Therefore, counseling may serve to prevent abuse in future rela-

1

tionships. Finally, counseling reflects the humane recognition that many abusive individuals are themselves deeply troubled by emotional instability, substance abuse, or the deleterious long-term effects of childhood trauma. Although debates remain as to whether such factors play a causal role in spousal violence, an underlying assumption of most clinical approaches is that these difficulties are potentially important contributing factors worthy of therapeutic attention.

Yet, despite their potential promise, it is important to ask whether counseling interventions for abusive individuals in fact promote victim safety by effectively altering abusive behavior. Several early studies showed that group counseling focused on anger regulation and communication skills training produced significant reductions in abusive behavior relative to no-counseling control groups (Dutton, 1986a; Palmer, Braun, & Barrera, 1992; Waldo, 1988). More recent, large-scale studies, in contrast, have indicated that group counseling may not contribute significantly to the reduction of partner violence beyond the effects of prosecution and probation monitoring (Dunford, 2000; Feder & Ford, 1999).

A recent review of more than two dozen outcome studies revealed very small average effects of group counseling for partner-violent individuals. Focusing on the simple dichotomous outcome of any physical abuse recidivism (vs. no physical abuse recidivism), the outcome difference between treated and untreated groups in randomized experiments averaged about 0.1 standard deviation units, using either official police reports or victim partner reports to measure abusive behavior outcomes. This difference translates into an average reduction in violence recidivism rate of about 5% for those who receive counseling (Babcock, Green, & Robie, 2004). For example, if 40% of control group (untreated) individuals engage in recidivist violence, then 35% of individuals receiving standard counseling services for partner violence would be expected to engage in recidivist violence. Not only is this magnitude of influence far less than desirable, it is also far smaller than the effects found in other areas of research on psychotherapy and behavior change (Bowers & Clum, 1988; Lambert & Bergin, 1994). In addition, to date, no specific type of intervention for partner violence has been found to be consistently more effective than any other intervention (Babcock & LaTaillade, 2000). These results (reviewed at length in Chapter 4) indicate that there is substantial room for improvement in the design, implementation, and evaluation of counseling programs for partner-abusive individuals.

During the 1990s two prominent task forces examining domestic violence both concluded that a wider range of intervention approaches was needed to address this complex problem. In 1996, the American Psychological Association Presidential Task Force on Violence and the Family asserted that "although many advocates believe that short-term psychoeducational programs are important to help stop physical violence immediately, recent studies suggest another promising approach: assigning different batterers to different types of ·short- and long-term programs, depending on their specific needs" (p. 87). Similarly, in 1998, the National Research Council and Institute of Medicine of the National Academy of Sciences recommended that treatment programs should "identify and develop program components that can address the needs of different types of batterers" (Chalk & King, 1998). Despite these recommendations, the widely available services for individuals who abuse intimate partners tend to be "one-size-fits-all" group programs (Healey, Smith, & O'Sullivan, 1998).

## THE PURPOSE OF THIS BOOK

This book was written in response to concerns about the efficacy of standard group counseling for abusive clients. It reflects our clinical experience and the growing research literature on partner-violent individuals, both of which suggest that abusive clients are a heterogeneous population with varied treatment needs. As far as we can gather, there are as yet no well-specified and standardized individual therapy interventions for abusive clients in the literature and precious little empirical research to date on such interventions. We decided to develop such an approach in order to promote further research and clinical developments. The resulting treatment contains a number of innovations, as detailed below.

### Individualized Treatment

There are many treatment manuals for working with partner-abusive clients, virtually all of which rely on the group format (e.g., Pence & Paymar, 1993; Stordeur & Stille, 1989; Stosny, 1995; Wexler, 2000). Groups have a number of advantages over individual treatment, most notably greater cost efficiency and the potential for constructive peer influence. However, groups also have several disadvantages. The first concern arises from group treatment research on delinquent adolescents (Dishion, McCord, & Poulin, 1999). For such individuals, group influence processes can produce negative treatment outcomes, such as increases in delinquent behavior relative to no-treatment controls. Apparently, peer reinforcement for deviant beliefs and behaviors can outstrip the prosocial messages provided by the treatment program (Dishion, Spracklen, Andrews, & Patterson, 1996). A recent qualitative analysis of poor outcome cases from Murphy's group cognitive-behavioral therapy (CBT) program for partner-violent men identified clustering of repeat recidivists within specific treatment groups characterized by problematic peer influence processes and resistance to therapist influence (Lynch, DeDeyn, & Murphy, 2003). For certain combinations of clients, the group format may reinforce negative thinking and abusive tendencies. Clinical observations suggest that this process may be accelerated by therapist behaviors or program philosophies that promote an "us versus them" mentality in the group.

A second concern with the exclusive reliance on the group format in the literature on partner-violence intervention involves the lack of flexibility in implementing these programs. For example, some abusive clients present with concerns, such as a history of sexual abuse in childhood, that they are simply unwilling to acknowledge or discuss in the group context. Others are difficult or disruptive in the group setting or unresponsive to group intervention. In addition, an individualized approach may be the only way to provide partner-violence interventions in small towns or rural communities where the number of cases is not sufficient to develop groups.

The third, and most important, concern with the group format involves an inherent limitation in the capacity to tailor interventions to the specific needs of each client. Within the traditions of cognitive and behavioral therapies, group treatments tend to be successfully employed under one of two general conditions, neither of which directly applies to the treatment of partner-abusive clients. First, well-specified and focused intervention methods that have been carefully developed and empirically validated in the individual treatment format can be adapted to the group format and used productively with a homogeneous client population afflicted by the same condition. For example, panic control methods have been successfully translated to the group format with little, if any, loss of efficacy because the active ingredients of treatment were well-understood and targeted toward a homogeneous population with few complicating factors (e.g., serious addictive disorders) to inhibit treatment (Craske & Barlow, 2001). The second effective use of the group format is as a therapeutic context for social difficulties. The best example here is the treatment of social anxiety disorder through group role-play interventions (Turk, Heimberg, & Hope, 2001). In this case, the group itself provides a context for exposure therapy. Although other examples of effective group treatments exist, we believe that the decision to use a group format should be very carefully and thoroughly informed by the nature of the treatment population and the type of intervention methods needed to alter the problem behavior.

Partner-abuse treatments stand in stark contrast to most successful adaptations of structured behavioral interventions to the group treatment format. Group treatments for abusive clients do not have the benefit of extensive prior efforts to develop and test interventions in the individual treatment format. Treatment development has been hampered by the simultaneous need to address social and political concerns regarding gender and power, complex group processes, and technical implementation of intervention methods. The result is often a loose adaptation of intervention techniques, such as relaxation training or cognitive restructuring, provided within a conceptual framework that is disconnected from the original formulation of the intervention technique and without sufficient technical knowledge of how, when, and whether such interventions will bring about therapeutic benefit for abusive clients.

In addition, partner-abusive clients are a very heterogeneous population in terms of motivations for engaging in abuse, co-occurring problems such as substance abuse and personality disorders, and motivation to change. Thus, it is very difficult to specify generic intervention strategies that will be effective in all or most cases. For example, one client may physically assault his partner exclusively to escape from conflict discussions, another in response to imagined infidelity, and a third in an attempt to force his partner to comply with his sexual demands. Although all may share certain beliefs that promote their use of interpersonal violence, a functional analysis of their abuse leads to quite different targets for shaping alternative thoughts and behaviors. Similarly, some abusive clients arrive at the clinic ready and willing to engage in active change, whereas others are angry, suspicious, and mistrustful toward the therapist and highly resistant to therapeutic influence. Distinct intervention strategies are needed for clients who are at vastly different points on the continuum of change.

Despite concerns about the lack of flexibility in exclusive reliance on the group format, potential negative peer influences, and the remarkable heterogeneity of abusive individuals, a number of states have adopted standards for the court-ordered counseling of abusive clients that either require it to be conducted in the group format, caution against the use of individual counseling for abusive clients, or state that individual counseling is "inappropriate" except in "special circumstances" (Austin & Dankwort, 1999). The "special circumstances" are not typically articulated.[2] As far as we can gather, there are no empirical data to support these standards, that is, no studies demonstrating that group intervention is more efficacious or safer than individual services for partner-abusive clients. Conversely, a recent controlled study found that an individual client intake approach based on the principles of motivational interviewing was more effective in stimulating abusive clients' subsequent involvement in treatment as compared to an intake approach that relied in part on the group format (Musser, Semiatin, Taft, & Murphy, 2005).

## Case Formulation Approach

In response to the heterogeneity of partner-abusive clients and their diverse intervention needs, the treatment described in this book relies on individualized case formulation. We provide detailed suggestions and advice regarding functional assessment of abusive behavior and how to develop a case formulation to guide intervention with each abusive client. This is a challenging clinical task, particularly in light of the difficulties in establishing a treatment alliance with angry and resistant clients (DiGiuseppe, Tafrate, & Eckhardt, 1994). Nevertheless, our clinical experience suggests that there is no substitute for a solid case formulation in directing treatment with this complex and heterogeneous population.

## Emphasis on the Collaborative Working Alliance

Clinicians working with partner-violent individuals are often reluctant to do the very things that are most likely to promote successful change in abusive behavior, namely to provide a high level of reflective listening, warmth, and empathy in order to facilitate the development of a collaborative working alliance. Clinicians often express the fear that collaboration equals collusion, that is, that by showing concern and understanding, the clinician will inadvertently support abusive behaviors and beliefs. In fact, nothing could be farther from the truth. The more the clinician truly understands how a client thinks and feels and the more accurately such understanding is communicated, the more likely the clinician is to formulate the proper targets of change and the more likely the client is to accept therapeutic influence. In line with these clinical observations, recent studies have found that a strong working alliance between client and therapist in the group context predicts lower posttreatment abuse (Brown & O'Leary, 2000; Taft, Murphy, King, Musser, & DeDeyn, 2003). In addition, when motivational interviewing, which involves a high level of empathic reflection, is conducted in an individual format during the intake process, it enhances therapist ratings of the working alliance and compliance with directive therapy strategies during subsequent group treatment for abusive clients (Musser et al., 2005). In line with these findings, this manual provides suggestions for establishing a collaborative alliance and conducting treatment in a collaborative fashion.

## Specification of Treatment Phases

Treatment of abusive clients progresses through some logically ordered phases, beginning with the outward manifestations of hostility and treatment resistance and moving toward underlying self-organizing principles that promote abusive and controlling styles of relating. Abusive clients vary widely in how rapidly they progress through these phases and in their need for attention to different treatment phases. Although the phases of treatment are not rigidly distinct, and movement back and forth between phases is expected in the change process, there is heuristic value in conceptualizing the major tasks of treatment along the lines of a four-phase model.

The first phase of treatment focuses on enhancing motivational readiness to change. The goals are to reduce client resistance to treatment, help the client resolve ambivalence about change, and establish collaborative goals and plans for the change process. The second phase of treatment focuses on enhancing safety and stabilization through understanding how and when abusive behaviors occur and implementing strategies to prevent the escalation of conflicts to abuse. In addition, this phase of treatment often focuses on helping clients stabilize chaotic or disrupted lifestyles. Examples include establishing sobriety, reducing risky substance use, solidifying the decision whether to separate from the relationship partner, promoting safe child visitation arrangements, addressing employment instability, and obtaining treatment for significant medical or psychiatric problems. The third phase of treatment focuses on enhancing relationship functioning through cognitive change and behavioral skills training. The main goal is to develop relationship beliefs and behaviors that provide an alternative to coercion and control, facilitating new strategies to resolve relationship problems and promote healthy interactions. The fourth phase of treatment focuses on relapse prevention and trauma recovery. The goal is to address concerns and difficulties that may inhibit long-term personal and family well being and that may facilitate a return to abusive behavior. For some clients, this phase is used to finalize a self-directed change effort and to promote active coping at the earliest stages of warning signs of return to abusive behavior. For many, this last phase of treatment also involves cognitive reprocessing of childhood trauma experiences that contribute to disrupted attachment relationships and underlying difficulties in establishing a secure bond with an intimate partner. Further information on the four phases of treatment is presented in Table 1.1.

## Empirically Based Approach

There are four key ways in which the current treatment is informed by empirical research. First, we used the research literature on cognitive, behavioral, and emotional features of partner-abusive individuals to articulate targets for clinical assessment and intervention, most notably studies that compare abusive men to men in distressed, but nonviolent, relationships. Chapter 3 reviews the clinically relevant characteristics of abusive clients based on this research literature. Second, we used the research literature on psychotherapy and behavior change to develop general guidelines for this intervention. Across a wide array of clinical problem areas and theoretical approaches, research consistently points to the importance of empathic listening, the collaborative working alliance, and strategies to facilitate self-directed change as crucial elements of successful intervention. Third, we used the research literature on cognitive and behavioral thera-

TABLE 1.1. The Four Phases of Cognitive-Behavioral Therapy
for Partner-Abusive Individuals

Phase 1: Stimulating and consolidating motivation to change

*Goals*: Decrease resistance; increase change talk (self-motivational statements);
establish a working alliance; develop goals for personal change

*Major techniques*: Motivational Interviewing, including reflective listening; affirming
autonomy; change planning

Phase 2: Promoting safety and stabilization

*Goals*: Eliminate the use of physically assaultive, sexually assaultive, and threatening
behaviors; stabilize life circumstances; identify and address major barriers to effective
treatment

*Major techniques*: Functional analysis of abusive behaviors; shaping of alternative
behaviors; cognitive restructuring of abuse-promoting beliefs; directed problem
solving; adjunctive treatment for substance abuse and severe mental disorders

Phase 3: Enhancing relationship functioning

*Goals*: Reduce distress-maintaining relationship cognitions; build relationship
communication and problem-solving skills; enhance positive attributions about the
partner and positive shared experiences; support responsible and effective parenting

*Major techniques*: Cognitive restructuring of problematic relationship assumptions
and hostile attributions; education about healthy relationships; relationship skills
training (active listening, nonabusive self-expression; problem solving); parenting skills
training

Phase 4: Promoting trauma recovery and preventing relapse

*Goals*: Reduce toxic effects of trauma history on relationship functioning; Consolidate
a self-directed change process; increase awareness of relapse process; prevent return to
abusive behavior

*Major techniques*: Cognitive processing of traumatic experiences; identification of
relapse pattern and relapse cues; promotion of active coping with relationship
concerns; booster sessions

pies, most notably for relationship distress, personality disorders, mood
and anxiety disorders, and trauma recovery, in order to inform the specific
cognitive-behavioral interventions proposed here. Adaptations of CBT
have been quite effective across a wide array of behavioral and emotional
problem areas. However, counter to the popular misconception that CBT
interventions must provide a rigid predetermined structure for each treatment session, modern CBT has evolved and expanded to treat complex
problems with the use of flexible treatment principles and individual case
formulation (e.g., Linehan, 1993a; Persons, 1989; Persons & Tompkins,
1997).

Fourth, we used the research on interventions for partner-violent men in order to support the need for an individual approach and, where possible, to identify specific treatment components that are likely to be effective with this population. Most notably, recent investigations have found that motivational interviewing (MI) can enhance involvement in active change elements of cognitive and behavioral treatment that are related in turn to successful violence cessation outcomes (Kistenmacher & Weiss, in press; Musser et al., 2005; Taft et al., 2003). MI was designed to reduce client resistance to change and to help clients resolve ambivalence about change, crucial tasks at the outset of treatment for most abusive clients.

In addition, group delivery of generic forms of CBT has been found to be no more successful in ending violence than unstructured supportive group treatment (Morrel, Elliott, Murphy, & Taft, 2003), process–psychodynamic group treatment (Saunders, 1996), or rigorous case monitoring (Dunford, 2000). Although several plausible explanations for these null findings exist, we believe that they indicate a need for more intensive delivery of cognitive-behavioral interventions that are tailored to specific individual problems and needs (e.g., Fruzzetti & Levensky, 2000).

Given the stark limitations of current knowledge about effective treatment for abusive clients, this book was written more to stimulate new research than to report on previous research. It is designed as a treatment manual to support clinical trials of individual CBT for abusive clients and as a guidebook for clinicians conducting individual work with this population. In the absence of a reasonable treatment manual, state-of-the-art intervention studies are not possible. A controlled investigation is currently underway using this book as a treatment manual to compare individualized CBT to standard group treatment as usual. Future studies may look at the combination of individual and group approaches, examine different components of CBT, or explore whether different approaches are more or less effective with distinct subgroups of abusive clients. In addition, referrals of women abusers are rapidly growing, and adaptations of treatment to gay and lesbian populations and diverse cultural groups are sorely needed. Thus, we see the current manual as a modest first step toward specifying treatments that can be studied in rigorous experiments and further developed and refined to maximize efficacy in ending partner abuse. As with any scientifically informed endeavor, it is inevitable that the recommendations and procedures outlined here will evolve to integrate new findings.

## Practical Advice

Following the scientist-practitioner traditions in clinical psychology, the treatment recommendations in this book are not only informed by empirical research, but are also the result of extensive clinical experience in treating partner-abusive clients and in training and supervising therapists who work with this population. For the past decade, Murphy has served as the director of an abuser intervention program that serves about 100 clients each year. The program is housed within a comprehensive, community-based domestic violence agency and focuses on the combined missions of clinical service, training, and research. Many of the recommendations presented here derive from trial-and-error, and a great deal of credit is due to the dozens of clinical staff and doctoral students who have worked with the program over the years, as well as discussions with colleagues from other abuser intervention programs and fellow researchers.

## Clinical Examples

In the spirit of promoting practical and procedural knowledge, we have provided clinical and case examples for many of the intervention techniques presented. Many of these examples were derived from audio recordings of treatment sessions conducted in research protocols, with editing to protect client anonymity and enhance the reading flow of spoken language transcripts. Some examples are hypothetical or an amalgam of statements drawn from different sessions. Throughout, we use clinical material to reinforce conceptual recommendations, realizing that there are no magical words or phrases and that the spirit in which an intervention is delivered and the intended goals of the intervention are more important than the precise verbalizations used by the therapist.

## SUGGESTIONS ON HOW TO READ THIS BOOK

In this fast-paced, information rich world authors can no longer maintain the conceit that readers will plow through a book like this from beginning to end. Therefore, we decided to provide some "quick read" suggestions for different categories of readers, hoping to stimulate further consideration of the core ideas and interventions presented. If you are among the large number of readers already convinced that individual treatment for abusive clients can't and won't work and believe that the authors are irresponsible for suggesting such folly, and you are looking for a few juicy tidbits to support your critique, we suggest that you focus on the material on individual case formulation, the collaborative working alliance, and the use of reflective listening and motivational interviewing techniques promoted in Chapters 6 and 7. These methods are most out of line with current trends in the field.

If you are a clinician who has worked in this field for a while and you are disillusioned with the standard group approaches, we also suggest that you begin by focusing on the material on individual case formulation, the collaborative working alliance, and the use of reflective listening and motivational interviewing techniques in Chapters 6 and 7. If these ideas strike your fancy, then we recommend that you read the chapters on assessment (Chapter 5) and specific cognitive and behavioral intervention strategies (Chapters 8–11).

If you are new to the field of partner-abuse intervention, but practice in other areas of mental health treatment, we suggest that you begin with Chapters 2–4, which describe the clinical phenomenon of abuse, traditions in the field, and characteristics of this treatment population. If we haven't lost you at that point, then the material on clinical assessment and case formulation should provide a good foundation for the subsequent chapters on intervention strategies.

If you are a researcher or practitioner searching for specific clinical topics or materials, if you are simply interested in getting the big picture quickly, or if you want to refer to key guidelines to facilitate treatment adherence, here is a rapid reading guide. The four phases of treatment are outlined in Table 1.1. Suggestions for functional and descriptive assessment of abusive behavior appear in Figure 5.1 (p. 78–85), and a general overview of the major areas for comprehensive clinical assessment of abusive clients appears in Table 5.2 (p. 107–108). The rationale for integrating motivational interviewing techniques with CBT is provided beginning on page 135 (in Chapter 7), and suggestions for implementing cognitive-behavioral interventions in the spirit of MI appear at the end of Chapter 7, beginning on page 161. Recommendations for how to conduct relationship skills training with this population begin on page 177. Common themes and variations in abusive thinking are provided in Table 9.1 (pp. 196–198), and a list of common cognitive distortions with examples is provided in Table 9.2 (pp. 205–206). Relapse prevention strategies are outlined on page 250–253. Trauma reprocessing techniques are discussed on pages 234–244. Although these materials outline the main ingredients of the treatment, as with most recipes the secret lies in the artful combination of ingredients and the nature and timing of the chef's ministrations.

### NOTES

1. Throughout the book, we use the terms "counseling," "therapy," and "treatment" interchangeably to describe psychosocial intervention for partner-violent clients. There have been controversies in the field over whether these programs are educational or psychotherapeutic in nature. In part, these controversies have been theoretical, concerned with whether a "therapeutic" approach excuses responsibility for violent behavior through analogy to mental health disorders or medical disease. And in part, these controversies have been practical, concerned

with whether only mental health professionals can administer these interventions, as terms such as counseling and psychotherapy are legally protected areas of professional practice in many states. From our perspective, all of the programs described to date have a psychotherapeutic quality to them, even when the program authors characterize the interventions as purely educational in nature. All are concerned with stimulating behavior and attitude change, most use behavioral and/or cognitive therapy methods to do so, and most operate under the expectation that participants will reveal deeply personal information about their lives, family histories, relationships, and/or personal beliefs. In addition, given that a sizeable number of partner-violent clients have other mental health concerns or substance use problems, we assert that mental health training is an important qualification for conducting these interventions and that they should be delivered within the spirit and guidelines of mental health practice.

2. The content and focus of state standards for abuser intervention are summarized in a National Institute of Justice publication (Healey et al., 1998) and reviewed in articles by Austin and Dankwort (1999) and Maiuro, Hagar, Lin, and Olson (2002). Interested individuals should consult their own state regulations to determine if there are any professional practice limitations on the format of treatment for partner-abusive individuals. More detailed information is generally available through state coalitions against domestic violence.

# / 2 /

# The Forms and Patterns
# of Abusive Behavior

Intimate partner violence is almost always part of a more comprehensive problem with coercive control and emotionally abusive behavior. Common forms of abuse include both moderate (e.g., pushing or grabbing) and severe (e.g., beating up or choking) forms of physical violence, threats and intimidating gestures, destruction of property, denigration and humiliation, hostile withdrawal, and efforts to monitor and limit the partner's activities and social contacts. Sexual coercion and forced sex are also common in abusive relationships. Legal definitions related to domestic abuse involve placing someone in fear of bodily harm (assault), unwanted physical contact (battery), and a variety of other partner-related offenses such as phone harassment, stalking, destruction of property, or trespassing. In addition to criminal case referrals, individuals may be sent to counseling from civil court proceedings involving orders of protection or may seek treatment when their partner threatens separation or leaves the relationship.

## LEGAL CONCEPTS OF PARTNER ABUSE

It is very important for clinicians working with partner-violent offenders to develop familiarity with the relevant legal terminology and legal concepts related to abuse. Some legal terms and concepts vary from state to state, and the legal practices with respect to partner violence prosecution vary considerably across local jurisdictions. A variety of criminal offenses may result in case referral to partner abuse programs. Many of those referred

13

from criminal court proceedings have received charges of battery and/or assault. In general terms, "battery" refers to unwanted physical contact, and "assault" refers to actions that put another person in fear of bodily harm. Interestingly, a review of charging documents often reveals alternative or additional charges beyond assault and battery. For example, an individual who calls a former girlfriend against her wishes on a number of occasions, goes to her house, enters when asked not to, and breaks some of her possessions may receive charges such as telephone harassment, breaking and entering, criminal trespass, and malicious destruction of property. Most states have new crime categories, such as stalking or strangulation, which may be charged in some cases of partner abuse.

## PHYSICAL ABUSE

The concepts used in partner abuse intervention tend to focus on the behaviors and relevant intentions rather than the legal concepts. To date, the predominant social and public health attention in the area of partner violence has focused on physical abuse. Physical abuse can be defined as coercive attacks directed against another person's body. The term "intimate partner violence" has become widely used in recent years. The term "intimate" is used to separate this type of abuse from other relationship categories, such as parent–child abuse, elderly abuse by caregivers, sexual harassment in the workplace, etc. The term "partner" reflects two well-established facts. The first point is that partner violence is common not only within legally recognized heterosexual marriages, but also in dating, cohabiting, and gay and lesbian relationships. The second point is that many couples experiencing abuse or violence do not live together in a domestic arrangement. Finally, the term "violence" is generally reserved for physical assault directed at the other person's bodily integrity and, in some contexts, is used to refer more specifically to aggression that is likely to produce physical injury. In the current book, we prefer the term "abuse" to "violence." Whereas violence usually implies physical attack, "abuse" is a more general concept that can reflect physical, emotional–psychological, and sexual dimensions. By using the term "abuse," we seek to indicate that the problem of intimate partner abuse includes a set of controlling and coercive behaviors that is broader than mere physical acts of violence. The treatment conceptualization of the functions and cues for abuse generally requires this broader perspective, notably with regard to the patterns of emotional abuse and controlling behaviors. A focus on these more subtle forms of abuse helps the clinician to form a coherent understanding of the behavioral, cognitive, emotional, motivational, and characterological dimensions of the individual's problems.

Beginning with the pioneering work of Murray Straus and colleagues in the 1970s, social scientists have distinguished severe forms of physical partner aggression from more moderate forms (Straus, 1979; Straus, Hamby, Boney-McCoy, Sugarman, 1996). Examples of severe aggression include weapon use, beating up, choking, hitting with hard objects, and punching. Examples of moderate aggression include grabbing, pushing, shoving, and slapping. Research findings are mixed as to whether severe and moderate violence are best conceptualized as part of the same underlying continuum or whether they are distinct forms of partner aggression (Barling, O'Leary, Jouriles, Vivian, & MacEwen, 1987; Pan, Neidig, & O'Leary, 1994a). Almost no one reports engaging in or experiencing severe forms of physical aggression without also reporting moderate forms of aggression (Straus, 1979). Whereas severe aggression carries a substantial probability of physical injury under any circumstance, moderate aggression is less likely to produce physical trauma. It is important to note, however, that serious injuries can be sustained as a result of all forms of physical partner aggression. For instance, a push, shove, or slap may send its recipient down a flight of stairs or into a door edge, bathtub, or piece of furniture, causing serious or even fatal injuries.

## EMOTIONAL-PSYCHOLOGICAL ABUSE

Although the distinctions may be subtle or irrelevant in many real-life contexts, physical aggression toward objects and threats of violence are often placed in a separate category from aggressive behaviors directed at the partner's body. These former behaviors are considered examples of psychological or emotional abuse. Psychological abuse involves coercive verbal and nonverbal acts that are not directed toward the partner's body. These acts are typically intended to produce emotional harm or threat of harm (Murphy & Cascardi, 1999). Subjectively, psychological abuse has several common effects on the recipient—often producing fear, promoting a negative self-image, and increasing dependency on the abuser.

Several common types of psychological abuse have been identified in research reviews (Marshall, 1994; Murphy & Cascardi, 1999). For the current purposes, we focus on four types of psychological abuse that differ in form and are presumed to have distinct interpersonal functions (Murphy & Hoover, 1999). The first type, labeled "dominance/intimidation," involves behaviors that share similarities to physical assault and appear intended to produce fear or submission in the partner. These include threats of violence or harm (e.g., threatening to hurt or kill the partner, one's self, or others), violence toward objects (e.g., punching walls, throwing things, or breaking objects that are highly valued by the partner), and intimidating looks or gestures (e.g., hovering over the partner in an ominous fashion during a conflict or disagreement).

The second type of psychological abuse, labeled "denigration," involves belittling, critical, and humiliating acts intended to attack or damage the partner's sense of self-worth. Examples include calling the partner stupid, ugly, or worthless, humiliating or belittling the partner in front of friends or relatives, and calling the partner crazy. Like dominance/intimidation, denigration tends to be highly correlated with physical partner aggression. These attacks on self-esteem create some of the most severe and lasting emotional pain experienced by victims of domestic violence (Follingstad, Rutledge, Berg, Hause & Polek 1990).

A third type of psychological abuse, labeled "restrictive engulfment," involves efforts to track and monitor the partner's whereabouts and isolate the partner from important social contacts or self-enhancing activities. Examples include checking up or spying on the partner, searching through the partner's personal belongings, listening in on the partner's phone conversations, trying to force the partner not to see friends or family members, undermining the partner's personal relationships, and negating the partner's efforts to obtain work or education. These behaviors appear designed to increase the partner's emotional or economic dependency on the abuser, to reduce perceived threats to the relationship from sexual rivals, and to enhance the abuser's influence over the partner by reducing or eliminating other sources of social influence. Restrictive engulfment has been associated with high levels of anxious—insecure attachment concerns in the abusive partner.

A fourth type of psychological abuse, labeled "hostile withdrawal," involves aversive escape or avoidance behaviors intended to help the abuser ignore the partner's concerns and punish the partner through withdrawal of attention or affection. Such behaviors often function to increase the partner's anxiety or insecurity about the relationship. Examples include acting cold and distant when angry, refusing to discuss things that are important to the partner, spending long periods of time away from the partner in a spiteful fashion, or otherwise withdrawing attention and contact and ignoring the partner's concerns.

These four forms of abuse have been validated by demonstrating that they form distinct factors in checklist measures of abusive behaviors and by examining their correlations with a range of problematic interpersonal styles (Murphy & Hoover, 1999; Murphy, Hoover, & Taft, 1999). All four types of psychological abuse are correlated with the tendency to be domineering and over-controlling in interpersonal relationships. However, these types of abuse vary in their correlations with interpersonal affiliation problems ranging from overinvolvement and intrusiveness to disconnection, coldness, and isolation. Dominance/intimidation and denigration represent two relatively "pure" forms of interpersonal problems with dominance and control. Hostile withdrawal, in contrast, reflects a tendency toward interpersonal avoidance and emotional coldness. Restrictive engulfment reflects a tendency toward intrusiveness and hyperaffiliation, including a fear of abandonment.

Some individuals are "generalists," engaging in all the different forms of emotional abuse at roughly similar levels. Others tend to specialize in one or two forms of emotional abuse. For example, one common pattern involves high levels of hostile withdrawal and denigration. This pattern reflects a distancing motivation and a lack of interpersonal warmth. Another common pattern involves high levels of dominance/intimidation and restrictive engulfment. This pattern reflects a dependency motivation toward affiliation and enmeshment and a fear of abandonment. Both of these patterns imply underlying personal concerns or self-esteem deficits, but with divergent strategies designed to alleviate them. In the former pattern, the individual asserts dominance and superiority by denigrating the partner and presenting the self as aloof or invulnerable. In the latter pattern, the individual asserts coercive and intrusive control while appearing needy or vulnerable. These examples illustrate how a careful assessment of emotional abuse can help the clinician to develop hypotheses about the underlying motivations, inadequacies, self-schemas, and relationship skills that need to be addressed to shift the abusive relationship pattern toward healthier forms of interaction and influence.

## SEXUAL COERCION AND VIOLENCE

A final important category of partner-abusive behavior is sexual coercion and violence (Frieze, 1983; Russell, 1982; Walker, 1984). These acts span the continuum from unpleasant pressuring to forcible rape. Some behaviors in this category combine sexual coercion with emotional abuse, for example in humiliating or denigrating comments related to attractiveness or sexual performance. Sexual jealousy, or sexually proprietary behavior more generally, is often intense in abusive relationships and is a common motivating factor in violent episodes and spousal homicides (Brisson, 1983; Dobash & Dobash, 1979; Wilson & Daly, 1998).

Aggressive, controlling, and aversive sexual behaviors are very common among partner-abusive men. In one early study, Walker (1984) found that about 60% of battered women reported that they were forced to have sex by their partners. Frieze (1983) reported that about one-third of battered women had experienced forced sex consistent with the legal definition of rape. In subsequent studies, researchers have described two types of sexually aggressive behaviors. The first type, labeled "sexual coercion," involves efforts to obtain sexual compliance or gratification through behaviors such as verbal pressuring, deception, denigrating comments, or threats to end the relationship. The second type, sometimes labeled "sexual violence," involves the threat of force or use of force in an attempt to gain vaginal, oral, or anal sex. These latter behaviors unequivocally constitute sexual assault or rape from a legal standpoint, whereas the former ("coercive") acts, may constitute sexual assault in some instances but not in others.

Using two different measures of sexual coercion in a mixed community sample of partner-violent men and nonviolent controls, Marshall and Holtzworth-Munroe (2002) found that 56% of women reported at least one act of sexual coercion during the previous year, and 14% reported the use of force or threat of force in the sexual context. In a marriage clinic sample, among those wives who reported severe physical partner violence, 55% reported experiencing sexual coercion and 11% reported threatened or forced sex in the year before treatment (Meyer, Vivian, & O'Leary, 1998).

The sexual dimensions of partner abuse are not limited to verbal coercion or forcible rape. Some victims report being pressured or forced to mimic acts from pornography, engage in sadomasochistic activities, have sex with multiple partners, or engage in painful or humiliating sex acts (Walker, 1984). Some abusive clients withhold sex in a denigrating and insulting fashion. If the partner refuses sex or is thought to show disinterest, some abusive clients will verbally berate the partner or withhold money or other resources as a punishment. Some abusive individuals pressure or coerce the partner to be sexually intimate in an attempt to alleviate their (the abusive individuals') obsessive jealousy. Abusive clients quite commonly report scenarios that indicate a blurry awareness of sexual consent. Their partners may ostensibly consent to engage in sexual activities with which they feel uncomfortable, displaying signs of shame, guilt, or anger as a result. The ability to say no or resist requests can be severely impeded by the presence of relationship violence and coercive control.

The available statistics and descriptions of sexual abuse provided by battered women paint an alarming picture. It is very clear that sexual coercion and violence must be carefully assessed in working with partner-abusive clients. Whenever possible, reports should be gathered from both the abusive client and collateral partner to obtain a full picture of this problem. Although some abusive men have difficulty recognizing or acknowledging the coercive aspects of their sexual relationships, studies to date have found that reports from perpetrators and victims are surprisingly similar (Marshall & Holtzworth-Munroe, 2002; Meyer et al., 1998). As discussed in detail in the chapter on clinical assessment, the therapist must be very careful to insure the collateral partner's confidentiality in securing reports of abuse experiences.

# / 3 /

# The Clinically Relevant Characteristics of Partner Abuse Perpetrators

Important research and scholarship on domestic violence has derived from a variety of disciplines. Historians, anthropologists, criminologists, sociologists, psychologists, social workers, legal scholars, nurses, psychiatrists, and other physicians have all contributed to our scientific and clinical understanding of this complex social, physical health, and mental health problem. Within a single intimate partner violence (IPV) case, it is common to find a number of people working together to end the abuse, including friends and relatives, victim advocates, counselors, attorneys, physicians, and representatives of the faith community. Appreciation of this wide array of perspectives can facilitate the clinician's understanding of partner abuse, and the ability to collaborate with a range of professional and nonprofessional helpers is an essential survival skill. Cross-disciplinary efforts should be approached with a sense of respect and collegiality. Clinicians must also realize that, on occasion, they may encounter steadfast resistance to a particular theoretical or clinical perspective. For example, some advocates may be resolutely opposed to the idea that mental health syndromes—such as mood disorders, personality disorders, or substance dependence—have any role in domestic abuse. Such challenges need not be seen in a negative light (e.g., as questioning the authority of mental health professionals), but rather as an impetus for careful empirical and theoretical justification of our ideas and interventions.

There is also an inherent difficulty in the prediction of behavior that, while having severe and damaging consequences, is relatively infrequent (Straus & Gelles, 1990). In all but the most extreme cases, physical partner

19

assault occurs, on average, less than once per month (although other forms of abuse may occur more frequently). Many perpetrators seen in IPV clinics have engaged in one or a small number of partner violence incidents. This is not to minimize the effects that even one IPV act can have on a victim, but to indicate an important dilemma from a risk prediction and prevention standpoint: The more rare and the more specific the criterion, the more difficult it is to predict. Thus, researchers examining the unique risk factors for IPV must address the question of how to predict relatively rare events enacted by a heterogeneous group of men across a wide range of situations, given the range of different backgrounds, different life experiences, different social and economic circumstances, and different attitudes about the acceptability of such behavior. Given this dilemma, it is somewhat surprising that a number of consistent risk markers have emerged from studies to date.

Further, it is important to note that this is an *emerging* area of inquiry with a relatively brief history. To use an analogy provided by Fincham (1994), the behavior of a toddler looks poorly coordinated and lacking in direction if the standards of adult development are applied. But if one considers this behavior with a developmentally appropriate perspective, it seems perfectly reasonable and informative. The same can be said of research on the characteristics of abuse perpetrators. We would be wise to consider this work in light of its early developmental stage.

In this chapter, we begin by noting that the search for characteristics that differentiate abusive from nonabusive men is heavily guided by the theoretical approaches outlined in the subsequent chapter. Thus, any conclusions about such characteristics are limited by the types of variables deemed important within a particular theoretical approach. Only recently have investigators attempted to construct more comprehensive theoretical models to capture the range of social, interpersonal, and intrapersonal factors that influence IPV perpetration (e.g., Holtzworth-Munroe & Stuart, 1994a).

In addition to a certain degree of theoretical myopia about what is, and what is not, an IPV risk factor, researchers have questioned whether a single set of factors can apply to the diverse population that has been variously labeled partner-assaultive men, maritally violent men, domestic violence perpetrators, batterers, etc. Are such men representative of a unitary subgroup of the male population, sharing a similar set of distinguishing factors? Or are these men a heterogeneous group such that their violence is associated with a host of factors that resist a singular, interpretable profile? Partner-violent women have also received attention in recent years, with most investigators presuming that somewhat different factors may explain their violence when compared to men's violence (Hamberger & Potente, 1994).

Given these complexities, our treatment approach is based on two general assumptions. The first is that there are a number of cognitive, affective, and behavioral correlates of IPV that are relatively common to this treatment population. These factors provide an empirically sound set of common treatment targets. The second assumption is that there are clinically important individual differences in the motivations for abuse, conditions under which it occurs, and functions that it serves. Therefore, the clinician cannot simply apply the same set of intervention procedures to all members of this heterogeneous treatment population. The remainder of this chapter is devoted to identifying common features of abusive clients. The remainder of the book builds on these general findings by promoting individualized conceptualization and treatment of IPV cases.

Several excellent qualitative and quantitative reviews of the research on IPV perpetrators have been published in recent years (Holtzworth-Munroe, Bates, Smutzler, & Sandin, 1997; Feldbar-Kohn, Schumacle, & O'Leary, 2000; Schumacher, Feldbar-Kohn, Slep, & Heyman, 2001; Tolman & Bennett, 1990). The current review is focused on variables that not only have been shown to be associated with IPV perpetration but that also have direct clinical relevance. For example, ample research indicates that lower socioeconomic status and younger age are risk factors for IPV perpetration. However, while clinically relevant to the extent that they may influence or modify intervention effects, these factors are not readily *modifiable* through psychosocial treatment and are not direct targets of change. Likewise, witnessed and experienced violence in the family of origin are important risk factors for IPV (Delsol & Margolin, 2004; Schumacher et al., 2001). Given that personal histories cannot be modified directly, the primary clinical import of these findings is to direct our attention toward factors that may mediate or moderate the intergenerational transmission of aggression, such as traumatic anger reactions, conflict avoidance, beliefs in the positive value of aggression to solve interpersonal problems, or a domineering and uncompromising interpersonal style. These more *proximal* factors are addressed clinically in light of their developmental origins, but with the primary emphasis on change in current relationship behavior.

Therefore, the current review emphasizes that subset of IPV risk factors that are clinically relevant, have proximal associations with IPV, and are potentially modifiable. These risk factors fall into three broad categories: (1) cognitive, (2) affective–psychopathological, and (3) relationship–behavioral. More distal factors, such as family history variables, social and cultural messages related to violence and gender, or even evolutionary factors, are thought to influence partner violence through their effects on these more proximal mediating variables that are present and activated in abusive situations (O'Leary, 1988). The clinical challenges are first to identify these factors in the individual case, and second to derive and test strategies to alter these factors.

## COGNITIVE FACTORS

From a variety of theoretical perspectives, including both feminist and modern behavioral approaches, cognitive variables have a direct and obvious link to IPV. It is plausible that some individuals who abuse a loved one make a simple choice to act in this manner and could choose to act otherwise if so motivated. A more common perspective in the available research is to assume that abusers endorse attitudes, beliefs, and points of view that support or justify their abusive behaviors. Thus, various cognitive models would indicate that abuse perpetrators know what they're doing, think it's an acceptable thing to do, and store a repertoire of abusive behaviors in memory for use in situations deemed appropriate for this type of action. For example, consider a man who strikes his wife following an argument as a function of a belief that she has been unfaithful. One may assume that he (1) engaged in an internal dialogue concerning her behavior (e.g., "I know the phone was busy because she was talking to that guy"), (2) formulated a strategy to deal with the conflict (e.g., "I'll show her she can't get away with this crap"), and (3) expected a positive outcome from the abusive action (e.g., "She'll never disrespect me again, that's for sure"). According to social information processing theories of IPV (e.g., Holtzworth-Munroe, 1992), cognitive variables may be influential in several ways, influencing selective attention to situational cues, interpretation of the meaning of social events, evaluation of response options, monitoring of the effectiveness of the response, alleviation of negative self-evaluations after abusive behavior, and integration of the various aspects of these experiences into a network of interpersonal and relationship schemas.

If abusive men are found to endorse attitudes, beliefs, attributions, or other cognitive products that are consistently related to the onset of partner-directed violence, such information could have substantial impact in at least two related areas. First, the presence of such discriminating cognitive characteristics would aid in the construction and validation of more comprehensive etiological models of IPV. A critical question facing researchers and practitioners is why some husbands, but not others, react violently to particular relationship situations. If we know that Joe and John have similar socioeconomic circumstances, grew up in similar small towns, and both report high levels of marital unhappiness, but only Joe physically assaults his wife, it would seem logical to investigate whether cognitive and attitudinal factors explain this difference between the two men. However, while existing models of IPV (e.g., Holtzworth-Munroe & Stuart, 1994a;

O'Leary & Vivian, 1990) have addressed *why* one would expect abusive men to think differently than nonabusive men, they have not firmly established *how* cognitions specifically and functionally relate to negative affect and aggressive behavior in close relationships.

The second benefit to investigating cognitive factors related to IPV, most relevant to the current purpose, is to provide potential target variables for change in clinical intervention. While more data are needed to answer the critical question of whether CBT compares favorably to other interventions currently used to treat abusive men (see Babcock et al., 2004), there is an important assumption underlying the promotion of CBT that needs to be addressed, namely whether there is sufficient evidence to implicate cognitive variables in the etiology and maintenance of intimate violence, and, if so, which are the most crucial targets of intervention? The following review considers the most widely studied cognitive correlates of IPV perpetration.

## Attributions

From a theoretical perspective, "attributions" refer to the explanations we make regarding the causes of events and responsibility for them. Social cognitive research indicates that individuals are most prone to make attributions in response to negative, unpleasant, or pain-inducing events. The premise underlying investigations of the attributional style of IPV perpetrators is that such men actively attempt to explain the causes of partner conflicts and to determine personal responsibility and blameworthiness for negative relationship events. While faulty attributions have been found to be directly related to relationship distress (e.g., Bradbury & Fincham, 1990), a primary concern within partner violence research is whether particular attributional styles uniquely and directly contribute to the occurrence of husband-to-wife aggression aside from the general association with relationship distress (Fincham, Bradbury, Arias, Byrne, & Karney, 1997). Thus, research has investigated whether IPV perpetrators explain the causes of their violence via internal factors (e.g., "I have a bad temper"), or external, circumstantial factors (e.g., "My wife was nagging me"; "I was drunk"). A related question is whether IPV perpetrators believe that their partners possess specific negative traits or hostile intentions that render the partners responsible for the violence they suffer (e.g., "She does those things just to piss me off"; "I told her not to do that anymore, but she kept on doing it, so what other option did I have?").

With regard to causal attributions, researchers have consistently found that IPV perpetrators believe that both aggressive and nonaggressive relationship conflicts are caused by their partner (e.g., Cantos, Neidig, & O'Leary, 1993; Shields & Hanneke, 1983). For example, Dutton (1986b) found that one-third of his sample of IPV perpetrators attributed the cause of their violence to their wives. While 21% "excused" their assault by attributing their violence to situational circumstances, 79% accepted personal responsibility but justified their violent acts by blaming the victim. Participants who thought their wives caused the violence were the most likely to minimize the extent of the violence and to justify the violence as a necessary conflict strategy. None of the studies, however, included a control group, thus making it difficult to determine whether these patterns are specific to IPV perpetrators, found in unhappy relationships in general, or perhaps found in most or all individuals under conditions of relationship conflict. This is particularly important given the "correspondence bias" (Gilbert & Malone, 1995), which refers to the general human tendency to locate the causes of other people's behavior in personality traits and the causes of our own behavior in the shifting events and situations we encounter.

Regarding attributions of blameworthiness for aggressive relationship conflicts, IPV perpetrators tend to blame the conflict or aggressive incident on perceived negative attributes and hostile intentions of their female partners. Holtzworth-Munroe and Hutchinson (1993), for example, asked maritally violent husbands (MV), maritally distressed–nonviolent (DNV) husbands, and maritally satisfied–nonviolent (SNV) husbands to imagine themselves experiencing nine vignettes depicting problematic marital situations. After each, they completed questionnaires measuring (1) the extent to which they believed that the wife had acted with negative intent and selfish motivation and deserved to be blamed for her actions, and (2) whether the wife acted according to five specific negative intentions (e.g., to make them angry, hurt their feelings, etc.). Results indicated that MV husbands were more likely than SNV husbands, but not more likely than DNV husbands, to attribute the cause of the imagined conflict to the negative intentions, selfish motivations, and blameworthiness of the wife. On the second measure, MV men were more likely than either comparison group to agree that their wives had specifically acted with hostile, negative intent (e.g., "She was trying to hurt me"), especially following situations involving jealousy, rejection by the wife, and potential public embarrassment. These data were replicated and extended by Eckhardt, Barbour, and Davison (1998), who reported that that MV men were more likely than DNV comparison men *spontaneously* to verbalize hostile attribution statements during a think-aloud anger-induction laboratory task consisting of imagined scenarios that involved their wives. Schweinle, Ickes, and Bernstein (2002) suggested that this tendency may be due to the "overattribution bias," an increased likelihood of inappropriately inferring harsh criticism and rejection when abusive men are asked to judge the intentions and feelings of not only their female partners but women in general. Using more traditional questionnaire methodologies, other researchers have also found that IPV perpetrators tend to blame their violence on the negative intentions of their female partners (Byrne & Arias, 1997; Fincham et al., 1997; Holtzworth-Munroe, Jacobson, Fehrenbach, & Fruzzetti, 1992; Rouse, 1984; Shields & Hanneke, 1983).

## Attitudes and Beliefs

Whereas the attribution construct concerns the determination of causal source and intent, attitudes and beliefs represent generalized cognitions regarding the way in which individuals interpret, represent, and/or perceive incoming information. The core feature of the attitude construct involves the evaluation of a stimulus, based on prior cognitive, affective, and behavioral information (Fazio, Sanbonmatsu, Powell, & Kardes, 1986; Fiske & Taylor, 1991). It is also assumed that attitudes can vary in "strength," or the degree to which an evaluation is automatically activated by a particular stimulus object. The more chronically the attitude is accessed in a particular context, the more likely it is to be activated without conscious deliberation when the context is present and, thus, the stronger the attitude (Fazio et al., 1986). As noted by Abelson and colleagues (e.g., Abelson, Kinder, Peters, & Fiske, 1982), this evaluation can vary according to affective intensity, such that attitudes may be "hot" (affect-laden evaluations about particular stimuli; e.g., "It is wrong for my wife to talk to other men!") or "cold" (simple judgments of preference; e.g., "I like watching television").

Researchers investigating the faulty or erroneous beliefs of IPV perpetrators consider this construct to represent specific thought components of a larger, more generalized attitude or schema. According to this conceptualization, an individual may endorse a particular set of beliefs about commonly encountered situations (e.g., "My wife should always show me respect"). Such beliefs may influence selective attention to specific aspects of a situation (e.g., focusing on the fact that the partner is looking away when he talks to her), the emotional reaction to the situation (e.g., anger and contempt), and response tendencies (e.g., raising his voice or saying something mean to get her attention). This closely corresponds to clinical–cognitive models of emotion (e.g., Ellis, 1962), whereby one's belief system mediates the relationship between activating environmental events and subsequent behavioral and emotional consequences. In this model, emotional distress and problematic interpersonal behaviors arise as a function of erroneous interpretations of the meaning of interpersonal events that are driven by irrational beliefs.

The earliest research on attitudes and IPV grew out of feminist theories of wife assault (e.g., Dobash & Dobash, 1979), which posit that Western society is built upon patriarchy, "a system of social organization that creates and maintains male domination over women" (Sugarman & Frankel,

1996, p. 14). Males are therefore socialized to hold attitudes that justify or support the patriarchal system. These attitudes and resulting behaviors, when combined with patriarchal practices in the legal system, religious institutions, and other social systems, result in the collective maintenance of male domination over women in the domestic sphere. From this perspective, the underlying ideology of male superiority gives rise to the specific appraisals of wrongful behavior by a wife or girlfriend and justifies the use of coercion and force to re-establish patriarchal power arrangements.

In a meta-analytic review of the role of patriarchal attitudes and wife assault, Sugarman and Frankel (1996) evaluated three attitudinal components of patriarchal ideology: attitudes toward violence within intimate relationships, gender-role attitudes, and gender schema. Among studies that examined these three attitudinal constructs, the largest effect size was for attitudes toward violence (mean $d = 0.71$), with IPV perpetrators reporting more positive attitudes toward the use of physical aggression within their relationships than nonviolent husbands. A moderate effect size was found for gender-role attitudes (mean $d = 0.54$), with a great deal of variability among studies. The gender-role attitude effect appeared to be a function of which spouse provided the data on the husband's attitudes: The effect was significant and large when wives reported on their husbands' attitudes (mean $d = 0.80$), but was virtually nonexistent when husbands reported on their own attitudes (mean $d = -0.14$). Abusive men's self-reported gender-role attitudes, on average, have not been significantly different from the self-reported gender-role attitudes of nonviolent men (mean $d = 0.11$). Finally, a weak mean effect size was reported for the IPV perpetrators' self-reported gender orientation on measures of masculinity and femininity ($d = -0.14$), with much variation among effects. IPV perpetrators appeared to endorse an undifferentiated gender-role orientation relative to nonviolent husbands. However, measures of masculinity and femininity appear to be confounded by self-esteem and the tendency to respond in a socially desirable fashion, so these findings are difficult to interpret in a gender theory framework. Overall, Sugarman and Frankel (1996) offered only partial support for the hypothesized influence of patriarchal ideology in the perpetration of wife assault. IPV perpetrators are more approving of violence in their relationships but do not necessarily avow more traditional gender-role expectations or greater masculine ideals when compared to nonviolent men. These results in and of themselves do not necessarily undermine feminist theories of partner violence because the goal of such theories is often to explain why men in general abuse women, rather than to explain which men in particular will be most likely to assault their partners. Nevertheless, the implication is that personal beliefs regarding the utility and acceptability of partner-abusive actions may have wider clinical relevance when compared to ideologies about gender roles, although the latter are likely to be important as well in some cases.

It also bears noting that the more severe (generally violent/antisocial) type of partner-violent men often endorse a stronger belief in male dominance when compared to other IPV perpetrators (Saunders, 1992). Some recent evidence indicates that the partner violence perpetrated by antisocial men may be more instrumental and premeditated in nature than other men's violence (Remington & Murphy, 2001). Such individuals use violence in a relatively cold or calculating fashion to promote their specific beliefs and goals. Recent research with homicide perpetrators likewise indicates that psychopathic individuals rarely commit impulsive crimes of passion and almost always commit instrumental homicides aimed at achieving specific criminal goals. Nonpsychopathic offenders, in contrast, are much more likely to commit impulsive homicides with no premeditation under conditions of extreme emotional arousal (Woodworth & Porter, 2002). Thus, the instrumental assertion of male dominance may be most characteristically involved in severe partner violence perpetrated by men with antisocial personalities. We have also noticed clinically that gender ideologies are often prominent in the abusive actions of men from cultures that do not adhere to egalitarian relationship ideals common in contemporary Western societies.

The investigation of marital beliefs has a relatively long history in research on marital satisfaction. Ample data support the notion that "partners are likely to become displeased and report negative communication when their marriages do not live up to what they think marriage should be" (Baucom et al., 1996, p. 210). Thus, it seems logical to presume that IPV perpetrators may have more rigid relationship *standards*, beliefs about the way marriages should be, along with more disturbed relationship *assumptions*, which represent beliefs about the way their relationships actually are. Holtzworth-Munroe and Stuart (1994b) administered measures of marital standards and assumptions to samples of MV husbands, DNV husbands, and SNV husbands. MV men did not distinguish themselves from their nonviolent but maritally distressed counterparts on either of the relationship belief measures, although both distressed groups had more disturbed assumptions and standards relative to SNV husbands. Our clinical observations suggest that this is an area in need of further investigation, as the disparity between extremely negative views of relationship partners and rigid or moralistic appraisals of how partners should behave are common targets for our cognitive interventions with partner-abusive clients.

Other researchers have examined hypotheses stemming from clinically oriented cognitive theories of emotional distress (e.g., Ellis, 1994). In a study by Eckhardt et al. (1998), the irrational beliefs of maritally violent (MV) husbands, maritally distressed–nonviolent (DNV) husbands, and maritally satisfied–nonviolent (SNV) husbands were assessed using two methodologies. First, participants completed a questionnaire measure of irrational thinking. Second, participants articulated their thoughts to anger-arousing and nonarousing audiotaped marital conflict scenarios using the "articulated thoughts in simulated situations" research paradigm (Davison, Robins, & Johnson, 1983). In this study, the investigators created audio-taped interpersonal scenarios involving the participant's "wife" that each man listened to through a pair of headphones. As he imagined each scenario, the tape stopped at particular intervals and prompted the man to talk out loud about whatever he was thinking or feeling during the previous segment of the scenario. He then articulated his thoughts for 30 seconds, after which the scenario continued for another minute, followed by another thought articulation pause, and so on. These articulated thoughts were later coded by trained raters (who were not aware of the abuse status of the participants) for the presence of irrational ideas. The scenarios involved the man (1) overhearing his wife talking about him to a female friend in harshly critical and personal critical terms and insinuating that she would soon leave him, and (2) coming home to overhear his wife having dinner with a male acquaintance who appears somewhat flirtatious.

While there were no significant differences between MV and DNV groups on the questionnaire measure of irrational beliefs, they differed considerably in their articulated thoughts. Actual quotes from participants appear in parentheses below. MV men were more likely than DNV men to demean others' worth or value (*self/other rating*, e.g., "Go to hell, you cold, heartless bitch"), to place absolutistic demands that people act appropriately (*demandingness*; "You've got to show me more respect when I walk through that door"), to arrive at conclusions in the absence of supporting evidence (*arbitrary inference*; "So you've been screwing him for years now, is that it?"), and to see events in black-and-white terms (*dichotomous thinking*; "If you're gonna talk about me that way, you can get your ass out of my house and you better keep on running"). In addition, severely violent men were more likely than moderately violent men to articulate thoughts reflective of demandingness and characterizing an event as the worst possible outcome (*awfulizing*; "This is just terrible, awful, and you're going to pay"). Noticeably absent from both MV men in general and severely violent men in particular were anger-controlling articulations ("Hey, let's calm down before things get out of hand"), which were more prevalent in SNV men. Thus, a higher level of irrational thinking appears to characterize the cognitive output of maritally violent husbands, but this difference is observed primarily when the emotional substrate of anger is present, and it is not readily observed on general measures of irrational thinking.

In sum, the cognitive data suggest that as a group, IPV perpetrators are prone to blame the causes of violent incidents on their wives/female partners and to assume that their female partners and perhaps women in general are prone to hostile intentions and harsh criticism. In addition, IPV perpetrators positively endorse the usage of physical aggression in their relationships. Finally, evidence suggests that abusive men are prone to distorted and biased cognitive processing, especially demanding/absolutistic beliefs, arbitrary inferences about the causes of negative events in their relationships, and a tendency towards black-and-white thinking in which people and events are viewed in an extreme manner.

## AFFECT, PERSONALITY, AND PSYCHOPATHOLOGY

Much controversy exists within the domestic violence field concerning the relevance of emotional and psychopathological variables in explaining or predicting IPV. One concern is that invoking internal mechanisms such as psychological disorders or disturbed emotions will lead to a "medical model" approach that will focus attention away from the social causes of partner violence, the community institutions that condone such behavior, and the need for individuals to be held accountable and responsible for their abusive actions. While it would indeed be counterproductive to ascribe all abusive behavior to internal factors or psychological problems, it seems equally unproductive to turn a blind eye to such factors if empirical evidence consistently demonstrates that they are risk factors for partner violence. The field benefits little from overly simplistic, univariate models of IPV risk, irrespective of whether the singular hypothesized causes are social or psychological, internal or external in nature.

Researchers and clinicians have long noted that at least some cases of domestic violence involve individuals with psychological, emotional, and behavioral disturbances. More recently, the focus has turned to the question of not only whether certain disturbances are correlated with men's violence toward women, but also which factors contribute to causal models of violence risk and which are useful change targets in counseling abusive clients. These factors are reviewed below.

### Emotional Disturbances

*Anger/Hostility*

On the surface, disturbances in anger and hostility are perhaps the most obvious risk factors for partner violence. Doesn't it follow that aggressive people also tend to be angry people? The scenario wherein an enraged husband explodes with verbal and physical aggression directed toward his spouse appears to have ample representation in media reports of IPV incidents, and clinical scholars have advocated the use of anger de-escalating treatments for men who abuse their partners (e.g., Hamberger, 1997). Likewise, the accumulated data suggest that problems relating to anger arousal are moderately consistent in discriminating domestically violent from nonviolent males (Eckhardt, Barbour, & Stuart, 1997; Schumacher et al., 2001).

However, many gaps remain in our understanding of the role of anger in partner violence (Norlander & Eckhardt, 2005). First, relative to the accumulated knowledge concerning other negative emotions such as depression or anxiety, the emotion of anger has been infrequently studied and poorly defined in clinical research in general and in IPV research in particular (Eckhardt et al., 1997; Eckhardt & Deffenbacher, 1995). A second problem related to the first stems from the confusion that exists whenever one tries to assess a construct that is poorly defined, namely that most anger assessment instruments suffer from a variety of psychometric inadequacies (for a review, see Eckhardt, Norlander, & Deffenbacher, 2004), hampering the ability to draw definitive conclusions about the status of anger and hostility as IPV risk factors. Finally, there is a persistent bias against the mere notion of anger as a correlate of IPV among many domestic violence advocates. In a widely cited paper presenting the case against anger control treatments for partner-violent men, Gondolf and Russell (1986) argued that such programs are ineffective and potentially dangerous because they focus on the emotion of anger, rather than the conscious desire for control thought to motivate battering. In fact, many state guidelines governing court mandated intervention for abusive clients explicitly caution against or proscribe the use of anger management interventions (Healey et al., 1998). The net result of this stance has not only been the opposition of anger-based interventions but, more important, a steadfast dismissal of anger as a potential risk factor for violent behavior. Regardless of one's theoretical bias, however, it is hoped that the available research evidence will provide the answer to this question

Is anger a worthwhile treatment target for men who batter? A good starting point is to review the available empirical research on anger as a risk factor for partner violence. In a qualitative review, Eckhardt et al. (1997) reported that the question of whether anger serves as a risk factor for domestic violence depends on two factors: the exact construct being measured and the method of measurement. Researchers using self-report, paper-and-pencil measures of anger with clearly defined control groups of nonviolent men have reported equivocal findings. While the majority of research studies have found partner-assaultive men to be higher in anger than nonviolent comparison samples (e.g., Barbour, Eckhardt, Davison, &

Kassinove, 1998; Beasley & Stoltenberg, 1992; Boyle & Vivian, 1996), some studies have found either no significant differences or *lower* anger scores in partner-assaultive men (e.g., Hastings & Hamberger, 1988).

Researchers utilizing marital interaction paradigms wherein husbands and wives are observed engaging in a conflict discussion have provided clearer findings, implicating high anger expression as a discriminating feature of IPV perpetrators. This research has shown that observational ratings of anger and anger-related verbal content (such as disgust, derision, and criticism) clearly differentiate violent from nonviolent couples (e.g., Burman, Magolin, & John, 1993; Jacobson et al., 1994; Margolin, John, & Gleberman, 1988). However, these researchers have tended to assess anger solely in terms of its expressive, behavioral component without reference to other dimensions of the anger construct, notably the experiential and cognitive components. For example, Barbour et al. (1998) found that while IPV perpetrators score higher than nonviolent–distressed husbands on measures of trait anger, they did not differ in their anger articulations (i.e., vocalization of anger synonyms) while imagining relationship conflicts. So, in many ways, the question of whether men with higher levels of anger are at risk for IPV perpetration is stuck on a fairly elementary question—what do we mean by "anger"?

Whereas anger is an emotional construct, *hostility* is a personality construct reflecting the general tendency to perceive others in a negative light and to act in line with these negative views. To date, it does not appear that researchers investigating hostility among partner-assaultive men have utilized clear, unambiguous definitions of this construct. In turn, researchers have not identified clear patterns of hostility that distinguish IPV perpetrators from nonviolent comparison groups. One notable exception was a study by Maiuro, Cahn, Vitaliano, Wagner, and Zegree, (1988) indicating that partner-assaultive men have higher self-reported hostility than nonviolent comparison men.

Recent quantitative reviews suggest that anger and hostility are associated with risk for IPV at a moderate level. Schumacher et al. (2001) reported a medium effect size in terms of the ability of anger- and hostility-related factors to discriminate between IPV and non-IPV samples ($r$'s ranged from .18 to .52). However, these authors did not address the issues raised above concerning problems with research investigating anger and hostility at both the construct and measurement levels. In another recent meta-analysis, Norlander and Eckhardt (2005) calculated 39 effect sizes from 28 different participant samples reported in 32 publications. Results indicated that self-report measures of anger and hostility in general ($d = 0.55$) were more effective in discriminating between IPV perpetrators and control groups than were observational methods in general ($d = 0.34$). Self-report measures of hostility produced the largest violent–nonviolent effects

($d$ = 0.57), and observational measures of anger produced the smallest effects ($d$ = 0.25). In summary, perpetrator anger and hostility appear to be at least moderately associated with risk for IPV, but not as strongly associated as would be expected from naïve assumptions about partner violence as a problem intrinsically linked to anger.

## Depression

We located five studies that examined the relationship between depression and IPV. Across these studies, the most central findings are that the presence of depressive symptoms (although not necessarily a mood disorder diagnosis) significantly increases the odds of both mild and severe IPV (Pan, Neidig, & O'Leary, 1994b; Schumacher et al., 2001). Interestingly, an investigation by Feldbau-Kohn, Heyman, and O'Leary (1998) suggested that only 11% of a clinic sample of IPV perpetrators were diagnosed with major depressive disorder. While this is several times higher than the male population prevalence (3%), their results indicated that levels of anger may have mediated the relationship between a diagnosis of depression and the presence of IPV. Thus, depression may be related to IPV via intervening psychological factors, such as trait anger. Conversely, the depressive symptoms observed among IPV perpetrators may reflect transient negative reactions to relationship separation and loss that are associated with interpersonal dependency (Maiuro et al., 1988; Murphy, Meyer, & O'Leary, 1994).

## Other Affective Psychopathology

Surprisingly little research has been conducted examining whether other Axis I disorders or other affective psychopathological factors relate to IPV. In fact, only a handful of studies have addressed factors other than depression and anger/hostility. Kessler, Molnar, Feurer, and Appelbaum (2001) examined data from the National Comorbidity Survey of more than 8,000 adults and found that psychopathology in males, but not females, predicted intimate partner violence. Specifically, minor violence during marriage or cohabitation was predicted by the presence of premarital major depression, alcohol dependence, generalized anxiety disorder, and nonaffective psychosis, whereas severe acts of violence were predicted by dysthymia, adult antisocial behavior, and nonaffective psychosis. Danielson, Moffitt, and Caspi (1998) found that risk for severe IPV was increased if perpetrators had any Axis I diagnosis, anxiety disorder, or nonaffective psychosis (Schumacher et al., 2001). Murphy, Meyer, & O'Leary (1993) reported that IPV perpetrators in a clinic setting had higher scores on Million Clinical Multiaxial Inventory (MCMI) bipolar disorder and thought disorder scales than nonviolent controls in discordant relationships. It seems plausible to suspect bipolar illness to be related to IPV, and our clinical observations suggest that 5–10% of IPV perpetrators have a diagnosis of bipolar disorder. Yet, it remains surprising that there has been little if any systematic research on this interrelationship. Other researchers have reported that IPV perpetrators scored higher on MCMI anxiety, hysteria, paranoia, and psychotic thinking scales (Hamberger & Hastings, 1991; McKenry, Julian, & Gavazzi, 1995). In total, however, there is a paucity of research on these psychopathological factors that merit closer research attention using reliable and valid diagnostic assessment methods.

## Negative Affectivity

One important consideration involves the conceptualization of negative emotions that may be elevated among partner-abusive clients. An extensive body of empirical research indicates that negative emotions, most notably anger, anxiety, and sadness/depression, tend to co-occur. Thus, individuals who experience high levels of one of these types of negative affect tend also to experience high levels of the other types of negative affect. This underlying tendency to experience negative emotions frequently and intensely has been labeled "negative affectivity" (Watson & Clark, 1992). Negative affectivity is a trait-like dimension of personality and has received various labels including neuroticism and general distress level. It is important to the current discussion because negative affectivity may subsume various findings on anger, depression, and anxiety problems in partner-violent men. Rather than expecting pure form versions of these negative emotions, most studies have revealed a complex array of negative affect that is consistent with the notion that partner-violent men have high negative affectivity (Maiuro et al., 1988; Murphy et al., 1993).

## Self-Esteem and Dependency

A number of studies have indicated that partner-violent men report lower self-esteem than nonviolent comparison groups (Goldstein & Rosenbaum, 1985; Murphy et al., 1994; Neidig, Friedman, & Collins, 1986). High levels of interpersonal dependency have also been found relative to discordant, nonviolent controls (Murphy et al., 1994). These studies suggest that emotional vulnerabilities related to poor self-image and intense investment in the primary relationship contribute to the high levels of interpersonal sensitivity and negative affect arousal that abusive partners experience in their relationships. Further discussion of self-esteem and dependency is subsumed under the material on attachment insecurities below.

## Attachment Insecurities

Attachment theorists (Bowlby, 1969) maintain that the emotional security one feels in a relationship and the associated emotion regulation strategies to maintain connection and independence have their roots in early experiences with caregivers. Researchers investigating the attachment model have indicated that adult IPV perpetrators are more likely than nonviolent counterparts to have witnessed interparental violence and/or to have experienced childhood abuse (e.g., Delsol & Margolin, 2004) and, as a result, may develop more dysfunctional working models of intimate attachments. Consequently, these individuals have difficulty regulating emotion in close relationships (Dutton, 1998), with problems such as intense dependence on the intimate partner and fears of partner abandonment (Holtzworth-Munroe, Stuart, & Hutchinson, 1997b; Murphy et al., 1994). To ward off perpetual fears of being abandoned by the partner, many abusive individuals display heightened awareness of signs that the partner may desire another's affection, need more autonomy, or want the relationship to end (Barnett, Martinez, & Bluestein, 1995; Dutton, Starzomski, & Ryan, 1996; Holtzworth-Munroe et al., 1997b). This bias in social information processing results in even the slightest hint of relationship discord being interpreted as a sign of impending abandonment, causing the individual anxious overconcern and anger hyperarousal (for a review, see Eckhardt & Dye, 2000).

As a result of developmentally based disturbances in adaptive emotion regulation, the individual may resort to controlling and coercive tactics in an attempt to resolve emotional distress. For some individuals, physically and emotionally abusive behaviors may serve to prevent the immediate threat of partner abandonment or may maintain emotional distance, providing a method for regulating intimate emotions. In the developmental framework, these behaviors are seen as "attachment protest," whereby angry and coercive expressions serve to elicit a caring response from loved ones.

To date, only a handful of studies have investigated the attachment construct with appropriate nonviolent comparison groups. These studies have yielded average effect sizes in the small to medium range, with insecure forms of attachment being associated with increased risk for IPV (Schumacher et al., 2001). It is important to note that there are theoretical debates in the field as to whether adult attachment security can be assessed with self-report measures, or whether subtle aspects of verbal discourse coded from interviews regarding childhood caregivers need to be used. Two studies using these labor-intensive interview methods have found very high rates of insecure and disorganized attachment among serious IPV perpetrators (Holtzworth-Munroe et al., 1997; Babcock, Jacobson & Gottman,

2000). Disorganized attachment is the most disturbed form and typically develops in the context of abusive or neglectful parenting. Individuals with disorganized attachment classifications tend to lack a consistent or coherent strategy for regulating intimate emotions, displaying intense approach–avoidance conflicts in their relationships.

An analysis of sequential conflict patterns preceding the escalation to physical violence conducted by Babcock and colleagues (2000) further suggested that the motivations for abusive behavior may differ for the two major patterns of insecure attachment. Individuals with preoccupied attachment styles were more likely to become violent following a partner's attempts to withdraw during an argument, whereas individuals with a dismissing attachment style were more likely to become violent following a partner's verbal defensiveness or criticism. These findings suggest that two common functions of abusive behavior—avoidance and control motivations—may relate to styles of attachment that have roots in early learning experiences (Waters et al., 2000). These functional distinctions are very important in case conceptualization, as discussed in later chapters.

## Personality Disturbances

### General Indications

Studies using objective self-report measures have found elevations on a wide array of personality disorder scales among IPV perpetrators. Using the MCMI or its second edition, the MCMI-II, a measure that emphasizes personality disorder symptoms, IPV perpetrators scored higher than nonviolent comparison men on the avoidant, self-defeating, aggressive–sadistic, passive–aggressive, antisocial, borderline, narcissistic, and paranoid personality disorder scales (Hamberger & Hastings, 1991; Murphy et al., 1993). Most effects were in the small to medium range. After controlling statistically for general negative emotionality, IPV men differed from nonviolent controls only on scales related to antisocial and aggressive personality problems (Murphy et al., 1993). Similarly, on the Minnesota Multiphasic Personality Inventory (MMPI), both the most common and average profile for partner-violent men contains elevations on scales 4 (Psychopathic Deviate) and 2 (Depression) (Flournoy & Wilson, 1991). This profile "usually indicates a psychopathic or antisocial personality, with depressive features that seem to be produced by specific situations and are often short lived" (Hale, Zimostrad, Duckworth, & Nicholas, 1988, p. 217). One study compared IPV perpetrators to nonviolent controls in discordant and satisfied relationships on a comprehensive test of normal personality, the California Psychological Inventory. Many significant differences emerged, with the IPV group displaying lower responsibility, socialization, self-control, tolerance, achievement via conformance, achievement via independence, good impression, intellectual efficiency, and psychological mindedness (Barnett & Hamberger, 1992). The authors concluded that the IPV group had problems in the three general areas of "intimacy, impulsivity, and problem-solving skills" (p. 15).

## Antisocial and Psychopathic Features

These general self-report studies suggest that antisocial personality features are relatively common among IPV perpetrators. Individuals with antisocial personality disorder display a pattern of rule violation and delinquency beginning in childhood or early adolescence. They are characterized as impulsive, prone to aggression, and generally unconcerned with the rights and welfare of others. Psychopathy is a more extensive and typically more severe variant of antisocial personality disorder that involves a cluster of additional personality features including emotional detachment from others, relative absence of anxiety, remorselessness, and a glib and callous interpersonal style often accompanied by a charming façade.

Diagnostic data support the hypothesis that antisocial personality problems are fairly common among IPV perpetrators. Elevated IPV risk has been found among individuals with a diagnosis of antisocial personality disorder (Danielson et al., 1998; Kessler et al., 2001). In contrast to nonviolent men, IPV perpetrators are more likely to have a diagnosis of antisocial personality disorder (Dinwiddie, 1992). The level of symptoms of antisocial personality disorder was also higher among male alcoholics with a recent history of partner violence than among nonviolent alcoholics (Murphy, O'Farrell, Fals-Stewart, & Feehan, 2001). Hart, Dutton, and Newlove (1993) found that 29% of a clinical sample of IPV perpetrators met diagnostic criteria for antisocial personality disorder using a structured interview. Two other diagnostic interview studies found rates of antisocial personality disorder in the 15–20% range among men referred to an IPV clinic (Remington, Murphy, Scott, & Simoneti, 1999; Remington & Murphy, 2001). These rates are roughly four to six times higher than general population norms. Indeed, the association with antisocial behavior does not seem confined to clinical and forensic samples. A recent prospective study of a large New Zealand birth cohort indicated that antisocial problem behaviors in childhood and adolescence, including substance abuse, were the most robust predictors of intimate partner violence in young adulthood (Magdol, Moffitt, Caspi, & Silva, 1998).

In contrast, psychopathy, the most extreme version of antisocial personality, appears to be quite rare among clinical sample IPV perpetrators (Huss & Langhinrichsen-Roling, 2001). The psychopathy diagnosis, as assessed by various versions of Hare's Psychopathy Checklist, contains both an antisocial behavior dimension and a personality dimension reflecting emotional detachment, lack of anxiety, lack of remorse, and extreme self-centeredness. There are several possible explanations for these findings. First, psychopaths may engage in forms of severe violence, both within and outside of relationships, that land them in prison rather than in treatment. Second, the partners of psychopaths may be so severely terrorized and intimidated that they are unwilling to involve the police or to take personal measures that would lead the psychopath into treatment. Third, psychopathic individuals may simply ignore the court order to attend treatment, as they tend not to fear further punishment and are generally not motivated to conform their behavior to the dictates of the law. Finally, it is possible that true psychopaths are not sufficiently emotionally invested in a primary relationship to end up in domestic violence clinics. The true psychopath often leads a parasitic lifestyle with respect to relationship partners but may have very little difficulty leaving a partner who is no longer seen as useful for meeting the psychopath's material needs. Ironically, the absence of romantic motivation and love may protect some psychopaths against partner violence, as partner-violent men typically display a high degree of emotional investment in their intimate relationships (Murphy et al., 1994).

## Borderline Personality Disorder

Dutton (1998) has developed a theory of partner violence based on the premise that the abusive personality is essentially the borderline personality. This model represents an effort to subsume research on childhood victimization, affective dysregulation, and cyclical violence expression with remorse and efforts at reconciliation under the diagnostic and conceptual framework of the borderline personality. Dutton and colleagues (1996) found that IPV was associated with borderline personality organization, a syndrome characterized by identity problems, poor reality testing, and primitive psychological defenses. In addition, borderline features are correlated with a number of other problems in abusive men, including attachment insecurities and emotional abuse levels.

Nevertheless, it remains unlikely that borderline personality organization will provide a comprehensive account of the psychological problems of IPV perpetrators. For example, Hart and colleagues (1993) found that 24% of clinical sample IPV perpetrators met criteria for borderline personality disorder on diagnostic interview, and about 50% did not meet criteria for any personality disorder. Our efforts to diagnose abusive men have revealed rates of borderline personality disorder lower than 20% (Remington & Murphy, 2001). Subtyping studies described later in this chapter indicate that individuals with borderline features may form one subgroup of partner violence perpetrators but are far from a majority of this population.

## Summary and Implications

To date, the clinical implications of personality disorder research remain fuzzy. Given that personality disorders are defined as stable over time and highly resistant to therapeutic change, one somewhat pessimistic view is that IPV perpetrators will not likely respond to treatment due to underlying personality dysfunction. The associated research evidence is mixed. One study found that IPV perpetrators with antisocial and/or borderline features had higher rates of abusive behavior after standard group counseling (Dutton, Bonarchuk, Kropp, Hart, & Ogloff, 1997). Other studies, in contrast, have found that antisocial disorders or related features do not predict significant variation in treatment outcome for this population (Gondolf & White, 2001; Kropp & Hart, 2000; Remington & Murphy, 2001). At the present state of knowledge, when assessing and treating abusive clients it seems prudent to remain mindful that significant personality disorder may be present without presuming that individuals with personality disorder symptoms cannot respond to intervention. In addition, given the somewhat abstract nature of the personality disorder constructs, it seems reasonable to assume that these general problems will influence partner violence through specific cognitive, behavioral, and relationship mechanisms that can be targeted for change. It is also likely that individuals with serious personality disturbances will need more extensive treatment, perhaps including efforts to resolve and reprocess childhood trauma and alter underlying interpersonal- and self-schemas.

## SUBSTANCE USE AND ABUSE

Alcohol abuse is among the most robust correlates of IPV. U.S. population surveys indicate a significant linear association between alcohol consumption and IPV prevalence (Kantor & Straus, 1987) and between alcohol-related problems and IPV (Cunradi, Caetano, Clark, & Schafer, 1999; Leonard & Blane, 1992). Clinical studies of men seeking treatment for alcohol problems reveal a one-year prevalence rate of IPV that is four to six times higher than the rate found in demographically similar, nonalcoholic men (Chermack, Fuller, & Blow, 2000; O'Farrell & Murphy, 1995). Over half the female partners of men seeking alcohol treatment have been targets of IPV in the year preceding treatment (Murphy & O'Farrell, 1996). In addition, among men seeking treatment for substance abuse, those who perpetrated IPV had more severe alcohol problems (Murphy & O'Farrell, 1994) and higher levels of illicit drug use (Bennett, Tolman, Rogalski, & Srinivasaraghavan, 1994; Murphy et al., 2001).

Clinical studies of men seeking treatment for partner violence likewise reveal a high prevalence of alcohol problems. In a review of early case-control studies, level of alcohol use emerged as a consistent risk marker for husband-to-wife violence (Hotaling & Sugarman, 1986). A subsequent review of studies in which battered women answered general interview questions about their partners' alcohol use revealed a prevalence rate of alcohol problems among partner-violent men of approximately 50% (Leonard, 1993). Although these early studies had methodological problems, such as the use of single-source collateral data and unstandardized assessment methods, more recent data likewise indicate high rates of substance-use problems in this population. In a recent investigation of men seeking treatment at a domestic violence clinic, Fals-Stewart (2003) found that 38% had a current alcohol diagnosis—23% met DSM-IV criteria for alcohol dependence, and 15% met DSM-IV criteria for alcohol abuse.

Alcohol problems have important implications for response to IPV treatment as well. In two separate studies, individuals with alcohol problems at program intake were more likely than other clients to engage in physical assault after treatment (DeMaris & Jackson, 1987; Hamberger & Hastings, 1990). The level of recidivism risk associated with alcohol and drug use is remarkably high. A recent study used prospective weekly diaries and quarterly interviews with men in an IPV treatment program and their partners in order to assess the day-to-day associations between alcohol consumption and physical assault recidivism. The odds of physical partner aggression were found to be eight times higher on days when the abusive man had consumed alcohol than on sober days. The odds of severe partner aggression were 20 times higher on days of heavy drinking (six or more drinks) than on sober days (Fals-Stewart, 2003). Another recent study found that men who binge drank on a regular basis were 3.5 times more likely than men who never or rarely drank to engage in recidivist violence after IPV treatment. Men who were drunk nearly every day were 16 times more likely to engage in recidivist partner violence than those who rarely or never drank (Jones & Gondolf, 2001).

There is some good news on the substance use and partner violence front as well. In several studies conducted in alcohol or drug treatment clinics, individuals who achieve stable sobriety show substantial reductions in partner violence and are much less likely to continue violence when compared to relapsed patients (O'Farrell & Murphy, 1995; O'Farrell, Fals-Stewart, Murphy, & Murphy, 2003). Taken in sum, these findings provide a compelling case for the assessment and treatment of substance-use problems among IPV perpetrators. Such work should be an integral part of any IPV program.

## RELATIONSHIP-BEHAVIORAL FACTORS

In this section we review research concerning the behavioral and situational context in which IPV occurs, including relationship factors, skills deficiencies, behavioral problems, and other situational risk factors. At the core, IPV is a behavioral problem, and the same factors that govern other forms of enacted behavior must be considered in treating IPV as well.

### Relationship Distress

A recent meta-analysis found that relationship discord is one of the most consistent correlates of IPV (Schumacher et al., 2001). Couples experiencing partner violence are characterized by high levels of relationship conflict and low levels of relationship satisfaction. Clinical observations and qualitative studies further suggest that physical violence typically occurs in the context of an argument, disagreement, or relationship conflict (Dobash & Dobash, 1984; O'Leary, 1999).

The directional link between relationship distress and partner violence raises interesting questions. Do couples end up experiencing relationship distress because of abuse and violence? Or is the distress present prior to the onset of abusive behavior problems? Sometimes data from the same study are not consistent in answering this question. Using data modeling strategies, O'Leary and colleagues found that relationship distress predicted IPV prospectively among a sample of newlyweds (O'Leary, Malone, & Tyree, 1994). However, a different analysis of data from the same longitudinal study, conducted after excluding couples who reported physical violence prior to marriage, found that verbal aggression predicted the first instances of physical aggression longitudinally, whereas marital distress was correlated with first instances of physical aggression cross-sectionally but did not predict it longitudinally (Murphy & O'Leary, 1989). This latter finding suggests that marital distress may emerge as a result of hostile and aggressive interactions and perhaps as a function of unresolved conflicts and poor problem solving that are linked to these aggressive interactions. Although the arrow may point in both directions, it seems safe to assume that hostile and abusive interactions can erode or degrade the sense of satisfaction and adjustment in a relationship.

Researchers have also suggested that it is critical to specify the type of marital outcome under investigation. For example, in a four-year prospective study of newlywed couples, Rogge and Bradbury (1999) found that while communication problems predicted marital *dissatisfaction* four years later, the presence of marital aggression predicted marital *dissolution* over the same time period. Other researchers have found similar results, with Quigley and Leonard (1996) reporting that wives whose husbands ceased their violence had stable (although low) rates of marital satisfaction over time, whereas wives of husbands who continued their IPV showed marked decreases in marital satisfaction over time.

Several clinical implications can be drawn from the research on relationship distress and IPV. Most importantly, the vast majority of IPV perpetrators are in highly distressed relationships. Therefore, many existing strategies for the treatment of relationship dysfunction can be productively adapted to this population. In addition, the available evidence indicates that abusive behavior can play an important role in the erosion of relationship satisfaction and/or the dissolution of relationships, points that are of considerable relevance in motivating abusive clients to seek treatment and change their behavior. Finally, it is reasonable to conceptualize emotional and physical abuse as extreme and pernicious versions of relationship dysfunction, whereas relationship adjustment can be thought of as a general barometer of the affective and functional state of the relationship.

## Power and Control

According to feminist-informed models of IPV (e.g., Dobash & Dobash, 1979, 1984), IPV reflects men's malevolent use of relationship power and control tactics. The central theme of these models is that the patriarchal society provides an enormously influential and reinforcing context for men to use power and control tactics to subjugate their female partners and promote male privilege. Aggressive manifestations of abuse are but one example of power and control tactics, as men may also utilize psychological/emotional abuse, economic coercion, and restriction of movement and social contacts to intimidate, isolate, and control their partners. Theories of relationship power separate this construct into three factors (e.g., Cromwell & Olson, 1975; Gray-Little & Burks, 1983; Huston, 1983; McDonald, 1980): power bases (resources that each spouse brings into the relationship that assist in the achievement of each partner's goals), power processes (verbal interactional behaviors that unfold during conflict resolution), and power outcomes (who has the final say on important matters). It is worth noting again that power and control constructs are the central basis of feminist-informed theories of IPV, which ascribe the primary causes of IPV to a need for power in close relationships and a proclivity toward coercive and controlling behaviors directed by men against women to assert male power.

Given that these theories form the basis of several widely used and standardized interventions for IPV (e.g., Adams, 1988; Pence & Paymar, 1993), what does the available evidence say about the relationships among IPV and power/control tactics? As noted in the previous chapter, cross-cultural research provides some support for the link between systematic oppression of women and wife abuse (e.g., Levinson, 1987). Suprisingly, however, research on power assertion as a psychological and interactional process has provided only limited support for the foundational ideas in most abuser intervention programs. According to a comprehensive review by Malik and Lindahl (1998), this literature is fraught with numerous methodological problems and a seeming inability to establish the construct validity of power and control assessments. "When rare efforts to examine construct validity are undertaken, expected correlations among the dimensions are not found, indicating that empirically, *power has yet to be validated as a construct*" (Malik & Lindahl, 1998, p. 412, emphasis added). For example, in the most sophisticated study of power and control to date (Babcock, Waltz, Jacobson, & Gottman, 1993), no relationships were found between power bases (e.g., education, income, socioeconomic status) and IPV, and the relationships among power outcomes (e.g., control over decision making) and IPV were minimal. More compelling was a pattern of interactional style (a power process), such that violent husbands reported greater pursuit and demand tactics during conflict discussions, while wives reported withdrawing or shutting down. This husband demand/wife withdraw communication pattern was also supported by Holtzworth-Munroe, Smutzler, and Stuart (1998). Thus, it may be the case that while the patriarchal power and control arrangements provide an important distal context for violence against women, there is very little consistent empirical evidence and much conceptual confusion with regard to the concept of power dynamics at the level of individual characteristics and relationship interactions.

Empirical findings and clinical observations further suggest that the motivations underlying partner-violent acts are usually complex, rather than simple or straightforward expressions of dominance and control. Abusive individuals typically perceive themselves to be the victims of their partner's negative actions. Underlying emotional insecurities such as feared abandonment by the partner are often present as well. A functional analysis of clinically violent incidents reveals that abusive behaviors sometimes produce compliance or other desired behavioral changes by the partner and, thus, have controlling effects in the short term. In the long term, however, abusive behaviors are generally self-defeating, as they erode relationship harmony and often lead to emotional estrangement by the coerced partner and eventual dissolution of the relationship. Abusive clients, therefore, rarely see themselves as possessing a high degree of power and control in their relationships and more often experience themselves as powerless over negative relationship events. While this powerlessness may not be *objectively* valid, its subject experience may influence when abuse occurs, the form it takes, and the short-term interpersonal effects it has. Thus, the cognitive and emotional elements of the experience of victimization and powerlessness are important targets of intervention in many partner-abuse cases, as well as the poor interactional skills that often give rise to conflicts and power struggles.

## Interactional Style

The findings on discord and power dynamics in abusive relationships remind us that partner violence involves behavior occurring between members of a couple. This does *not* mean that victims of IPV are somehow to blame for the abuse they receive. But it does imply that a complete understanding of IPV requires knowledge of the context in which it occurs, and this context includes the behavior of both partners (Jacobson, 1994). Thus, we may attempt to change the male's abusive behavior using any number of counseling approaches only to find our attempts at behavior change fall short when the context switches from a counseling room to the couple's residence. Lingering resentment or outright hatred toward an intimate partner spill over into the content and style of couples' communications, and the origins of such resentment and hostility are often a combination of distorted thinking and just cause in both partners. Therefore, it becomes critical to understand the usual ways that couples with a violent partner interact about matters both mundane and serious and to integrate this information into effective clinical interventions.

Central to this understanding are research findings based on a microanalysis of the sequential behavioral patterns associated with IPV. In the typical research paradigm, the couple is asked to discuss a topic of considerable conflict or disagreement in a laboratory setting for 10–15 minutes, typically with the instruction that they should attempt to solve the problem. This interaction is videotaped and later coded by trained raters for the presence of specific verbal and nonverbal behaviors. Researchers have found that relative to nonviolent couples, violent couples exhibit more offensive negative behaviors during conflict discussions as well as more reciprocal patterns of negative communication (Berns, Jacobson, & Gottman, 1999; Burman et al., 1993; Cordova, Jacobson, Gottman, Rushe, & Cox, 1993; Jacobson et al., 1994; Margolin et al., 1988). In particular, violent couples seem to be locked in a pattern of reciprocal belligerence, contempt, disgust, and overt hostility, with each partner responding to the other's negative behavior with similarly negative reactions. This back-and-forth, "negative reciprocity" sequence is longer lasting and involves more negative behaviors in violent couples than in nonviolent couples. While few differences were observed in these variables between husbands and wives within violent couples (i.e., wives "gave as good as they got"), Jacobson et al. (1994) reported that violent males did not desist this negative communication pattern even after their wives exhibited fear or otherwise attempted to terminate the conflict. These data stand in stark contrast to a stereotyped image of the domestic violence victim as passive and shrinking and suggest that among many couples experiencing male-to-female IPV both partners are likely to be negative, reactive, and locked in battle.

These findings should not be taken to imply that individuals are somehow absolved of personal responsibility for their aversive or abusive behaviors because their partner is behaving likewise. In fact, this assumption is a very common belief of abusive clients that needs to be effectively challenged during treatment. Rather, the communication findings point out that abuse and violence are typically acted out in the context of heated conflicts, with considerable stimulation toward aggressive actions and reactions. A clinician's denial of this fact is often experienced by the client as a failure in empathy. In response, the client typically redoubles efforts to convince the clinician of how terrible the partner's behavior truly is. As the working alliance is established, the clinician can increasingly help the client to understand his own role in conflict escalation and facilitate the client's ability to react in ways that reduce the probability of negative reciprocity from the partner.

Research on mutual aggression further illustrates the importance of contextual factors in abusive behavior. When one partner has been physically aggressive in a relationship, it is highly likely that the other partner has been physically aggressive as well (Archer, 2000). Levels of verbal and emotional abuse also tend toward parity within couples. Although some of this mutual aggression reflects self-defense (Saunders, 1988), population surveys reveal that women report being about equally likely as their male partners to strike the first blow (i.e., initiate physical aggression) during conflict situations (Stets & Straus, 1990).

Although the perpetration of relationship behaviors such as slapping, pushing, and shoving is roughly equal for men and women (Archer, 2000), the consequences of violence are not gender-neutral. Due to average gender differences in size, strength, and aggression training, and in line with cultural systems that support male dominance, women overwhelmingly bear the brunt of the negative effects of violence in heterosexual relationships. Intense fear, traumatic stress symptoms, hopelessness, economic hardship, and physical injuries are all predominantly experienced by women in abusive relationships and appear to be relatively rare experiences for men in these situations (Cascardi, Langhinrichsen & Vivian, 1992). Nevertheless, clinicians need to acknowledge sensitively the abusive client's complaints about the partner's aggression, rather than assuming that these complaints are fabricated, exaggerated, or otherwise irrelevant. The therapist can gently encourage the abusive client to focus on how he or she copes with the partner's aggression and then subsequently on how he or she contributes to the escalation of hostilities and conflicts. In our experience, clients typically experience this approach as empowering as they come to realize that there are positive and nonabusive strategies for addressing relationship conflicts and influencing the partner.

## Behavioral Skills Deficits

A fairly obvious inference from the preceding review is that IPV perpetrators, in general, are unskilled communicators in close relationships. Beyond those data already presented, ample research supports this inference. For example, a key relationship skill is assertiveness, or "the ability to express one's feelings or wants, particularly as it relates to refusing requests from others, making requests of others, or initiating contact with others" (Schumacher et al., 2001, p. 328). The research examining general assertiveness among IPV perpetrators is inconsistent, with some data suggesting that IPV men are less assertive, and other data suggesting no differences in general assertiveness between violent and nonviolent males. However, *spouse-specific* assertiveness problems are more consistently associated with IPV, with two studies showing that IPV perpetrators exhibit lower spouse-specific assertiveness than nonviolent men in discordant relationships (Dutton & Strachan, 1987; Rosenbaum & O'Leary, 1981) and one study showing a difference between partner-violent and maritally satisfied–nonviolent groups (O'Leary & Curley, 1986).

Other research has found that partner-violent men have consistent difficulties with the appropriate expression of feelings and in the general competence of their reactions to conflict. Researchers (Barbour et al., 1998; Eckhardt, Jamison, & Watts, 2002) have found that during anger induction, violent males articulated significantly fewer statements reflective of anger and annoyance relative to nonviolent males, even though self-report measures revealed that they indeed felt angrier than nonviolent controls. Instead, partner-violent men appear to skip over the affective communication step and go directly to verbal insults, threats, and other forms of belligerent communication styles, perhaps in an attempt to win the interactional battle. Others have found that during imaginal marital conflicts, the coping responses of partner-violent men were significantly more incompetent than the responses of nonviolent men (Holtzworth-Munroe & Anglin, 1991). Specifically, while imagining a scenario wherein another man is flirting with the participant's wife, partner-assaultive men were more likely than nonviolent men to indicate that they would threaten the other man or the wife and less likely to handle the conflict in a socially appropriate manner. Other studies have found that across a wide range of imagined wife behaviors, violent husbands were more likely than nonviolent husbands to offer negative responses (argue with spouse; say nothing at all) and less likely to offer supportive behaviors (Holtzworth-Munroe & Smutzler, 1996).

These skill deficits appear to reflect generalized problems with social skills, although the deficits are particularly pronounced in the relationship domain (Anglin & Holtzworth-Munroe, 1997). Studies to date indicate that the skills deficits are most prominent under conditions of affective arousal.

## Clinically Relevant Subtypes of Partner-Abusive Clients

Several recent reviews have argued that perpetrators of IPV are not a homogeneous group and do not possess a unitary set of diagnostic traits (e.g., Holtzworth-Munroe & Stuart, 1994a; Johnson, 1995). The issue remains complicated, however, as quantitative studies have variously identified two (e.g., Chase, O'Leary & Heyman, 2001; Hershorn & Rosenbaum, 1991), three (Gondolf, 1988; Hamberger, Lohr, Bonge, & Tolin, 1996; Saunders, 1992; Waltz, Babcock, Jacobson & Gottman, 2000), or four (Holtzworth-Munroe et al., 2000a) different subtypes of abusive men. Clinical authors have identified as many as five different clinical types, typically involving combinations of control, dependency, and emotional stability (e.g., Elbow, 1977). Nevertheless, it seems clear that IPV perpetrators can be separated into at least two groupings. Those in the first cluster are aggressive only within the family or primary intimate relationship, typically showing signs of relationship discord but otherwise appearing relatively normal on psychological testing. Individuals in the second cluster have generalized problems with anger and/or aggression, possessing signs of serious deficits in impulse control and associated personality problems including antisocial and/or borderline traits. Not surprisingly, members of this more disturbed cluster (or clusters) perpetrate more frequent and severe IPV and have more associated clinical concerns such as substance abuse and childhood histories of violence exposure (Holtzworth-Munroe et al., 2000a; Saunders, 1992; Waltz et al., 2000).

Some studies have further subdivided the more disturbed cluster into two groups: generally violent–antisocial (GVA) versus borderline–dysphoric (BD) (or "pathological") subtypes. Empirical studies, however, have revealed relatively few differences between these two groups (Holtzworth-Munroe, et al., 2000a; 2000b; Waltz et al., 2000). Both the GVA and BD subtypes tend to differ from other IPV perpetrators on measures of the extensiveness or frequency of partner-abusive behavior, impulsivity, and levels of antisocial, psychopathic, and borderline traits. Some evidence has indicated that the BD group members display more evidence of attachment insecurity than the generally violent group members on variables such as fear of abandonment, dependency, jealousy, and anxious/ambivalent attachment. Individuals in the GVA group tend to have more generalized violence, more frequent IPV, and criminal involvement. However, in the studies to date, these two relatively pathological groups have not differed significantly from one another on the vast majority of measures, including measures of borderline and antisocial personality traits and dysfunctional anger (Holtzworth-Munroe, et al., 2000a; 2000b; Saunders, 1992; Waltz et al., 2000).

At present, it remains unclear whether it is more accurate to assume that there are different types of IPV perpetrators or to think of the different types as reflecting points along a continuum of case severity (O'Leary, 1993). A case-severity model maintains that correlated problems with impulse control and interpersonal dysfunction are increasingly probable as one progresses along the continuum of IPV case severity. Cases lower on the IPV problem continuum are presumed to have similar issues with impulse control, interpersonal skills deficits, and anger dysregulation, albeit in more muted and less obvious forms. A related notion is the diathesis stress (or liability–severity) model, under which individuals are thought to vary in their predisposition to partner violence based on a range of variables including genetic/physiological factors, learning history, and traits such as impulsiveness. Those who are high on this liability dimension will require very little stimulation to become aggressive, as they are generally lacking in the self-control mechanisms that normally quell aggressive impulses. These individuals will be more frequently and severely violent and prone to violence in all of their relationships. Aggressive behavior appears more or less in character based on the severity of their problem. Those who are low on the liability dimension will require a high level of stimulation to become aggressive, typically in the form of intense, escalating partner conflicts, physical aggression from the partner, and perhaps high levels of other life stress (e.g., unemployment, financial problems, etc.). Partner violence for these individuals will seem out of character and should be much less frequent and severe based on their possessing self-control mechanisms that break down under high environmental push.

The subtype construct may work well as a shorthand clinical descriptor of the patterns of dimensions or attributes that seem to interrelate among certain IPV perpetrators. As such, subtyping schemes may prove useful in the context of clinical practice. First, although its value has been questioned in recent years, there is a longstanding distinction in psychology between instrumental and hostile aggression (Bushman & Anderson, 2001). Hostile aggression is hypothesized to occur under conditions of high emotional arousal and to be mediated by sympathetic nervous system activation (i.e., the fight or flight response). Instrumental aggression is hypothesized to occur in the relative absence of sympathetic arousal and is directed toward a tangible functional goal (e.g., the completion of a robbery or torture of a political prisoner). A related clinical typology involves the distinction between proactive and reactive aggression (Dodge, 1991).

Under this model, reactive aggression is very similar to defensive rage reactions and involves "an impulsive retaliation or defense to perceived threat, provocation, or frustration," with "intense anger or other increased negative affectivity and/or physiological arousal due to interpartner conflict and/or perceived aversive partner behavior" (p. 572). Proactive aggression, in contrast, involves "effortful cognitive processing prior to and/or during the violence," such that the violence is "goal-directed, planned, calculated, or otherwise purposeful," along with evidence of limited negative affect arousal or a reduction in arousal associated with the violence. Chase and colleagues (2001) analyzed detailed descriptions of IPV episodes to categorize male IPV perpetrators into proactive versus reactive aggression groups. The reactive aggression group accounted for the majority of cases (62%), even though to be included in this group, individuals had to show no evidence of proactive aggression. In contrast to the reactive aggressors, proactive aggressors had higher levels of antisocial and psychopathic traits and were more dominant and less angry during a videotaped problem discussion with the relationship partner (Chase et al., 2001).

Another recent study found evidence that IPV offenders with a diagnosis of antisocial personality disorder were more likely than other IPV cases to report engaging in preparatory behaviors prior to aggression, such as shutting the blinds, unplugging the phone, and closing the doors (Remington & Murphy, 2001). In addition, they were also more likely to report positive emotions after engaging in partner violence, endorsing terms such as "pumped up," "justified," and "energized." These findings are consistent with the working hypothesis that the partner violence of those with antisocial personality disorder is more proactive–instrumental in nature and may involve arousal mechanisms associated with excitement and dominance, as opposed to threat-induced rage reactions.

Biological researchers characterize this distinction as defensive rage versus predatory aggression (George, 2003). These two aggressive behavior patterns are well documented in animals, and they have distinct underlying brain and hormonal mechanisms (George, 2003). The perception of threat and an initial freezing and fear reaction are key features of defensive rage. Interestingly, George and colleagues (2000) found that serious IPV perpetrators tended to respond with high levels of fear and/or rage reactions to a blood infusion of sodium lactate. Lactate infusion induces a panic attack in most individuals who have panic disorder but produces only minor unpleasant physical sensations in normal controls. These findings suggest that IPV perpetrators have abnormal sympathetic nervous system reactivity, tend to label sympathetic arousal as anger and rage, are experiencing defensive rage in response to perceptions of threat, and therefore engage primarily in arousal-mediated aggression. These researchers have also described recent brain imaging research using position emission tomography scans that further isolated deficient connections between a number of cortical structures and the amygdala in IPV perpetrators (George, 2003). The amygdala is a key brain center for the processing of threat and danger cues. It provides the initial evaluation of environmental threat, which is subsequently overridden by the more elaborate and subtle processing of stimuli in the cortex. George (2003) has argued that these findings demonstrate a biological deficit in the cortical control of threat perception, which is associated with dysregulated fear and rage reactions.

The cognitive and behavioral interventions presented in this book are hypothesized to work by strengthening the control by higher brain centers involved in rational thought and planned action over the more primitive processing of threat cues and defensive reactions. The client is helped (1) to reduce the appraisal of threat in relationship situations and relabel threat cues as benign relationship events, (2) to develop alternative relationship behaviors that prevent threatening interactions by promoting a more cooperative relationship atmosphere, and (3) to develop self-regulatory coping skills to prevent the escalation of rage reactions once negative emotions are experienced.

Taken in sum, the research and theory on subtypes of IPV perpetrators support the need for a functional analysis of abusive behavior in the individual case in order to accomplish these goals. Important variation across individuals is found with respect to the forms and patterns of partner-abusive behavior, the situational cues under which abuse occurs, and the interpersonal functions of abusive actions. These variations have important implications for devising an effective treatment plan, as described in the subsequent treatment recommendations.

# / 4 /

# *Intervention Models and Research*

There are several prominent intervention models for abusive clients, including feminist, social learning, trauma/psychopathology, and relationship systems approaches. Each of these models is reviewed here with respect to supportive evidence, strengths, and weaknesses because our treatment approach integrates elements from all of these perspectives while relying primarily on the social learning, cognitive-behavioral framework. Research on treatment compliance and outcome from group intervention models demonstrates a serious need for improvements and innovations in this area of clinical practice. Coordination with the criminal justice system may also enhance treatment effects.

## OVERVIEW OF EXISTING TREATMENT APPROACHES

### Feminist-Sociocultural Approaches

The feminist–sociocultural approach has received the greatest attention in the clinical and educational literature on interventions for abusive men. This fact is not surprising given that the early intervention programs were strongly associated with the battered women's shelter movement, which had strong roots in the women's movement of the 1970s (Schecter, 1982). This approach is best exemplified in the work of David Adams and the EMERGE collective from Boston (Adams & McCormick, 1982) and in the popular Duluth Model program (Pence & Paymar, 1993).

The fundamental principles of the feminist–sociocultural approach are that (1) domestic abuse is a systematic process of gender oppression; (2)

men batter women to enforce their dominance and get their way, or in response to perceived transgressions by women of their assigned roles and rights, (3) important social systems support the abuse in a number of ways, most notably by treating it as a private matter that is not worthy of public intervention, and (4) abuse is normal male behavior, and therefore is not a sign of psychological problems and not the result of dysfunctional relationship dynamics. Feminist scholars were instrumental in documenting various forms of psychological abuse that are often used along with physical assault to exert control over battered women (Pence & Paymar, 1993; Walker, 1984). Perhaps the most essential assertion of the feminist perspective is that partner abuse is a social and historical problem, not merely a psychological or biological problem. "Men who assault their wives are actually living up to cultural prescriptions that are cherished in Western society—aggressiveness, dominance, and female subordination—and they are using physical force as a means to assert that dominance" (Dobash & Dobash, 1979, p. 24). Attempts to find the origins of partner abuse in psychological disorders, personality traits, traumatic childhood experiences, substance abuse, or brain dysfunction are considered suspect. Such explanations are thought to excuse personal responsibility for abusive behavior, medicalize the problem, or focus attention away from the key social change agenda of advocating for women's rights and against male dominance of the domestic sphere.

Clinically, the feminist–sociocultural approach relies on an educational model with group interventions designed to increase men's consciousness of gender oppression and promote personal change in line with a larger agenda of social change. The mainstay of the approach is education focused on changing attitudes, most notably beliefs that support male privilege and dominance, the justification of power and control tactics such as violence and intimidation, and the deflection of personal responsibility. For example, one widely used treatment manual instructs the group facilitators as follows: "an abuser will often admit that he 'shouldn't have hit her but . . . ' That 'but' is reinforced every time it is not challenged" (Pence & Paymar, 1993, p. 95). Some feminist approaches combine this re-education approach with behavior therapy techniques such as training in relaxation and anger management skills and cognitive interventions focused on beliefs about gender roles, rights, and privileges (e.g., Saunders, 1996).

There is a good deal of supportive evidence for the gendered analysis of partner violence from sociological, anthropological, and historical sources (Murphy & Meyer, 1991; Yllo & Bograd, 1988). For example, cross-cultural studies reveal that wife abuse is more prevalent in societies where women can't own property and have very low status relative to men (Levinson, 1987). Further support derives from analysis of the inadequate responses provided by key social institutions, including medical, criminal justice, and religious systems, that have traditionally viewed partner abuse as a private family matter (e.g., Heggen, 1996; Micklow, 1988; Stark & Flitcraft, 1996). Qualitative analyses of interviews with battered women reveal the pervasive nature of abusive control and social barriers that prevent solutions to the problem (e.g., Dobash & Dobash, 1979; Walker, 1984). At nearly every turn, the social arrangements seem stacked against the battered woman who would seek help from family and extended family, religious leaders, the legal system, and the medical community. Traditional mental health providers have likewise been criticized by feminist scholars for not attending to the ways in which theories and interventions disempower women and blame victims for abuse (Adams, 1988; Bograd, 1984).

In contrast to the sociological and cross-cultural support for the feminist analysis of partner violence, to date there is only limited empirical support from psychological and relationship-level analyses for the feminist assumption that power assertion is the core cause of partner abuse (Malik & Lindahl, 1998). In part, this is because relationship power takes on many forms and is difficult to define and measure. Resource imbalances in factors such as income, education, and occupational status have been linked to partner violence in some studies (e.g., Hotaling & Sugarman, 1986; Hornung, McCullough & Sugimoto, 1981; Smith, 1988). Typically, risk for violence is elevated for couples in which the wife has higher income, education, or status than the husband, although power imbalances favoring husbands are also sometimes correlated with partner violence (e.g., Claes & Rosenthal, 1990). Imbalances in decision-making power and power transactions involving demands by one partner and withdrawal by the other have also been associated with partner violence (Babcock et al., 1993).

Some scholars and researchers have raised important challenges to the feminist perspective. First, partner abuse is quite prevalent in lesbian and gay male relationships, a fact that is difficult to explain if abuse is a purely gender-based system of oppression (Burke & Follingstad, 1999). Second, survey research has revealed that women are about equal to (or slightly higher than) men in their display of physically and verbally aggressive acts toward relationship partners (Archer, 2000), although the impact of women's aggression in producing injuries, fear, or emotional distress is substantially lower than the impact of men's aggression (Stets & Straus, 1990; Cantos, Neidig, & O'Leary, 1994; Cascardi et al., 1992). Aggression by women toward men is somewhat difficult to explain from the feminist perspective in which partner violence is purely an expression of male power and control. Third, recent literature reviews indicate that men in treatment for domestic abuse are not more likely than nonabusive men to endorse sexist beliefs in male privilege or regarding women's roles and rights, as indicated by over a dozen case control studies (Eckhardt & Dye, 2000;

Sugarman & Frankel, 1996). Thus, while the feminist model is a compelling and intuitively appealing account of the causes of domestic violence, many complexities remain with respect to the supporting research.

The clinical and educational techniques used by programs like the Duluth model (Pence & Paymar, 1993) can also be criticized on several grounds. First, these approaches are often quite confrontational in nature, as the counselor is instructed to address, square on, any potential instance of victim blaming or risk colluding with the abuser's negative beliefs (Pence & Paymar, 1993). Persistent confrontation and forceful disputation of the client's beliefs early in treatment may fail to promote the nonspecific conditions of therapeutic change, most notably a strong working alliance between client and therapist reflecting agreement on the goals of counseling and the tasks needed to attain these goals (Murphy & Baxter, 1997). Recent studies indicate that the therapeutic alliance is an important predictor of abusive behavior outcomes in group interventions for partner-violent men (Brown & O'Leary, 2000; Taft, Murphy, King, Musser & DeDeyn, 2003). Although proponents of these approaches typically assert that they are conducting education rather than counseling or therapy, a cursory review of the techniques used indicates that they are psychoeducational in nature, require extensive self-disclosure, and are oriented toward the promotion of personal transformation and behavior change (Murphy & Baxter, 1997).

Second, these models may be overly narrow in their focus on beliefs about gender roles, particularly given that such beliefs have not been convincingly linked to the perpetration of partner abuse. In the absence of evidence that misogynistic attitudes are activated during the expression of partner abuse or are uniquely elevated among abusive individuals rather than a consequence of general sex-role socialization, the predominant focus given these factors during treatment may be somewhat misplaced. Other cognitive factors may warrant greater attention, including beliefs in the utility and correctness of aggression and violence and hostile attributions of the partner's intent. Although in some cases these cognitive biases may be linked to more global ideologies regarding gender roles and women's rights, it is dangerous to assume that such links are invariably present and salient in all cases.

Third, important questions arise from the strong stance taken by these programs regarding the unimportance of psychological factors in partner violence. Feminist authors have expressed serious concerns about theories postulating psychological factors as causes of IPV, arguing that such theories provide abusive individuals with ready-made excuses for their violence, thus preventing the assumption of personal responsibility for abusive behavior (e.g., Adams, 1988; Bograd, 1984). Therefore, conditions that may influence impulse control and aggressive behavioral tendencies, such as traumatic brain injuries, bipolar disorder, and the abuse of alcohol, cocaine, and other drugs, are often considered to be irrelevant to interventions for partner-violent individuals. Mounting evidence on the influence of head injuries, executive (frontal lobe) functioning, and psychoactive substance abuse problems indicates that this stance may be seriously misguided (e.g., Leonard, 2002; Rosenbaum, Hoge, Adelman, & Warnken, 1994; Cohen, Rosenbaum, Kane, Warnken, & Benjamin, 1999). Although many abusive individuals account for their violence in ways that externalize responsibility or excuse the wrongfulness of abusive actions (Dutton, 1986b), it is not clear that psychological explanations of abuse or attention to possible contributing factors at the individual level will exacerbate the tendency to diffuse personal responsibility. In fact, for many abusive clients it may be a step forward to acknowledge the presence of personal problems or difficulties, as this move redirects blame toward the self and away from the victim.

Finally, it is not clear from the feminist perspective how motivation to change is possible other than through the fear of incarceration and other legal punishments. If men batter women to accomplish important personal goals, and this practice is supported and approved by the culture, then why would individuals stop this practice willingly on the basis of education about gender issues? Given that counseling or therapy is not equivalent to coercion and punishment, its role in the change agenda remains consigned to the social and cultural level, despite being directed at the individual level. Even in the absence of highly confrontational intervention techniques, by conveying the message that the client deserves to be punished for his actions and that such actions cannot be explained by personal or psychological factors (other than a desire for power and control), it is not clear how program staff can foster clients' investment in behavior change.

## Social Learning Approaches and the Cognitive-Behavioral Model

Whereas the feminist approach looks for the causes of partner abuse in the society at large, the social learning approach focuses on the interaction of the individual with the social and interpersonal context. The fundamental principles of the social learning model are that (1) aggressive and controlling behaviors are acquired and maintained through classical conditioning, operant conditioning, and observational learning, (2) the processing of social information in partner-violent men is systematically distorted toward negative interpretations of others' behavior and positive interpretations of the outcomes of aggression, and (3) partner-violent individuals have a deficient repertoire of basic relationship skills, including communication and problem solving, that could supplant the use of abusive and controlling behaviors. The social learning model allows for complex, individual learning histories, including the socialization processes discussed by feminist theorists, such that no specific cause is necessarily expected in all cases, yet a number of sources may be common to many cases. The social learning model assumes that abusive and violent behavior patterns can be unlearned and replaced by more adaptive and healthy ways of relating.

The supportive research evidence for the social learning model of partner violence is very extensive. One prime example is the high prevalence of both witnessed and experienced abuse in the childhood histories of partner-violent men (Delsol & Margolin, 2004). These experiences provide an important learning context for the use of violence in the home. In the social-cognitive domain, partner-violent men respond to relationship conflict scenarios with more negative thinking and less self-regulatory thinking than nonviolent counterparts (Eckhardt et al., 1998), and they make more hostile and negative attributions about the causes of negative partner behaviors (Holtzworth-Munroe & Hutchinson, 1993). Finally, abusive individuals display social behavior deficits with respect to interpersonal problem solving and nonhostile communication of feelings and desires (Cordova et al., 1993; Holtzworth-Munroe & Anglin, 1991; Margolin et al., 1988). Thus, while both the feminist and social learning models make extensive use of socialization processes as causes of IPV, the social learning model views these factors as *distal* causes of violence, with distortions in social cognition, behavioral skills deficits, and contextual variables serving as *proximal* factors.

Challenges to the social learning model have derived from the alternative views considered here. Feminist scholars have argued that the social learning model is not sufficiently sensitive to gender issues and that it may not adequately explain the motivations for interpersonal control in relationships. Those advocating a more psychopathological and/or psychodynamic approach have indicated that social learning may provide an overly shallow analysis of the personality problems of abusers, especially their global difficulties with emotional regulation, insecurity, and attachment anxieties (e.g., Dutton, 1998). Most relationship systems theorists would argue that a greater focus on dyadic and multiperson processes is needed to understand and treat abuse, perhaps with less emphasis on individual social information processing and individual learning histories (e.g., Neidig & Friedman, 1984).

Intervention from the social learning perspective emphasizes cognitive restructuring, emotion regulation, and skills training. The cognitive focus is on undermining assumptions and beliefs that help promote and maintain abusive behavior, such as negatively biased attributions about partner behaviors and overvaluation of aggression as a means of solving interpersonal problems. Emotion regulation techniques often focus on reduction of anger arousal through relaxation procedures and cognitive restructuring of anger enhancing thoughts. While there exists ample data supporting the notion that IPV perpetrators present with problems related to anger arousal, anger management interventions are quite controversial (e.g., Gondolf & Russell, 1986). Some state standards prohibit or caution against interventions that are based primarily or exclusively on anger management for court-mandated abusive clients (Austin & Dankwort, 1999; Healey et al., 1998). Opponents of anger management interventions suggest that batterers may use anger control problems (e.g., "I just have a bad temper") as an excuse from taking personal responsibility for their actions. Some have argued that anger-based interventions begin with the presumption that the victim did something wrong to cause the batterer to feel angry.

Behavioral skills training focuses on building relationship skills such as active listening and nonviolent assertiveness. Given that social learning models do not prescribe one specific causal pathway to partner abuse, it seems apparent that interventions should be tailored to the specific needs and deficits of the individual case. Strangely, however, social learning–based interventions in the field thus far have been conducted almost exclusively in groups, as indicated by both the available treatment manuals (e.g., Stordeur & Stille, 1989; Russell, 1995; Wexler, 2000) and research studies (e.g., Dunford, 2000; Morrel et al., 2003; O'Leary, Heyman, & Neidig, 1999; Saunders, 1996).

## Trauma and Psychopathology Approaches

Another group of approaches can be generally categorized under the heading of trauma and psychopathology models, often involving personality trait and attachment explanations. Although there are several versions of these perspectives, the fundamental principles are that (1) partner abuse results from underlying personality dysfunction that usually derives from a history of unresolved trauma, (2) the key features of the abusive personality involve attachment insecurity and mood cycling commonly associated with borderline personality organization, (3) other psychological problems such as antisocial and narcissistic personality, bipolar and other mood disorders, and panic proneness are also commonly associated with partner violence, and (4) there may be different types of abusers with differences in personality and psychopathology. These approaches are not necessarily related to a particular theoretical orientation, but it is common for the proponents to use concepts from psychodynamic, attachment, and biopsychological theories and to use officially recognized diagnostic labels from Axis I and II of the *Diagnostic and Statistical Manual of Mental Disorders* (American Psychiatric Association, 1994).

There is substantial supportive evidence for the trauma and psychopathology perspective. For example, personality disorder characteristics are consistently elevated among partner-violent men, although the majority may not have diagnosable levels of these disorders (Gondolf, 1999; Hamberger & Hastings, 1991; Murphy et al., 1993). Perhaps most notable are antisocial, borderline, and narcissistic features. Childhood trauma histories are also prominent among partner-violent individuals, with about half of clinical sample abusers reporting that they witnessed or experienced abuse in childhood. These experiences are interpreted more broadly within the trauma and psychopathology perspective than within most social learning models. They are thought to alter internal working models of attachment relationships, producing emotional dysregulation often manifested in a cyclical, "Jekyll and Hyde" dynamic in the abusive personality (Dutton, 1998). Studies have supported the hypothesis that abusive men, relative to nonviolent controls, have more disorganized and insecure styles of attachment (Babcock et al., 2000; Holtzworth-Munroe, Stuart, & Hutchinson, 1997), low self-esteem, high depressive affect, and high interpersonal dependency (Maiuro et al., 1988; Murphy et al., 1994).

Challenges to psychopathological models of partner violence derive from the finding that the majority of abusers probably do not have diagnosable mental health disorders (Gondolf, 1999). For example, roughly 15–30% meet the diagnostic criteria for antisocial or borderline personality disorders (Hart et al., 1993), although somewhat more may have subclinical features of these conditions such as borderline personality organization (Dutton, 1998). Likewise, a sizeable number report no serious traumatic history. Thus, these approaches may provide important insight with respect to the severe end of the partner violence continuum (O'Leary, 1993), perhaps reflecting characteristics associated with what Johnson (1995) termed "patriarchal terrorists." However, a focus on psychopathology and trauma may be less informative when it comes to the more normative, lower-level forms of abusive behavior, reflecting what Johnson (1995) termed "common couple violence."

In addition, it remains unclear whether associated psychopathology such as borderline personality organization should be the main focus of treatment rather than the abusive behavior, or whether some type of dual intervention is needed to address both problems. Initial clinical writings have provided a diverse set of recommendations for interventions that may address emotional and psychological difficulties in abusive clients. Examples include a process–psychodynamic group approach that involves structured review of traumatic experiences (Browne, Saunders, & Staecker, 1997), an attachment–psychodynamic approach focused on patterns of insecurity as expressed in the therapeutic relationship (Sonkin & Dutton, 2003), a psychoanalytic psychotherapy approach designed to address core conflictual relationship themes (Cogan & Porcerelli, 2003), and a supportive group approach relying on the principles of client-centered therapy

(Jennings, 1987). However, with the exception of Stosny's (1995) compassion workshop, which has a unique focus on self-regulation, the trauma/psychopathology perspective has not, as yet, produced a predominant conceptual model to guide intervention work nor a core set of intervention techniques.

Although the available research data are quite limited, initial efforts to examine clinical approaches derived from the trauma/psychopathology perspective have shown them to be no less effective than more common group treatments based on power and control or social learning theories. When compared to a feminist cognitive-behavioral group program, process–psychodynamic groups (Browne et al., 1997) produced similar rates of violence cessation with significantly lower dropout from treatment (Saunders, 1996). A supportive group therapy model derived from Jennings's (1987) approach and designed to muster the therapeutic factors of group experiences as outlined by Yalom (1995), was as effective as a group cognitive-behavioral program, with some evidence of greater increases in self-efficacy for abstaining from aggression in the supportive therapy condition (Morrel et al., 2003). In addition, an initial study of Stosny's compassion workshop found somewhat better outcomes when compared to standard agency treatment as usual (Stosny, 1995). Although these initial studies have methodological problems that limit strong conclusions, the results nevertheless suggest that alternative treatment models oriented toward resolution of childhood trauma experiences, promotion of supportive therapeutic group processes, and development of compassion are no less effective than standard group interventions and may be more accepted by abusive clients.

Recently, clinical researchers have begun to experiment with the application to partner-violent men of dialectical behavior therapy, a treatment approach originally developed for borderline personality disorder (Fruzzetti & Levensky, 2000; Waltz, 2003). This approach targets abusive behavior and safety issues, problems in establishing and maintaining the therapeutic relationship, and problems in affect regulation. Initial, uncontrolled case reports appear favorable, but as yet no data are available from controlled outcome studies on the effects of dialectical behavior therapy for partner-violent individuals. Along with the intervention presented in this book, these efforts reflect some of the very first attempts to provide more individualized treatment services for partner-violent individuals.

## Relationship Systems Approaches

One of the earliest approaches described for treatment of partner violence involves working with the dyad in a group setting, using similar principles to those outlined for the treatment of general marital distress, with some adaptations to the specific problem of partner abuse (Neidig & Friedman, 1984). This relationship systems approach was used extensively with military personnel and has been subjected to empirical investigation in recent years. The fundamental principles are that (1) partner abuse is an outgrowth of coercive dyadic exchanges, i.e., escalating mutual conflicts, and (2) both partners are involved in stimulating and maintaining aggressive interactions. Emotional and physical abuse are seen as an extreme form of dyadic conflict, in need of special clinical procedures but not qualitatively different from other, less destructive patterns of relationship conflict.

The supportive evidence for this approach is also quite extensive. First, while a controversial topic, the collective evidence suggests that men and women perpetrate partner IPV at a roughly equal rate (Archer, 2000), although the negative effects in the form of injury, coercion, and fear are considerably more prominent for men's aggression (Stets & Straus, 1990; Cantos et al., 1994; Cascardi et al., 1992). There is also considerable evidence to support a mutual escalation theory of partner violence, deriving from diverse samples including community surveys and marriage therapy clinics. Most notably, the correlation between the levels of aggression reported for two members of a couple are very high, often in the .6 to .7 range, indicating that both members of a couple tend to engage in corresponding rates of aggression. Stated otherwise, if one partner is frequently aggressive, the other partner also tends to be frequently aggressive. Some evidence indicates that self-defense accounts for a good deal of the mutual violence reported by battered women seeking treatment (Saunders, 1988). However, women in a community survey reported a different picture, indicating that they were about as likely as their partners to initiate the physical conflict in the most recent aggressive incident (Stets & Straus, 1990).

The most compelling support for the relationship systems theory derives from studies in which couples are asked to discuss a prominent relationship problem with one another in a controlled, laboratory setting. These interactions are recorded on audio- or videotape and then coded for a range of communication variables, including defensive and hostile communication behaviors. One stereotyped portrait of a battered woman is someone who shrinks from conflict in fear of a violent reprisal, is quick to back down from an argument, and is overly accommodating of the abusive man's need for dominance. However, these studies have revealed that in couples that have experienced husband-to-wife violence, *both partners* engage in more critical, aversive, defensive, and hostile communication behaviors, on average, when compared to partners in distressed, but nonviolent relationships (Cordova et al., 1993; Jacobson et al., 1994; Margolin et al., 1988; Murphy & O'Farrell, 1997). Such patterns were also revealed in a study that had couples describe and then enact a typical conflict in their home while being observed and videotaped by research assistants (Burman et al., 1993). Interestingly, not only do both members in aggressive couples engage in more negative, angry, and coercive communication patterns, they also tend to *reciprocate* negative communication more reliably. That is, when one partner says something critical or nasty, the other partner is much more likely to return a negative comment when compared to nonviolent dyads (Burman et al., 1993; Cordova et al., 1993; Murphy & O'Farrell, 1997). In brief, support for the mutual escalation model is quite extensive, encompassing data on aggressive behavior frequency, mutual partner aggression, and negative dyadic communication in couples with an aggressive husband.

On the other hand, findings on communication and mutual aggression should not be interpreted to mean that victims do not experience fear or traumatic reactions as a result of partner abuse exposure. A recent study found that 82% of the partners of men in an abuser treatment program reported at least one symptom of posttraumatic stress disorder (PTSD) as a function of their partner abuse experiences, with 70% reporting intrusive memories of the abuse, a key re-experiencing symptom. At the pretreatment assessment, about half (52%) of the partners met DSM-IV criteria for the diagnosis of PTSD in response to the male client's abuse. This rate declined to about one-third at the end of the man's scheduled group treatment (32%) and at follow-up 6 months after treatment (29%) (Taft, Murphy, King, DeDeyn, & Musser, in press). Other studies have likewise found high rates of PTSD symptoms among women exposed to partner violence (e.g., Astin, Ogland-Hand, Coleman, & Foy, 1995; Kemp, Rawlings, & Green, 1991). The emerging picture of the domestic violence victim is someone who may have anger and communication problems as well as fear and traumatic stress reactions. Clinically, it is crucial to remember that group averages apply only probabilistically to individual clients, and therefore the level of problems with communication, anger, aggression, and traumatic reactions should be evaluated for each individual case in order to make appropriate treatment recommendations.

Relationship systems interventions for partner abuse are based on a variety of theoretical assumptions drawn from structural and strategic family therapies (e.g., Cook & Franz-Cook, 1984; Stith, Rosen, & McCollum, 2002) and social learning (e.g., Heyman & Neidig, 1997; O'Leary et al., 1999). Despite some diversity in conceptualization of relationship dynamics, these approaches promote joint treatment of both members of the dyad. Approaches based on social learning theory (e.g., Heyman & Neidig, 1997; O'Leary et al., 1999) employ intervention strategies that are often similar to those used in group cognitive-behavioral treatment of abusive men, such as training in time out, listening skills, emotional expression skills, compromise, negotation, and restructuring of anger-enhancing cognition. The implementation and emphasis is quite different, however, focusing on change in both members of the couple and skills practice in the dyadic context. Interventions based on strategic and structural schools of family therapy tend to focus less on skills training and practice and more on establishing healthier boundaries and altering dysfunctional role enactments (e.g., Cook & Franz-Cook, 1984; Stith et al., 2002).

A number of significant objections have been raised about relationship systems approaches to partner violence, including concerns about victim blaming and safety (Bograd, 1984). By claiming that both parties participate in the mutual escalation of conflicts, are relationship systems theorists removing accountability from partner-violent men for their coercive acts and instead shifting responsibility to victims? Likewise, critics have asserted that conjoint interventions may place victims at increased risk for future violent episodes, either because conflicts discussed in session will carry over and escalate outside the consulting room or because conjoint therapy will encourage the victim to remain in the relationship to work things out rather than leaving the abuser. In addition, it can be argued that a gender-neutral systems perspective distorts the experiences of battered women by denying their unequal risk for exposure to coercive domination, isolation from social contacts, fear, physical injuries, and partner homicide.

There are also a number of practical challenges to implementing relationship therapies with partner-violent individuals. First, a sizeable proportion of those referred by the courts for partner violence counseling are no longer together with the victim at the time they present for treatment, so there is no current partner to include in conjoint therapy. Second, given that the criminal justice system normally identifies a perpetrator and victim, efforts to mandate treatment services for victims of violent crime raise important civil liberties issues. Finally, proponents of the conjoint model have an arduous path to market this intervention for court-mandated clients in the United States, given that many states (at least 20) have standards or guidelines that explicitly prohibit couples counseling with partner-violent offenders (Healey et al., 1998).

Despite these practical challenges, the commonsense hypothesis emerging from systems theory is that relationship interventions will be more effective than interventions addressing only one member of the dyad because both members of the couple are learning new relationship skills and altering problematic interactions. An extension of this hypothesis is that separate treatment of the two partners will also be less effective than conjoint treatment, which can intervene more directly into the problematic interaction styles that give rise to violence. Interestingly, these hypotheses have not been supported by empirical studies to date. Two investigations have compared couples group treatment to gender-specific group treatment for couples in which the man has engaged in partner violence. One study solicited voluntary treatment-seeking couples from the community (O'Leary et al., 1999), and the other sampled court-mandated clients (Brannen & Rubin, 1996). In both studies, gender-specific treatment was equally as effective as couples treatment in reducing physical and emotional abuse, with no clear added benefit from conjoint session work. A third study compared group treatment of the abusive man only to couples' group treatment in a sample of U.S. Navy personnel (Dunford, 2000). This study found no differences in outcome between these two treatment models and no better outcomes for either model relative to a minimal-treatment control group. Partner attendance at the conjoint meetings was very low (on average, only two partners attended each group meeting for every five abusive men who attended), suggesting either relatively low investment in treatment by partners in this sample or poor treatment delivery strategies that failed to engage the partners.

On the other hand, the severe cautions put forth by critics of couples' therapy for partner abuse have also received little if any support in the studies to date. The fear that conjoint treatment will enhance women's perception of personal responsibility for their partners' aggressive behavior has not been supported. Conjoint groups have been shown to increase men's perceptions of personal responsibility for their own aggression (O'Leary et al., 1999). There is also no evidence from weekly assessments that the material discussed in conjoint sessions was more likely than material discussed in gender-specific sessions to produce a violent argument outside of the treatment setting (Brannen & Rubin, 1996; O'Leary et al., 1999). One study found that couple arguments related to things discussed in treatment sessions escalated to physical aggression about 2% of the time in both couples' and gender-specific treatments (O'Leary et al., 1999). Although this is a relatively low percentage, nevertheless safeguards should be considered for session content that produces high anger arousal.

In one of the couples' therapy studies, men who had alcohol problems had better outcomes in the dyadic treatment condition as compared to the gender-specific condition (Brannen & Rubin, 1996). This latter result has interesting parallels in research on couples' treatment for individuals with alcohol and drug problems. Behavioral couples' therapy has been shown consistently to produce higher substance-use remission when compared to individual therapy for alcohol-dependent men (e.g., O'Farrell, Cutter, & Floyd, 1985) and drug-dependent men (e.g., Fals-Stewart, Birchler, & O'Farrell, 1996) as well as for drug-dependent women (Winters, Fals-Stewart, O'Farrell, Birchler, & Kelley, 2002). Ongoing relapse-prevention with the couple appears to enhance these effects (O'Farrell, Choquette, & Cutter, 1998). In addition, partner violence is substantially reduced when alcoholic patients attain stable remission of their substance abuse problems (O'Farrell et al., 2003; O'Farrell & Murphy, 1995; O'Farrell, Van Hutton, & Murphy, 1999). Finally, perpetration of partner violence has been found to be lower during the year after substance-use treatment for men who received conjoint couples' therapy in addition to individual and group treatment for drug problems as compared to men who received individual and group treatment only (Fals-Stewart, Kashdan, & O'Farrell, 2002). Taken in sum, these findings suggest that behavioral couples' therapy may be a helpful adjunct to substance-use therapy in reducing partner violence for drug- or alcohol-addicted clients.

## Summary Comments on Treatment Models

In summary, each intervention model for partner-violent individuals has some links to supportive research on the causes and correlates of partner violence. Yet, with the exception of couples' interventions for individuals with alcohol and drug problems, none of the existing treatment models has proven to be more or less effective than other approaches in reducing or ending partner-abusive behavior. Notably, each model has important conceptual limitations, and some also have important practical limitations on their use with court-mandated clients. A more integrative synthesis is needed to address the range of difficulties present among partner-violent clients.

To date, every treatment intervention study for partner-violent cases that we could locate in the published literature has used the group treatment format. As detailed throughout this book, however, partner-violent individuals are a very heterogeneous population with respect to several key clinical variables, including their motivational readiness for treatment, generality of problems with aggressive behavior, underlying personality dynamics, and motivations for engaging in partner aggression. The behaviors and reactions of their intimate partners are also diverse. The group format has a number of well-described benefits (Yalom, 1995), providing clients with an opportunity both to give and receive help and offering the potential for peer influence of individuals who are not responsive to authority figures. Nevertheless, our experience indicates that the group format seriously impedes the clinician's ability to address the specific individual problems and concerns of this heterogeneous and often challenging population. In addition, the influence of group members on one another's change process, although positive in many cases, can be quite negative in others.

## RESEARCH ON TREATMENT EFFECTIVENESS

For scientist practitioners, the most pressing question is whether any of the aforementioned interventions are in fact efficacious in altering the target problem behaviors of physical and emotional abuse. Given that some form of treatment program is a very common postadjudication outcome for partner-abusive individuals, one would expect that there are sufficient data to support this intervention strategy in general and to guide more specific choice of interventions that are best suited for particular cases. However, the available data on the effectiveness of standard group approaches for partner-violent men fail to provide satisfactory answers to the issues. Babcock and colleagues (Babcock & LaTaillade, 2000; Babcock et al., 2004) have summarized the available research on the efficacy of group treatment for partner-violent men using both qualitative and quantitative methods. The literature to date, which includes approximately 20 experimental and quasi-experimental studies, supports several conclusions:

1. Violence recidivism rates are only slightly lower, on average, for individuals who are assigned to group treatment when compared to individuals who are assigned to control groups that receive little or no counseling (Babcock et al., 2004).
2. Roughly two-thirds of cases in control groups who receive only monitoring over a period of approximately one year will *not* reassault as reported by victims (partners).
3. A relatively small proportion of abusive individuals, roughly 5–15% of cases, show very poor response to treatment as reflected in the continuation of frequent and/or severe physical aggression (Dunford, 2000; Gondolf, 2002).
4. No specific treatment approach has been shown convincingly to be more effective in reducing physical or emotional abuse than any other approach in head-to-head comparison studies or average effects across studies of single approaches.
5. Rates of treatment dropout are very high (usually 30–60%) and may be lowered by using methods that promote a collaborative working relationship (Taft, Murphy, Elliott, & Morrel, 2001).
6. Individuals who have serious co-occurring problems with substance abuse and ongoing abuse of alcohol are less responsive to intervention (have higher recidivism rates) than other partner-violent individuals (Fals-Stewart, 2003; Gondolf, 2002; Murphy, Morrel, Elliott, & Neavins, 2003).
7. The severity of the partner violence problem, as indicated by factors such as engagement in severe forms of partner assault, injurious violence, sexual violence, and extensive psychological abuse, predicts

recidivism after treatment (Murphy et al., 2003; Kropp & Hart, 2000). However, predictors of general criminal recidivism (such as psychopathic traits) have not in general predicted postcounseling partner violence recidivism (Gondolf, 2002; Kropp & Hart, 2000; Remington & Murphy, 2001).

8. Process factors that are associated with successful outcome in other areas of psychosocial treatment, such as the collaborative working alliance between therapist and client, group cohesion, and compliance with the assigned tasks of treatment, are associated with better outcomes (lower rates of posttreatment abuse) in group treatment for partner-violent individuals as well (Brown & O'Leary, 2000; Taft et al., 2003).

The effect size of group counseling for partner-violent men, expressed as Cohen's $d$ statistic (i.e., in standard deviation units of difference between treated participants and untreated control groups), has ranged from approximately –0.7 (Harrell, 1991) to 0.7 (Waldo, 1988). The average effect size of treatment derived from true experiments using random assignment to treatment versus control groups, was only around 0.10 (Babcock et al., 2004). This figure translates into a roughly five percentage point decrease in recidivism associated with standard group treatments used in the field. For example, if 40% of the untreated control group members engaged in physical partner aggression during the follow-up period after treatment, the expected average recidivism rate for those who attended group treatment would be about 35%. The most encouraging estimate of treatment effects derived from quasi-experimental studies of cognitive behavioral therapy, most of which compared treatment dropouts to treatment completers, with the average effect size of 0.55 (Babcock et al., 2004). However, this figure almost certainly overestimates the impact of group treatment, as dropouts are more likely to possess a number of characteristics that increase their risk for recidivism independent of treatment exposure, such as low motivation to change, substance-use problems, and a lack of investment in conforming to legal requirements (cf. Jones & Gondolf, 2001).

It may be enlightening to examine these effect sizes relative to other areas of research on psychotherapy and behavior change. The original meta-analyses indicated that, on average, psychotherapy produces effect sizes of about 0.8 to 1.0, many times larger than the effects observed for partner violence counseling programs to date (Lambert & Bergin, 1994). A meta-analysis of well-described behavioral therapies further indicated that the overall effect size could be broken down into nonspecific aspects of treatment (the psychological equivalent of a placebo effect), with the associated $d$ of approximately 0.25, and the specific effects of behavioral therapy procedures, with the associated $d$ of approximately 0.55 (Bowers &

Clum, 1988). In brief, if services for partner-violent men are conceived of as a form of psychosocial therapy, studies to date suggest relatively limited or marginal efficacy.

Nevertheless, the synthesis of quantitative studies on the effects of standard group interventions for domestic violence offenders is not entirely discouraging. First, it should be noted that given the high rate of serious partner violence in the population (around 3–4% of married couples annually; Straus & Gelles, 1990), and given that large numbers of abusive spouses are mandated to counseling, then even a five percentage point reduction in abuse can translate into thousands of prevented incidents per year. Second, there is substantial variation in the effects from different studies, suggesting that there may be meaningful differences among abusive clients or treatments that promote violence reduction. An early study by Waldo (1988), for example, showed effects more in line with traditional psychosocial interventions for other problems. Interestingly, Waldo's intervention was modeled after relationship enhancement approaches developed for the prevention of marital distress, with group sessions focused largely on training in communication skills through careful coaching and repetitive role playing. In another promising early study by Palmer and colleagues (1992), the intervention was a flexible application of cognitive and behavior change principles used in response to the situations and issues brought in by the clients, i.e., with substantial client direction in the treatment process. Finally, given that roughly two-thirds of cases in no-counseling control groups will not reassault during a normal follow-up period, interventions must have strong and specific treatment effects to produce significant results.

A careful analysis of variation in the results of studies conducted thus far raises several hypotheses that are consistent with recent theory and research on the process of treatment involvement and change for abusive clients. Note that these are framed as hypotheses rather than definitive findings at the present time:

1. A "strength-based" emphasis on building positive relationship behaviors, conflict management skills, and responsible family behavior may be more important than an emphasis on deficiencies and negative attitudes.
2. Interventions should provide training and practice to facilitate relationship skill acquisition for behaviors such as active listening, nonabusive self-expression, negotiation, compromise, and problem solving.
3. Interventions that invoke shame or defensiveness in abusive clients are unlikely to achieve desired effects.

4. Interventions that promote a collaborative working alliance between client and therapist will promote greater involvement in treatment, lower dropout, and better outcomes (Taft et al., 2001; 2003).
5. The promotion of a client-directed change process, including a high level of client involvement in setting the goals and agendas for session work, may circumvent negative reactions to direction and authority that are common among partner-violent clients (Musser et al., 2005).

## CASE FACTORS THAT PREDICT TREATMENT OUTCOME

As detailed in the previous chapter, partner-violent individuals form a heterogeneous treatment population. Several key factors predict relatively poor response to standard intervention programs, most notably the severity of the abusive behavior problem and the presence of ongoing substance-abuse issues (e.g., Gondolf, 2002; Murphy et al., 2003). The evidence is less consistent with regard to antisocial or other personality disorder traits, with some studies finding that narcissistic or antisocial traits predict poor treatment response (e.g., Dutton et al., 1997; Hamberger & Hastings, 1990), and other studies finding that antisocial or psychopathic traits do not predict differential response to intervention (Kropp & Hart, 2000; Remington & Murphy, 2001). Recent findings indicate that individuals with antisocial characteristics tend to have lower motivation for behavior change which, in turn, influences their capacity to establish a collaborative working alliance with treatment providers (Taft, Murphy, Musser, & Remington, 2004). Recent studies have provided rather shocking statistics on the association between problematic consumption of alcohol and postcounseling recidivism. In one large scale investigation of four large, urban batterer-treatment programs around the United States, Gondolf (2002) found that when compared to individuals who rarely or never drank alcohol, individuals who drank to excess occasionally were 3.5 times more likely to reassault their partners during the follow-up period, and individuals who were intoxicated nearly every day during the follow-up period were 16 times more likely to reassault their partners. Using weekly diaries gathered from both partners, Fals-Stewart (2003) likewise found that physical assault during the year after batterer counseling was 8 times more likely on days when drinking occurred in contrast to sober days, and severe violence was 20 times more likely to occur on days of heavy drinking in contrast to sober days. It is also very important to keep in mind the simple fact that past behavior predicts future behavior. Individuals who have engaged in relatively more frequent, severe, or injurious violence before treatment are much more likely to engage in violence after treatment (Murphy et al., 2003). Likewise, individuals with an extensive history of violence toward multiple relationship partners should be considered at risk for future violence even if they terminate the current relationship.

In addition to individual difference factors, a number of treatment process factors may be important predictors of outcome. Session attendance quite consistently predicts lower violence recidivism. As noted above, individuals with a stronger working alliance as reported by the therapist have been shown to have lower posttreatment violence as reported by collateral partners. In addition, greater compliance with homework assignments given during cognitive behavioral treatment has also been associated with positive treatment outcomes (Taft et al., 2003).

## THE EFFECTS OF COORDINATED COMMUNITY RESPONSE TO INTIMATE PARTNER VIOLENCE

Psychosocial interventions are part of a community response to intimate partner violence. Although this book promotes a therapeutic approach, treatment is most likely to be effective if supported by important systems in the community context. Motivations for behavior change can be both intrinsic and extrinsic. The perception that abuse is inappropriate can be substantially bolstered through the efforts of a coordinated criminal justice response as well as other important systems in the community such as medical professionals, the clergy, the schools, other mental health providers, and the media. From a behavioral perspective, negative social sanctions can push the individual toward the consideration of personal change.

Most of the social activism and research to date in this arena has focused on the criminal justice response to intimate partner violence. Research results have been complicated and somewhat confusing with respect to the efficacy of criminal justice interventions for partner violence. For example, whereas a well-publicized early study found that arresting and incarcerating individuals reduced the likelihood of partner violence recidivism (Sherman & Berk, 1984), subsequent attempts to replicate these findings showed no overall significant effect of arrest on recidivism. In fact, unemployed individuals had somewhat elevated rates of recidivism in the arrest condition (Schmidt & Sherman, 1993). Likewise, studies of civil protection orders and vigorous prosecution policies have yielded inconclusive findings (Buzawa & Buzawa, 1996).

Nevertheless, there are also studies that point to the added benefit of a coordinated criminal justice response to intimate partner violence. One investigation conducted in Baltimore revealed lower criminal recidivism for partner-violent men who had been more extensively involved in the coordinated intervention system (Murphy, Musser, & Maton, 1998). This study pointed to a cumulative benefit from the combined effects of successful prosecution, probation monitoring, and court-ordered counseling. Unfortunately, however, only a small percentage of cases were exposed to all of these elements of the intervention system. This and other studies decry the need for effective communication between treatment providers and representatives of the court and probation systems, as well as a need for further research on combined effects of legal and psychosocial interventions on partner violence.

# / 5 /

# *Clinical Assessment*
# *of the Abusive Client*

Clinical assessment provides the foundation for case formulation and individualized intervention. The initial assessment should provide a detailed set of hypotheses about the extent and nature of the presenting problems with partner abuse, including information about the situational and contextual cues for abusive behavior, the forms, nature, and extent of abuse, hypothesized interpersonal functions of abuse, and motivation for change. In addition, the initial assessment should provide screening information on common associated problems such as generalized anger and violence, substance abuse, mood disorders, and personality dysfunction. A good assessment of partner-abusive clients requires information from multiple sources, most notably from the identified relationship partner(s) as well as the abusive client. Police reports of violent arrest incidents are also helpful and can usually be obtained from referral sources in court-mandated cases.

This chapter provides a treatment-oriented overview of key areas in need of assessment, key strategies for obtaining the necessary information, and relevant clinical issues. Examples are provided in the subsequent chapter of how assessment information is used to develop a case formulation, prioritize treatment targets, and select intervention strategies. The primary focus is on the clinical interview. Relevant details and suggestions are provided with respect to pencil-and-paper assessments of partner-abusive behavior, and recommendations are made regarding a comprehensive initial assessment of these clients. Special attention is given to the assessment of anger and hostility, as these factors are helpful in formulating targets of intervention. Detailed information on the psychometric properties of available instruments is available in works devoted to the assessment of partner violence (e.g., Rathus & Feindler, 2004), anger and hostility (e.g., Lipkus & Barefoot, 1994; Eckhardt et al., 2004), and marital discord (O'Leary, 1987).

The intervention approach described in this book was developed within the general traditions of CBT. One key element of CBT is behavioral assessment. As outlined by Rathus and Feindler (2004) with respect to partner abuse, the behavioral assessment approach has several unique features. Behavioral assessment tends to prioritize (1) observable behaviors (over inferred characteristics), (2) present and recent events (over historical or developmental factors), (3) environmental and situational determinants of behavior (over intrapsychic determinants), (4) idiographic, individual analysis (over nomothetic, or normative analysis), (5) multiple sources of assessment data (over single-source information from the client), and (6) ongoing or continuous assessment (over one-time assessment).

As with many good ideas, these recommendations can be taken too far. For example, the focus on present versus historical issues should not be used to downplay the importance of learning history in the development of aggressive behavior nor should it be used to avoid a careful and thorough assessment of relevant childhood variables, such as the experience and witnessing of abuse, which can prove very important in understanding and altering abusive relationship schemas. Likewise, the preference for environmental and contextual determinants of behavior over intrapsychic factors and traits needs to be carefully balanced against the need to assess cognitions that promote abuse and the broader, trait-like distortions in interpersonal behavior and self-regulation that are common among abusive clients.

## SPECIAL CONSIDERATIONS: WORKING WITH COURT-MANDATED CLIENTS AND ADDRESSING SAFETY CONCERNS

Before detailing specific assessment methods, it is important to review some issues involved in assessing and treating clients who are court-ordered to attend counseling. Cases referred from criminal court have usually either been found guilty of a criminal offense or have been offered some type of deferred prosecution agreement. If counseling or therapy is ordered as a condition of deferred prosecution, then the prosecutor should move for a trial if the individual does not comply with the order. If counseling is ordered after a guilty verdict, failure to comply usually results in a violation of probation and may place the individual in jeopardy of completing a suspended jail sentence. Legal sanctions for noncompliance with court-mandated counseling vary across jurisdictions. Within jurisdictions, judges and prosecutors may vary in the extent to which they see counseling non-compliance as an issue that warrants a serious response from the court. It is also important to note that criminal prosecution often proceeds without the victim's consent or testimony. Vigorous prosecution strategies have been widely adopted in cases of intimate partner violence due to concerns that abusers may coerce victims not to press charges or testify and in response to the criticism that the legal system has not traditionally treated partner violence as a serious crime.

In some jurisdictions, referrals are also common from civil court proceedings that involve no criminal charges. Typically, these involve a petition by the victim for a civil order of protection, which may be variously called a stay away order or no-contact order. If granted by a judge or magistrate with only the victim present, this order may be called an "ex parte" ("in the absence of the party"). Orders granted solely on the basis of one party's testimony are usually short-term and temporary. The standard of evidence used in civil protection order cases is less stringent than the reasonable doubt standard applied in U.S. criminal law. In many locales, an individual may be recommended or ordered to receive partner violence counseling from a protection order hearing. The violation of a civil protection order is normally treated as a criminal offense. Individuals who fail to comply with a counseling order from a civil court proceeding are usually held in contempt of court, although there may be a specific criminal offense for this situation in some states.

Regardless of the specific referral process, it is incumbent when accepting legal case referrals to establish and maintain good communication with the referring parties. This communication must include an explicit understanding with both the referring party and the client of the types of information that will and will not be shared with the referral source. Appropriate releases of information must be secured from the client. Perhaps most important, the clinician must work to establish clear boundaries between the legal system and treatment and a clear role in this system. The clinician faces a difficult balancing act in establishing a therapeutic alliance with the client while promoting safety for those who may be victimized by the client and ensuring accountability to the referring parties and relevant legal processes. Safety should always be the clinician's number-one concern.

The system of case referral and legal accountability can break down in many ways. Although treatment providers should never place themselves in the role of police or probation officers, and every effort should be made to distinguish treatment from punishment, therapists should also avoid efforts to circumvent legal consequences that clients may face as a result of their abusive actions. It is crucial for therapists to convey a respectful attitude toward judges, prosecutors, probation agents, and other representatives of the legal system. Therapists should make special efforts to understand the other key players in the community intervention system by exploring their roles, responsibilities, and perspectives on the problem of intimate partner violence.

Sensible and effective policies for handling court-referred cases can help promote victim safety and prevent complications in clinical decision making. Clients should be provided with a treatment contract that is written in clear and simple language and that covers confidentiality, attendance and fee policies, communication with victim partners, and communication with referring sources. Clear and reasonable guidelines for session non-attendance are particularly important, as some abusive clients will frequently cancel or fail to attend scheduled sessions and yet perceive themselves to be in compliance with court-mandated counseling because they attend occasionally. Providers should review with referral sources the nature and type of information that they expect to receive on compliance with court-ordered counseling and should develop standard forms or letters to report on treatment compliance.

As representatives of traditional mental health disciplines, providers must uphold high standards for ethical practice, including both the protection of client confidentiality and the duty to protect potential victims of violent clients. In discharging these duties, it is very helpful to establish and maintain contact with the relationship partners of abusive clients. The purpose of such contact includes (1) provision of information regarding shelter, counseling, legal advocacy, and other services available to victims of partner violence in the community, (2) assessment of the client's difficulties from the partner's perspective, (3) provision of information regarding the nature, focus, and scope of services being offered to the abusive client, and (4) provision of safety planning suggestions when appropriate and necessary. Assessment of dangerousness includes gathering of information from the partner about the frequency, severity, extent, and nature of the client's abusive behavior. Such assessment should cover the extent to which the client has ever injured the partner, the partner's level of fear, the availability of weapons, threats of suicide or homicide, and other relevant safety information. Structured danger and risk assessment instruments are discussed later in this chapter.

The therapist should engage in safety planning with victims whose partners pose significant risk. The therapist should inquire whether the victim or potential victim has some place to go in the case of danger or impending abuse and, if necessary, should encourage the victim to gather and hide relevant documents, identification, checks, money, or credit cards, car keys, clothing and personal effects, and similar materials for the children for use in the event of a rapid escape. Partners should be informed about the legal remedies available to them, including civil protection orders and procedures for filing criminal charges. It is very important for treatment providers to establish working relationships with local domestic violence agencies, to be well-informed regarding the services available for victims of domestic violence, and to support the efforts of community organizations that address partner violence. Although in some cases victim outreach can complicate the treatment relationship with abusive clients who deny or minimize their problem behavior, on balance we feel that routine partner contact is a crucial element in ethical practice with this treatment population.

When conducting partner contacts, the treatment provider should be sensitive to the concerns and difficulties often faced by victims of partner violence. Some partners may want little or nothing to do with anyone providing services to the abusive client (for example, after they have separated). Questions may remind them of traumatic experiences that they would rather forget. Other partners may feel coerced by the abusive client into cooperating with treatment providers or may believe that communication with the treatment provider compromises the victim's safety. Some may become highly invested in the abusive partner's treatment or develop unrealistic expectations about change. In addition, it is important for the treatment provider to remember that many victims of partner violence have posttraumatic stress symptoms, substance-abuse problems, depression, or other difficulties that require sensitivity and concern on the treatment provider's part.

The victim partner should be provided with full assurance of confidentiality and informed of the legal exceptions to this policy such as child-abuse reporting. Victim partner information should never be used to confront an abusive client, as this can invoke defensiveness and may stimulate retaliation. However, for intact couples that are living together, we sometimes request permission from the victim partner to discuss specific information or appraisals with the client, usually only after the client has been in treatment for a while and the therapist has had multiple phone contacts with the partner. For example, the partner may report that the client has been making progress in some areas (e.g., stopping conflicts from escalating) but needs to work on other areas (e.g., avoiding discussions of the partner's concerns). In such cases, the therapist may decide to ask the partner whether these impressions can be shared with the client to help shape treatment goals or strategies. In such cases, the therapist should be very clear and explicit with the partner regarding the material that will be shared with the client. As a general rule, the therapist should only ask for such permission if it would add information to help direct treatment and is not likely to stimulate defensiveness in the abusive client. This is most common when the discussion with the partner reveals both evidence of progress and areas in need of further work. When handled effectively by the therapist, such communications tend to strengthen the bond with the client because they provide external validation of the client's efforts and help focus the goals and strategies of treatment on issues that are of direct relevance to the client's relationship.

## ASSESSMENT OF DANGEROUSNESS AND RISK

At the early stages of the assessment process, it is important to conduct a general evaluation of the level of risk and dangerousness presented by each specific client, including an informed conclusion regarding the risk of future violence. This effort should be informed both by our understanding of general violence risk prediction and by recent advances in the specific risk prediction of partner violence. While research over the past 30 years has been somewhat discouraging in terms of how well clinicians are able to predict acts of future violence in general (Monahan & Steadman, 1994), some important conclusions are nevertheless warranted. First, predictions of future violence are best done with empirically derived methods (see Monahan et al., 2001). Objective, actuarial methods of violence prediction have routinely outperformed clinical judgment in study after study, and clinicians would be wise to rely on such methods, rather than intuition, when trying to predict dangerousness in their clients. That said, just as the meteorologist can alter a sunny forecast after noticing rain falling outside the office window, so, too, can the clinician modify specific predictors of future violence by incorporating clinically derived information into risk assessment. Important areas of concern may include direct or indirect threats of harm, recent change in clinical status (e.g., onset of a manic episode), recent unwanted separation, and suicidal thoughts or a history of suicidal behaviors. Second, there is no one single factor that predicts violence. Rather, a variety of objective indicators must be incorporated into a model of violence risk, a strategy exemplified in several recently developed multidimensional tools for predicting general violence, including the HCR-20 (Douglas & Webster, 1999), the Violence Risk Appraisal Guide (VRAG; Harris et al., 1993), and the iterative classification tree (ICT) variables from the MacArthur Risk Assessment group (Monahan et al., 2001).

In the context of judging the likelihood of whether an abusive client will reassault an intimate partner in the near future, three potentially useful IPV prediction instruments exist. The Danger Assessment Instrument (DAI; Campbell, 1986, 1995) is a 15-question interview concerning risk factors for spousal homicide. Items are scored "yes" or "no" with the total number of "yes" responses summed to achieve a total DAI score. While the DAI is typically administered to female partners of abusive clients, the items refer to perpetrator behavior and thus may provide information relating to dangerousness during interviews with abusive clients. The DAI has shown to have fair internal consistency and strong stability coefficients over a one-week period. DAI scores positively correlate with other validated measures of severe violence, and discriminate among samples of women of varying degrees of abuse severity. The Spousal Assault Risk Assessment Guide (SARA; Kropp, Hart, Webster, & Eaves, 1995) is a clinician-completed checklist of 20 risk factors concerning risk for spousal violence. The first 10 items refer to criminal history variables and general violence risk factors (prior assaults, lifestyle instability, substance use, mental illness, homicidal/suicidal ideation), while the second set of 10 items address spousal violence risk factors (frequency and severity of recent assaults, minimization/denial of abuse, violence-endorsing attitudes, weapons use, violations of protective orders). Items are scored on a 0–2 scale to yield a variety of continuous scale scores as well as several critical item indices. While these items can be scored solely on the basis of case/file review, the authors advocate the use of interview-derived information as well. The SARA possesses good psychometric properties and has been shown to discriminate between recidivistic and nonrecidivisitic spouse abusers at the completion of their probationary term (Kropp & Hart, 2000). However, at the current time ongoing studies to evaluate the predictive validity of either the DAI or the SARA using prospective datasets are not yet available in published form.

A third instrument, the Partner Assault Prognostic Scale (PAPS; Murphy et al., 2003) was developed to predict violence recidivism risk for men entering partner violence counseling. The PAPS does not require any specialized training or clinical judgment to administer. It was modeled after Campbell's DAI and questions used in a previous risk prediction study by Weisz, Tolman, and Saunders (2000). The PAPS requires baseline assessment data from both the abusive client and the collateral relationship partner. It contains 17 risk indicators derived from a small number of structured interview items along with factors (e.g., presence of injuries in past six months, history of sexual violence in the relationship, etc.) derived from standard self-report instruments—the Revised Conflict Tactics Scale (Straus et al., 1996) and the Alcohol Use Disorders Identification Test (AUDIT; Babor, de la Fuente, Saunders, & Grant, 1992; Bohn, Babor, & Kranzler, 1995). Initial findings revealed significant prediction of postcounseling physical assault, severe violence, and criminal recidivism. At the current time, the PAPS is recommended for research use, for example as a balancing factor in clinical trials. Further research is needed to validate specific cutoffs for the detection of high-risk cases in clinical practice.

# CLINICAL INTERVIEW

Carefully conducted clinical interviews with the partner-violent individual and the relationship partner are essential in the assessment process. To date, none of the available pencil-and-paper assessment instruments provides sufficient case-specific information on the context in which abuse occurs, the cognitive factors associated with abusive actions, the sources of relationship conflict, the process of conflict escalation, and the short-term and long-term consequences of abusive behavior. Together with structured assessment results, these factors can be used to develop a case formulation that guides the selection and implementation of intervention strategies for the individual. The process of case formulation is described in detail in Chapter 6.

One major clinical task in assessment is to use standardized measures and general concerns along with the idiosyncracies and unique problems of the individual client in order to inform treatment planning. Figure 5.1 presents an outline for a semistructured clinical interview to gather information that is relevant to the case formulation. The interview proceeds by gathering both general information about relationship problems and abusive patterns and specific, detailed information on one or more abusive incidents. Flexibility is required in the clinical assessment of partner-violent individuals, depending on their readiness for change and the extent and nature of their problems with abuse. Some individuals describe an extensive history of abusive acts and have begun to identify patterns and contributing factors. Highly motivated clients who acknowledge serious problems with abuse may be ready to complete all aspects of this clinical interview when they first present for treatment. Others minimize or deny their abuse, report little or no physical aggression, and may resist the interviewers' efforts to obtain relevant details. For these individuals, the clinical assessment of abusive behavior may take place over the course of several sessions that are infused with supportive interventions to enhance motivation to change. Such individuals require considerable encouragement to examine a specific incident that resulted in their referral to treatment or to explore common disagreements or arguments in their relationships. A number of common therapist traps in working with "resistant" clients (i.e., those in early stages of change) are described in Chapter 7, along with strategies to avoid falling into them.

The foremost principle is to promote a collaborative working alliance by meeting the client where he or she is in the change process and gently assisting him or her to move further along in this process. Efforts to rush the exploration of abusive behavior by uncovering the relevant facts and details may alienate hostile clients who blame others for their problem

**FIGURE 5.1.** Functional and descriptive interview to assess abusive behavior.

## GENERAL DIRECTION

The following outline for a semistructured clinical interview is designed to facilitate the development of hypotheses regarding:

1. The contextual and situational cues for abusive behavior.
2. The cognitive antecedents to abusive behavior.
3. The short-term and long-term consequences of abusive behavior.

The clinician must use considerable skill and judgment to gather the relevant information. Some general advice:

1. Provide a high level of empathy and active listening skills.
2. Allow the client to describe events or stories in his or her own terms and preferred style.
3. Whenever possible, use the client's own terms to describe behaviors, situations, and events and avoid terms that the client rejects (words like "violence," "abuse," "batterer," and "therapy" evoke negative reactions in some clients).
4. Look carefully for signs of client resistance or negative reactions; when present, inquire about the client's reactions and address relevant concerns.
5. Empathize with the client's perspective without affirming it as the only way to experience and respond.
6. Gently encourage elaboration and detail through nonverbal gestures and open-ended questions (e.g., "Tell me more about that"; "What was happening before that?"; "What happened after that?").
7. Remember to inquire about background factors in the person's life at the time of abusive incidents, arousal-inducing factors (e.g., stress, other recent problem situations), contextual and situational antecedents, disinhibiting factors (e.g., alcohol, drugs, sleep deprivation, etc.), and consequences, both short- and long-term.
8. Assess cognitive antecedents by asking questions like "What did that mean to you?", "How do you view or interpret what happened?", "What about that was most troubling to you?", "What did you assume your partner was trying to do?", etc. Questions such as "What were you thinking when . . . ?" may confuse clients because they are tapping event-based memories rather than general beliefs and assumptions.

## HANDLING RESISTANCE

Common signs of resistance are the client justifying or defending actions as if being judged by the therapist, skipping over obvious segments of events, punctuating the sequence of events at specific points in order to create a positive impression of self or a negative

*(continued)*

**FIGURE 5.1.** *(page 2 of 5).*

impression of the partner, directly challenging the interviewer, overtly or covertly implying that the interviewer doesn't understand the client's situation, lumping the interviewer together with the criminal justice system or with others that the client feels victimized by, and harboring or expressing concerns about whether the information will be used against the client.

### Some Ways to Address Resistance in the Interview

This depends on the specific nature of the resistance, the context in which it occurs, and the client's style of relating:

- At the outset, clarify confidentiality and note that even though some of the things asked about can be personal or even embarrassing, people often feel relief from getting things off their chests.
- State explicitly that you are not here to place blame or pass judgment. Your job is to help people stay safe from experiencing or causing physical harm, cope with difficult situations in the best ways they can, and improve the quality of their relationships with partners, family members, or other important people in their lives.
- Make it clear that you realize relationships can be very difficult, and other people often do not act the way we think they should. Do not take sides against the client. During the assessment, avoid pointing out others' perspectives unless explicitly asked to do so by the client.
- The fundamental principle here is to get inside the client's head, to find out what is bothering the client; when, how, and why abusive actions occur; and how the client feels about these issues.

### REVIEW OF SITUATION(S)

I usually start by saying something like the following to a court-ordered client. Please use your own style and words to convey similar messages.

*Our first task is to talk about the things that brought you in here. This includes both any events or situations that occurred and, most important, **your** view of these events. Before we start, I want to clarify my role. I am not here to judge you or to place blame. If you were ordered to come here by a court, the only thing that we are required to tell the people who sent you here is whether your involvement in our program is "satisfactory," which means that you are attending the required sessions and paying the required fees. The judges and attorneys recognize that counseling requires a confidential relationship. They know when they send someone here that we won't violate a client's confidence against that person's will, except in the conditions that we already talked about as the limits to confidentiality when you signed the confidentiality forms.*

*Personally, I can't really do much to get you **into** or **out of** trouble for things that have happened in the past. That's really up to you and your attorney if you have one. Attending our program consistently and working with us does help some people resolve their legal*

*(continued)*

**FIGURE 5.1.** *(page 3 of 5).*

*situation. Our job is to provide a place where you can discuss things that are important to you. We will try our best to understand and help. We see it as our job to help you cope with things that may be causing you distress or upset and to help understand things that may have caused you to get into trouble with the law. Our biggest goals are to help people have good relationships with partners and family members and to help them avoid doing things that might get them into further trouble with the law.*

Before proceeding, I discuss these issues and any concerns the client may have with the client. Often this involves an explicit statement that the client may not feel totally comfortable with this arrangement and a request that the client let me know of anything that I can do to help him or her get something positive out of this situation.

*OK, so the place I would like to start is with your reasons for coming in to see me, including any things that have happened that led to your being sent here, your personal reasons for coming in, and anything that you might be interested in getting out of a program like this, if you have thought about that.*

- Inquire about the target incident if there was an arrest, etc.
- If there was no specific target incident, inquire in general about reasons for being referred or seeking services.
- If the client is self-referred, after initial inquiries about reasons for coming in, inquire about the most difficult or worst argument or fight that the client has had in recent months.

Gather information in the following categories by examining one or more situations. The following categories of potentially relevant information are listed in chronological order for clarity. In general, however, the assessment proceeds in a different order, usually beginning with the situation or event and then proceeding backward and forward in time. In other words, it is usually easiest to begin with the client's view of the situation or events, then help the client elaborate the details of the situation, the events that led up to the situation, and the effects and aftermath.

**A. The background context (e.g., life events, daily hassles, stressors, etc., happening around the time of the event)**

*Example questions and prompts:*
- What things were going on in your life around this time?
- Were you experiencing any stress at work? With your family or in-laws?
- Were you or your partner having any problems with money, health, or other important issues?
- Do you recall if anything else happened that day that may have influenced your mood or reactions?

*(continued)*

FIGURE 5.1. *(page 4 of 5)*

## B. The situational cues surrounding the event

*Example questions and prompts:*
- So what happened just before the [argument, fight, incident—try to use the client's own words] began?
- Where were you at the time [in which room]?
- When was it?
- What were you doing before it started? What was your partner [or name] doing?
- Was there something in particular that was said or done that initiated the argument?
- What is your view on how or why this all started?

## C. Any specific things that were said or done that escalated the conflict

*Example questions and prompts:*
- What happened next? What happened then?
- What did you say or do next?
- What did you say or do when your partner did that?
- Go back to when x happened, do you recall what happened just before that?
- Was there something in particular that was said or done that made the [argument] escalate [get worse; become physical; get ugly]?

## D. The client's interpretation of the meaning of the cues and escalating stimuli

*Example questions and prompts:*
- What in particular about that bothered you [or bothered you the most]?
- How did you view what was happening?
- How did you look at what your partner said or did?
- What did that mean to you when . . . [x happened; your partner said x; did x, etc.]?
- What makes that in particular tough to handle?
- People often see things in different ways, depending on their history together . . . I'm wondering how you interpreted what your partner said [or did]?

## E. The extent and severity of aggression

*Example questions and prompts:*
- How bad did the [argument, conflict, fight] get?
- What was the worst thing you did?
- What was the worst thing your partner did?
- What other things did you do?
- How aggressive did you become?
- Did anyone get physically injured, bruised, scraped, or anything like that?
- Did you say things that now, looking back on it, maybe you didn't mean?
- Did you threaten to do things like harm your partner, the children, your self, or your partner's friends or relatives?
- How does your partner view what happened? What do you think your partner would say was the worst thing that happened during this event?

*(continued)*

81

**FIGURE 5.1.** *(page 5 of 5)*

**F. The immediate effects, especially the reactions by the partner and other witnesses to abusive or violent acts, and the client's personal reactions to the event**

*Example questions and prompts*:
- How did your partner react to x [the event or specific acts]?
- What did your partner do afterward?
- Did anyone else see or hear what happened? If so, how did they react? What did they say or do?
- Were the police involved? If so, how did they become involved, and what did they say and do?
- What effect do you think these actions had on your partner?
- What effect do you think these actions had on others who saw or heard what happened?
- How did you feel immediately afterward [or right after doing x]?
- What were your personal reactions to this event?

**G. The longer term "aftermath" of the event, including effects on the partner, witnesses to the event, legal consequences, and personal reactions**

*Example questions and prompts*:
- What effect do you think this event (or other ones like it) have had on:
  Your partner?
  Your relationship?
  Your children?
  Your relatives [or your partner's relatives]?
  Other people who may know what has happened?
- Were there legal consequences, and if so, what are they [probation, suspended jail sentence, fines, lawyer bills, loss time from work, fear of further punishment, etc.]?
- How do you feel personally about this event [or about situations like these]?

behaviors and mistrust the treatment staff. During these early sessions, the therapist must strike a balance among providing supportive empathy, gathering relevant information to formulate the case, and stimulating the client to articulate motivations for change. The primary goal is to help the client articulate the desire for change and meaningful goals for change. The intervention is most likely to succeed if the client is an equal, active, and consenting participant. The vast majority of clients, even hostile and resistant ones, can be engaged in the assessment process after some initial motivational interviewing to empathize with their concerns about being coerced into treatment. As motivations for change come into focus, then the therapist should shift toward gathering the relevant information necessary to specify the targets for behavioral and cognitive change.

In court-ordered cases, it is crucial for the therapist to address some common client wishes and misconceptions before embarking on an extensive assessment process. First, it should be made clear that the therapist cannot exonerate the client in a legal or moral sense. Many clients assume that if they answer the assessments the "right way," they may get out of trouble or influence legal proceedings toward some desired outcome. Assuming that the clinician is not conducting a forensic assessment at the behest of the court or the client's attorney, then this point should be firmly established at the outset. Similarly, it is important to convey a clear separation boundary between therapy and the court system for mandated clients. In our program, we clarify that the judge (and/or probation officers and prosecutors) holds the cards with respect to legal action and prosecution of the client. Therapists are not, and should not be, in a position to determine whether the client goes to jail, pays fines, gets custody or visitation with children, etc. In fact, we try very hard to influence those decisions and processes only through influencing the client's behavior and attitudes. In other words, we try to limit communication with referring agents to general information about whether the client is attending and participating in treatment (with exceptions made for normally required violations of confidentiality for the duty to protect, child abuse, or imminent suicide). The following transcript from a clinician's early introductions with a court-ordered client provides an example of efforts to clarify roles:

"Before we get going, I wanted to give you a little information about my role here and our program's relationship to the court system. The most important thing is that it is *not* my job to get you out of trouble, or to get you into trouble. Those things are up to you and your attorney. It *is* my job to help you look at your situation and to assist you in making changes that you see fit and that may help you to avoid doing things that could get you into trouble in the future. I'm not here to pass judgment on you in any way, and I don't have the power to punish you or to take away punishments that a judge might give. For example, if someone is ordered to come here by a judge, I can't undo that order. I will be happy to provide a letter or attendance sheet acknowledging your participation in our program at your request.

"So what *can* I do? Well, everyone has problems at times getting along with our relationship partners or family members. Sometimes arguments and disagreements get carried away, and things may be said or done that are hurtful or harmful to one another. Sometimes relationships sort of turn sour for reasons we might not fully understand. The bottom line is that working to improve how we relate to our partners can have a lot of benefits for us and for others around us. If our relationships are on track, and we are handling problems effectively, then it is very unlikely that things will get to a point where anyone would feel the need to involve the police or courts.

"So this situation is kind of like a carrot and stick. The courts, judges, and probation agents hold the stick. They're the ones that can punish you, send you to jail, fine you, extend your probation, or take you off probation, and so on. Our program has more of a carrot to offer, ways to help you improve your relationships, to solve problems that come up, manage stress, and other things that we hope will help you feel better about important areas of your life. But a lot of that is really up to you. We find that counseling is like a lot of things in life— the more someone puts into it, the more likely they are to get something out of it."

(The therapist then elicited the client's reactions to these statements, discussed confidentiality and its limits, showed the client an example letter and form that is used to communicate with the courts, and obtained releases of information to talk to the client's partner and the referring source.)

As in behavioral therapies more generally, assessment here is conceptualized as a continuous, ongoing process that both informs and is informed by intervention efforts (Bellack & Hersen, 1998). The initial assessment provides the outlines of a map that will guide intervention efforts. As each new issue or problem is addressed in treatment, further assessment is used to fill in the details for that area of the map. Stated differently, the initial case formulation provides a general set of hypotheses regarding the individual's problems and their potential resolution, and subsequent clinical efforts test and further elaborate these hypotheses. For example, the initial assessment should suggest some general cognitive themes associated with the escalation of relationship hostilities and abuse, such as distorted perceptions of being disrespected or unappreciated by the partner, unrealistic appraisals of threat to the relationship from the partner's associations with friends or relatives, catastrophic thoughts about being controlled by the partner or trapped in the relationship, or a rigid need always to be right or perfect. As intervention moves to address these general cognitive themes, greater detail will emerge to elaborate the specific conditions that elicit problematic thinking, the specific automatic thoughts and interpretive biases that arise, the nature of underlying beliefs or relationship standards that give rise to the problematic thoughts, and the coping strategies used to manage the associated emotional distress. As the therapist begins to educate the client about these problematic thought patterns and assist the client in challenging them, further assessment information emerges on the nature and type of cognitive interventions that are most helpful for this individual.

Given the legal complications, mistrust, and hostile outlook of many abusive clients, it is also occasionally necessary to readminister initial assessments when the client feels motivated to work on a particular area and acknowledges that responses to the initial assessment were altered in an attempt to look good. When this occurs, we try to normalize the process and take a matter-of-fact approach to rectify the problem. For example, the therapist might say something like the following:

> "We find that a lot of people who come here to see us are a little suspicious at first. We ask a whole lot of personal questions and many people worry that their answers might be used against them in some way with their partners or in court. This is a very understandable reaction, because nobody wants to get in more trouble with the law, and a lot of people feel that they weren't treated fairly by the police or court system. After coming here for a while some people think, 'Hey, maybe I can get something out of this counseling.' After they see what this is like, a lot of clients realize that we aren't trying to use this information against them, but we need it to help understand what has happened so we can help them avoid these problems in the future. I have the feeling that your view has kind of changed over the last few weeks. If this is true, it may be helpful for us to go over some of the same questions we asked when you first came here to get some additional information to help us with our work. What do you think about this idea?"

A semistructured clinical interview like that presented in Figure 5.1 covers several important topics that can inform the initial case formulation. Before administering the clinical assessment, it is important to remind the client that there are no right or wrong answers, that the information is kept confidential and will not be shared with others without the client's written permission, and that the information will be used to figure out how best to help the client. If additional services may be required or recommended from the assessment, it is important to inform the client of this fact up front (perhaps by providing some examples) to avoid undermining trust. Unfortunately, such information may in some cases bias responses on assessments of alcohol or drug use or mental health symptoms, again confirming the importance of obtaining information from the relationship partner whenever possible.

In addition to gathering general assessment and screening information, the clinical assessment interview needs to focus in-depth on one or more specific relationship conflicts. One area of inquiry concerns the background and context in which the abusive conflict erupted. Questions involve factors going on in the client's life at the time of the incident, including stressors such as work-related problems, illnesses, or other concerns that may heighten one's background level of arousal or limit one's impulse control. It is important to remember that many abusive incidents involve a confluence of factors such as life stress (e.g., problems at work), serious relationship problems (e.g., the discovery of an affair), and factors that limit impulse control (e.g. substance use). A confluence of factors is particularly likely when aggressive incidents are very rare and seem out of character for the individual client. On the other side of the continuum, aggression may occur with very little apparent stimulation for individuals who have generalized problems with aggression, poor impulse control, and a history of frequent or severe partner abuse.

A second area of inquiry concerns the precipitating conflict that escalated to partner violence. What was the nature or topic of disagreement? How did the conflict or argument begin? Is this a common source of difficulty for the couple, or is it a new or unusual topic? The overwhelming majority of partner violence incidents occur in the immediate context of an argument or disagreement. The nature and thematic content of the disagreement often provide clues to the underlying beliefs that need to be changed in treatment and the relationship skills deficits that need to be remedied. For example, one individual became violent after his wife had taken his truck to a family gathering that he had refused to attend, planning instead to play poker with his buddies. Further examination revealed assumptions about the partner's motives ("she did it so I couldn't go out with my buddies") and justifications for the use of violence ("I need to show her she can't get away with this crap"). In addition, the assessment indicated a seriously problematic history of interactions regarding in-laws and difficulties in compromising and problem solving around issues related to time with extended family and time for personal pursuits.

A third area of inquiry involves the process of conflict escalation. What was happening at the time the argument became physical? Were specific things said or done just prior to the escalation of aggression? How long did the conflict last, and did it progress through predictable phases (e.g., rising voices, insults or name calling, attempts to leave or withdraw met with resistance from the partner, etc.)? Was there a point of no return when the client no longer cared about the consequences of abusive actions? This type of information can be very helpful in finding safety strategies to prevent violence escalation, particularly if there is a period of conflict escalation prior to abusive or violent behaviors that can be used to signal the need for alternative coping methods, such as a brief time-out or appeal to calmer discussion. Some individuals report a clear set of phases for the conflict escalation that can be used to develop a set of coping strategies for each phase that are designed to prevent the escalation to the next one and that form a series of treatment targets.

A fourth area of inquiry, alluded to above, involves the uncovering of automatic thoughts, appraisals, and other cognitions arising during the initiation and escalation of relationship conflict. Clinical methods for eliciting such thoughts are subtle. For example, many clients will be unable to answer the question "What were you thinking when . . . ?" Some respond better to prompts such as "What did that mean to you when that happened?" or "At that time, why did you think your partner did or said that?" Early on in assessment and intervention, it is usually easier to access attributions than other types of cognitions. For example, most clients will offer spontaneous negative attributions about their partner's motives and intentions (e.g., "She does that to piss me off"; "She doesn't want me to see my kid"; etc.). As a general rule, a richer set of cognitive material is revealed by inquiring about clients' beliefs and explanations of relationship events rather than by asking them to reflect on and report specific thoughts that occurred in specific situations, although this latter approach can also be productive in some cases. The therapist often has to infer underlying beliefs and assumptions from the client's view of events.

It is very important not to challenge the client's assumptions too forcefully or directly during the early assessment phase. The therapist is better off simply trying to uncover and understand what the client thinks and feels using open-ended questions and reflective listening. If this is done effectively, without criticism or punitive judgment, clients often spontaneously challenge their own behavior or thinking. If the therapist sounds critical or judgmental by challenging too directly and too soon, most abusive clients will rationalize and defend their problematic thoughts and actions or will clam up rather than reveal their true beliefs. To promote client involvement in the change process, the therapist should begin using cognitive restructuring techniques only after an initial working alliance has been formed (with some agreement on the goals of treatment) and the CBT model has been explained to the client. Early therapist cognitive interventions tend to address the evidence for and against specific assumptions and attributions or the heuristic value of maintaining certain relationship beliefs. These intervention techniques are presented in detail in Chapter 9.

A fifth area of inquiry involves the short-term consequences of the abusive behavior. How did the partner react to specific abusive or aggressive actions? Did the abuse bring about some form of concession or compliance? Did the escalation of aggression cause the partner to stop doing something that the client found aversive? Were other people brought in to the conflict, such as children or in-laws? Often a careful analysis reveals interpersonal functions of aggression that need to be addressed through the development of alternative behaviors or cognitive restructuring. For example, individuals commonly report that physical aggression puts an end to an escalating conflict they feel has become intolerable. Intervention needs to identify and shape alternative strategies to end an escalating conflict, for example by conceding certain points in a disagreement, refusing to talk until the partner stops yelling, or leaving the argument temporarily to calm down and address the relevant concerns.

A sixth area of inquiry in the clinical interview involves the dynamics of influence and control in the relationship. It is important to identify which aspects of the client's relationship problems and abusive behavior are relatively frequent or characteristic behaviors, and which aspects are relatively infrequent or uncharacteristic. Generally speaking, it is more productive to focus interventions on the common, recurrent problem behaviors, as resolution of these difficulties will usually prevent the escalation to more severe and less common problem behaviors. Many clients resist the detailed analysis of an abusive incident that ended up in their being arrested or referred to treatment because they believe that it is a very unusual, isolated incident that will not recur. In some cases, this belief is supported by a long history of nonviolent relationship behavior, whereas in other cases it is not. In either case, one goal of the assessment is to discern how the incident fits into a broader pattern of relationship problems and coercive control. Important to this pursuit is an analysis of the general topics and themes in the relationship conflicts. For example, we use a structured questionnaire that asks the individual to endorse the extent to which different relationship problem areas are difficulties for him or her. It is very important to examine ways in which the violent incident is similar to and different from other relationship conflicts. Was the initial disagreement over a topic that is a common source of relationship distress? Were there factors or behaviors during this event that are common to their conflicts (e.g., one person leaves the situation, threatens to end the relationship, etc.)? Are there common beliefs or assumptions that help escalate negative emotions, for example a specific way of interpreting the partner's actions that pervades the client's relationship difficulties?

## QUESTIONNAIRE MEASURES
## OF PARTNER-ABUSIVE BEHAVIOR

Questionnaire measures provide an efficient addition to an assessment based on the clinical interview, and many have well-documented psychometric properties. With regard to the detection of abuse, research in a marital clinical context has revealed that a brief, pencil-and-paper measure yielded considerably higher detection rates of physical partner aggression when compared to two other assessment methods: (1) a spontaneous list of relationship problems provided by each spouse, and (2) questions about hitting and aggression administered in separate interviews with each spouse (O'Leary, Vivian, & Malone, 1992).

Table 5.1 lists several widely used pencil and paper measures of partner abuse. Some of these measures, such as the Conflict Tactics Scale (CTS; Straus, 1979), can be administered either via pencil-and-paper format or through structured interview. Each of these measures contains a list of abusive acts and asks the respondent to report on the frequency or level of occurrence during some specified time interval. Typically, individuals report on the 12-month period prior to intake, but time frames can be adjusted for various needs. Questionnaire measures provide a quick and handy tool for ongoing assessment and can be administered every week or every month to check for abusive behavior during these briefer intervals of time. In addition to reporting on the frequency of each abusive act in the time frame, it is very helpful to ask whether the behaviors have ever occurred in the relationship if they have not happened in the specific assessment interval.

The use of a relatively objective list of abusive acts has important benefits when compared to subjective interpretations of terms such as "abuse." That is, a respondent need not infer that any particular behavior is abusive in order to respond to the item. Clinical experience reveals that some individuals, in fact, feel that there is nothing wrong with many of the behaviors on these instruments, in particular the various forms of emotional and verbal abuse. Even with the most objective questionnaire items, however, the respondent must make subjective appraisals, for instance whether a particular action was a "hit," a "slap," or a "push." In addition, these instruments typically ask respondents to report on a lengthy interval of time and, therefore, are subject to memory distortions, problems recalling when certain events occurred, and inaccuracies resulting from mental arithmetic in estimating the frequency of various behaviors (e.g., "How often in the past 12 months did your partner call you names?").

The scales use different response formats. Some, such as the CTS and Multidimensional Measure of Emotional Abuse (MMEA), inquire about the numeric frequency of each behavior in the specified assessment interval

TABLE 5.1. Pencil-and-Paper Measures of Partner-Abusive Behaviors

| Measure (total no. of items) | Domains assessed (no. of items per domain) | Citation/availability | Brief comments |
|---|---|---|---|
| Conflict Tactics Scale (CTS-Form RC) (19) | Physical Aggression (9) Psychological Aggression (7) Reasoning (3) | Straus (1979) | Widely used, including U.S. national surveys. Limited assessment of psychological aggression. Several forms and adapted versions available. Has been criticized for ignoring the context, motivations, and impact of aggression. |
| Revised CTS (CTS-2) (39) | Physical Assault (12) Psychological Aggression (8) Sexual Coercion (7) Injury (6) Negotiation (6) | Straus et al. (1996) | Expanded, revised version of CTS. Each subscale contains moderate and severe items. Item order is random. |
| Severity of Violence against Women Scales (46) | Serious Violence (9) Moderate Violence (3) Minor Violence (5) Mild Violence (4) Threats of Serious Violence (7) Threats of Moderate Violence (4) Threats of Mild Violence (4) | Marshall (1992) | Scale construction designed to discriminate the severity of different forms of abuse. Response format may be vague (e.g., "many times"). Excludes most forms of emotional abuse. The violent acts items can be combined into a total score. |

| Instrument (items) | Subscales (items) | Citation | Comments |
|---|---|---|---|
| | Symbolic Violence (4)<br>Sexual Violence (6) | | |
| Abusive Behavior Inventory (30) | Physical Abuse (10)<br>Psychological Abuse (20) | Shepard & Campbell (1992) | Some confusion over items that were moved from the psychological to the physical scales (threats).<br>Designed to be consistent with a feminist analysis of abuse. |
| Measure of Wife Abuse (60) | Physical Abuse (15)<br>Psychological Abuse (15)<br>Verbal Abuse (15)<br>Sexual Abuse (15) | Rodenburg & Fantuzzo (1993) | Assesses severe forms of abuse with graphic terms.<br>Wording is aimed at victims only, but is gender-neutral.<br>Assesses both frequency and impact of abuse. |
| Psychological Maltreatment of Women Inventory (58) | Dominance–Isolation (20)<br>Emotional–Verbal (28) | Tolman (1989) | Extensive list of emotionally abusive acts.<br>Doesn't break down into presumed functions or styles of abusive behavior.<br>Developed for severe domestic abuse samples. |
| Multidimensional Measure of Emotional Abuse (28) | Restrictive Engulfment (7)<br>Hostile Withdrawal (7)<br>Denigration (7)<br>Dominance–Intimidation (7) | Murphy et al. (1999) | Contains distinct factors of emotional abuse.<br>Can be useful in case formulation.<br>Assesses relatively common behaviors. |

[a]Nine items from the PMWI were not included on either of the two subscales, but are included in the total score calculation.

(e.g., 3–5 times; 6–10 times). Others, such as the Psychological Maltreatment of Women Inventory (PMWI) and Severity of Violence Against Women Scales (SVAWS), use response terms such as "rarely," "often," or "many times." Whereas the former instruments are subject to estimation errors, the latter are subject to variations due to the interpretation of response option terms. At any rate, clinicians and researchers should exercise caution in inferring that the responses reflect an exact report of the frequency of abusive behaviors. This having been said, meaningful variation is revealed on these scales with respect to at least three dimensions of abusive behavior—the frequency, severity, and range or variety—and clinical assessment should take each of these dimensions into account.

The most notable criticism of scales such as those outlined in Table 5.1 is that they ignore the context, meaning, and impact of aggressive actions. A partner who pushes a violent spouse in a self-defensive fashion would still be considered physically aggressive on these scales. Likewise, a "grab" from a 120-pound woman yields the same score as "grab" from a 250-pound man. The logical answer to these valid criticisms has been to include additional questions, either on the questionnaire or through a follow-up interview, to assess these other features of abuse, including the conditions under which it occurs and its physical and emotional consequences (Straus, 1990).

Research on the psychometric properties of these pencil-and-paper measures of partner abuse has yielded some interesting findings. First, these instruments in general appear to have adequate internal consistency reliability (Straus, 1990). In addition, the original CTS had high reproducibility as a Guttman scale (Straus, 1979). The CTS items were ordered in severity such that individuals were very unlikely to indicate engaging in an aggressive behavior further up the scale unless they had endorsed all of the items lower down on the scale. For example, few individuals report having beaten up their partner if they haven't already reported having pushed, grabbed, or shoved the partner, thrown things, etc. Straus (1979) also reported pretty good convergence between college students' reports of their parents partner aggression on the CTS and parents' own reports. Pencil-and-paper measures have proven to be quite helpful in detecting partner abuse in samples that were not specifically referred for partner violence treatment (e.g., O'Leary et al., 1992) and in demonstrating a broad range of correlations with abuse in community samples (e.g., Magdol et al., 1998; Straus & Gelles, 1990).

Recent research has suggested that the agreement between spouses' reports on the CTS is low after correcting for chance agreement and that this poor inter-reporter concordance threatens the validity of pencil-and-paper measures of partner aggression (Schafer, Caetano, & Clark, 2002). A review of relevant studies suggests that caution is warranted in examining or combining abuse reports from clients and collateral partners. Disagreement may be particularly common in clinical settings where one or both individuals perceive some type of social or legal benefit from minimizing reports of abusive behavior. However, considerable interspousal agreement beyond chance has been found in studies to date (e.g., Jouriles & O'Leary, 1985; Szinovacz, 1983), and follow-up studies indicate that abusive clients sometimes reveal recidivist violence that collateral partners do not reveal (Gondolf, 1997). The most conservative approach for clinical practice and research is to err on the side of caution and safety by assuming that any partner's positive endorsement of abuse is valid and, where disagreement is found, to use the higher report.

## SELF-MONITORING

A daily record of situations, emotions, thoughts, and actions can provide an important adjunct to assessments administered within the clinic setting. Self-monitoring serves several important purposes that help determine when it should be used by the clinician. The first is in tracking the frequency and timing of specific behaviors or events that may be overlooked or distorted on retrospective reports. For example, clients in distressed relationships will often underestimate the frequency of positive or neutral interactions with the partner. Some clients may underestimate their use of critical or hostile comments toward family members. Daily recordings can be used to get a more accurate accounting of such events, which in turn can be helpful in directing the client's attention toward problem behaviors or in altering the client's appraisal of the strengths and weaknesses of relationships. A second purpose is to track changes in the frequency of certain relationship events or problem behaviors over time. For example, it may be very helpful to have the client record for two to three weeks at the outset of treatment the frequency of angry, hostile, or critical interactions with the partner and the client's use of verbally or psychologically abusive behaviors (using a standard checklist or one developed specifically with the client and targeted toward common problem behaviors). Reassessments can then be conducted later in treatment to determine how much the weekly frequency of negative relationship interactions has declined and to illustrate areas in need of continued change. A third purpose is to assess certain behaviors or events that are more accessible "on line"—close in time to when they occur—and less accessible in the clinic setting. Notable examples are the automatic thoughts associated with escalation of anger or other negative emotions and the "softer" emotions such as hurt feelings, fear, or sadness that are often covered up by anger. Ongoing self-monitoring of such variables may aid not only in the assessment of targets for change, but also serve as an intervention to stimulate self-regulation by enhancing the client's ability to track and challenge problematic thoughts or to reduce anger by labeling and experiencing a broader range of emotions often associated with anger reactions.

From a clinical perspective, clients with problems related to aggression, anger, and hostility often lack a clear sense of the functional relationships between situational cues and the experiential and behavioral elements of their outbursts (Eckhardt & Dye, 2000). As discussed by social cognition researchers (e.g., Bargh, 1997), ample evidence indicates that preconscious exposure to certain situational cues is sufficient to alter subtly emotion, thought, and behavior (e.g., Bargh, Chen, & Burrows, 1996), although the individual is unable to identify the stimulus conditions that prompted such changes. Thus the use of self-monitoring strategies may help to "de-automatize" the individual's anger arousal tendencies, as the individual works to track the frequency and intensity of anger reactions to naturally occurring events. Although distortion can influence the validity of self-monitoring data, this method usually provides a rich, current sample of affect based on real-life events, rather than post-hoc discussions of past events or reports about general tendencies. Moreover, self-monitoring also provides a transition into application of the coping skills and self-control strategies addressed in treatment sessions and can provide a crucially important bridge between treatment and everyday life.

The target behaviors of self-monitoring should, in general, emerge from the idiographic case formulation in light of some common behavior change goals. The target of self-monitoring may change or expand over the course of treatment as progress is made and new behavior change goals are addressed. Greater complexity can be added over time. For example, the individual may at first simply record specific emotions and the situations in which they occur, subsequently adding tasks to instill a greater differentiation of emotional/physiological, cognitive, and behavioral reactions, to distinguish external and internal prompts for specific emotions and behaviors, and to track covarying conditions (e.g., stress at work, fatigue, hunger, children's behavior, etc.) that may increase the probability of abusive actions. The client and therapist should regularly review the self-monitoring information to abstract themes and issues to address, monitor progress, refine intervention targets, and uncover hidden strengths and resources that might be generalized to other situations. Self-monitoring of anger reactions has been shown to have adequate test–retest reliability over a 10-week period without treatment. Highly angry individuals have been shown through this method to experience more intense, lengthy, and interfering anger than their low-anger peers (Deffenbacher, 1992; Deffenbacher, Demm, & Brandon, 1986; Deffenbacher & Sabadell, 1992; Desnoes & Deffenbacher, 1995). Thus, self-monitoring appears promising in assessing reactions to situational prompts of anger and provides clarity and richness to question-naire responses.

The most common target for self-monitoring involves situations that produce anger and provide risk for physically or emotionally abusive behaviors. We recommend that individuals keep a record of any situations in which they engage in such behaviors or feel compelled to for at least two to four weeks near the beginning of treatment. Obviously, education on the definitions and forms of abuse, particularly emotional abuse, is crucial for this task. A more general record of negative emotions is often helpful for individuals who struggle with general dysphoria and affective dysregula-tion. When the treatment focus is on relationship skills, such as communi-cation and problem solving, the individual can be asked to self-monitor positive behaviors by the partner (this has been called "positive tracking" by marriage therapists; Jacobson & Margolin, 1979) and personal use of specific skills such as active listening or compromise. Most clients appreci-ate and benefit from self-monitoring targets that are not singularly nega-tive, i.e., tasks that include tracking of effective coping and the use of posi-tive skills.

Clinicians should be aware of several useful formats for self-monitoring. Some clients like to keep their records on full-size paper in a three-ring binder. Others prefer a small notebook or notecards that can fit in their purse or pocket. Individuals who have handheld computers (personal data assistants) can be encouraged to use these for self-monitoring tasks by cre-ating memo files with the relevant prompts and using a daily calendar or alarm to signal the need for self-monitoring. Some individuals may prefer to use a personal organizer or calendar book. Digital voice recorders or audio recorders can be used while driving. The prompts either have to be memorized by the client or recorded on a file that can be replayed when necessary (which is easier to do with digital recorders than tape recorders). The bottom line is that the therapist should become familiar with a range of formats and should adapt the self-monitoring task to the clients' life con-text to enhance compliance.

Figure 5.2 provides a basic example of an anger self-monitoring form that we use in our intervention program. This is a very helpful tool for edu-cating the client about the cognitive-behavioral model during early treat-ment sessions. It asks clients to track situations, thoughts, bodily sensa-tions, anger level, other emotions, and actions in order to illustrate the connections among them. In the buzzing confusion of everyday life, most individuals experience all of these things simultaneously and have trouble separating the situation or events from their interpretation of the meaning of the events and their resulting emotional reactions and behavioral responses. This simple technique provides a method to analyze events into their component reactions, highlighting the potential cognitive and behav-

**FIGURE 5.2.** Self-monitoring form for anger.

## DIRECTIONS

This activity involves keeping a diary or record of situations that made you angry, including your thoughts, feelings, and actions. In addition to angry emotions, you can also use this form to keep track of other difficult or stressful situations. The goal is to help you learn more about the things that make you angry or upset, how these situations begin, how anger builds, and how you cope with anger. Keeping an anger log will help you notice patterns that you can change.

Begin by choosing a time when you got angry and go through the following steps. For your first one, think back to a time when your anger got you in trouble, like an arrest or a time when you did or said things that you later regretted. Try to record at least one situation or event each day for 2–3 weeks. If you did not get angry that day, think back to a situation from the past.

1. Write the date and time of the event or situation in the far left column. Give your best guess if you are not sure.
2. Describe the situation in the second column. Where were you? What happened that made you angry?
3. Describe your thoughts in the third column. What were you thinking at the time you first became angry? What thoughts were in your mind as your anger grew stronger? What about this situation made you most upset or angry?
4. Describe your bodily sensations in the fourth column. How did your body feel when you became angry? What sensations did you have?
5. Rate your level of anger in the fifth column. Use a scale from 0 to 100, where 0 is totally calm and 100 is the angriest you have ever been.
6. In the sixth column, list the other emotions you felt. Before or during your anger, did you also feel things like fear, jealousy, disappointment, or hurt?
7. Describe your actions in the last column. What did you do when you first became angry? What did you do once your anger built up to a high level?

**SELF MONITORING FORM FOR ANGER**

| Date/Time | Situation | Thoughts | Bodily Sensations | Anger Level | Other Emotions | Actions |
|---|---|---|---|---|---|---|
| | Where were you? What occurred? | What went through your mind? What about this situation made you most upset or angry? | What bodily feelings did you have (e.g., heart racing, tension in your chest, etc.) | Rate your level of anger on a scale from 0 to 100, where 0 is totally calm and 100 is the angriest you have ever been. | What other feelings did you have? Was anger covering up "softer" feelings like fear or hurt? | What did you do when the situation began? What did you do as you became more angry? |
| | | | | | | |
| | | | | | | |

ioral targets of change. This form presumes that the emotional reactions to angry situations are often complex, involving not simply anger but other emotions as well. The anger log format is particularly helpful for clients who acknowledge difficulties with their anger or temper.

Occasionally, the anger log baffles clients who deny anger or suppress the experience and labeling of angry emotions. They may report that "there was nothing to record this week," or "I didn't get angry at all this week." For such clients, more general self-monitoring strategies focused on negative emotions may be more helpful because they avoid the implication that the client is frequently angry. A good example is the Daily Record of Dysfunctional Thoughts presented in the manual for cognitive therapy of depression (Beck, Rush, Shaw, & Emery, 1979, p. 403). Typically, after a week or two of self-monitoring negative thoughts or emotions, such clients begin to recognize that anger is an important part of their reactions to difficult situations.

It is generally important when using self-monitoring strategies to include alternative or coping thoughts and behaviors as part of the task. Figure 5.3 presents a coping responses form that can be used after the client has been self-monitoring anger situations successfully. This form is useful in the intervention phase of treatment to facilitate self-reflection and the development of nonabusive coping strategies for difficult situations.

The biggest challenge for the clinician in using self-monitoring strategies is to establish and maintain compliance. Compliance with self-monitoring appears to be heavily influenced by when and how it is introduced. If, for example, the busy clinician simply hands the client a self-monitoring form near the end of an early treatment session and asks the client to fill it out during the week, the majority of clients simply will not do it (or will not understand the task). In such cases, it is crucial that the therapist complete one or more examples on the self-monitoring form together with the client in session before asking the client to do this task alone outside of session. For example, the therapist might choose a situation or event that has been discussed in session and record it on the anger self-monitoring form (see Figure 5.2), prompting the client to help provide the material and using the client's own words as much as possible. As a general rule, the client should watch the therapist make a sample entry on the form. Then the therapist should watch the client make an entry on the form (perhaps instructing the client to think out loud while completing the task) before instructing the client to do it outside of session. It may be helpful to make up some sample completed forms or to save copies of completed forms (with permission) from previous clients and use them to illustrate the task.

In addition to explicit instruction in filling out the self-monitoring form, the rationale and use of the information must be carefully and thoroughly explained to the client. The client's explicit agreement should be secured before assigning this task. Once this shared understanding of the purpose and nature of the task is in place, the therapist should anticipate along with the client exactly how and when the self-monitoring is likely to be completed. Will the client fill it out at the end of the day, and if so, when during the evening routine? How will the client be reminded to complete the self-monitoring task? If the client brings the form along during the day, when would be a good time to jot things down? It is a very good learning experience for therapists to engage in self-monitoring tasks themselves and to experiment with different formats and strategies for complying with this assignment (Watson & Tharp, 1997). Given the challenging nature of self-monitoring, the therapist should be prepared for minimal or marginal performance by the client during the first week or two. Therapists should be very encouraging of all client efforts to complete the task. Whenever possible, it is very important each week to discuss with the client examples from the self-monitoring form or, at a minimum, briefly to acknowledge the task completion and note examples for individuals who have been complying with the task for many weeks. These discussions not only reinforce the client's self-monitoring behavior, but they facilitate generalization of the therapeutic work to the natural environment. Finally, the therapist should be prepared to troubleshoot with the client any difficulties or problems in completing the task, as the initial plan for when and how to complete the self-monitoring often falls through. Changes in assessment format, revisiting of the value of the task, or other supportive strategies to encourage self-monitoring often pay off in the long run.

The other main factor to consider in the use of self-monitoring assessments is timing. There are at least two good times to introduce this task. One is when the client is contemplating the need for change; the task can raise awareness of the problem and enhance focus on the targets for change. A second good time is when the client has accepted and articulated the desire for change. Self-monitoring can seem like a tedious and time-consuming task, and therefore successful compliance usually requires some motivation toward self-understanding or behavior change. In general, it is better to delay the use of self-monitoring by a week or two until the client is more "on board" than to assign this task and have the client fail to comply, do a half-hearted job, or comply begrudgingly without obtaining intrinsic benefit from the task.

As a final note, it is very important not to overwhelm the client with too many self-monitoring tasks at once or with unrealistic expectations about the level of self-monitoring that is possible or even necessary to facilitate treatment progress. We attempt to use some self-monitoring strategies with almost every case, recognizing, however, that not all individuals are willing or able to comply with it.

**FIGURE 5.3.** Coping responses form.

## DIRECTIONS

Coping with anger and difficult situations requires new attitudes and new behaviors. The Coping Response Form is like the Anger Self-Monitoring Form, but it asks you to think about ways to cope in order to change your thoughts and actions.

To fill out a Coping Response Form, choose a time when you got angry and go through the following steps. For your first one, take a situation from one of your anger logs.

1. Record the date and time of the event or situation in the first column.
2. In the second column, note whether the situation could have been avoided or prevented and, if so, how.
3. In the third column, write down some coping thoughts that could replace or limit the angry thoughts. What could you think in this situation to help you stay calmer? Are there different ways to look at the situation that would prevent your anger from escalating?
4. In the fourth column, describe some ways that you might handle feelings other than anger, for example fear, jealousy, disappointment, or hurt. How could you cope with these feelings so that they don't increase your anger?
5. In the fifth column, describe the actions that you could take to cope with this situation effectively. What alternative actions are possible?
6. In the sixth column, describe the likely effects or consequences of handling the situation this way. For excample, how others might respond.

Remember that coping doesn't require perfection. Everyone gets angry and has other bad feelings. It is important to be thoughtful and flexible. Sometimes we think that there is only one right way to handle a difficult situation, only one way to look at it, and only one way to act, but there are really many alternatives to cope with the things that make us angry.

As with the anger self-monitoring form, try to complete one coping responses form every day for 2–3 weeks. If you don't have any angry situations that day, use one from your anger self-monitoring forms.

## COPING RESPONSES FORM

| Date / Time | Situation | Alternative Thoughts | Coping with Other Emotions | Alternative Actions | Effects and Consequences |
|---|---|---|---|---|---|
| | Could you have avoided or prevented this situation from occurring? If so, how? | What could you think in this situation to help you stay calmer? What are some different ways to view this situation or event? | How could you cope with other feelings (such as fear, hurt, jealousy, etc.) that came up? | What are some ways to handle the situation? What would be a good way to cope or a constructive course of action? | What might be the effects of handling the situation in this way? |
| | | | | | |

## ASSESSMENT OF ANGER AND HOSTILITY

As discussed in the preceding chapters, the role of anger in partner violence is a controversial issue, with some experts asserting that anger is an important predictor of general violence (Monahan et al., 2001) or is an important cue for abusive behavior and a key treatment target (e.g., Barbour et al., 1998; Boyle & Vivian, 1996; Maiuro et al., 1988; Sonkin, Martin, & Walker, 1985), and others asserting that anger is an excuse to delimit personal responsibility for violent acts and a misguided target of treatment (e.g., Gondolf & Russell, 1986). Ultimately, this controversy raises empirical questions that must be answered through careful assessment and investigation. Although the evidence thus far indicates that problems with anger and hostility are strongly correlated with partner violence (reviewed by Norlander & Eckhardt, 2005), the efficacy of anger management interventions in reducing partner violence remains less clear in research to date. By emphasizing an individualized approach that targets key contributing factors in each case, the current intervention model is consistent with cognitive-behavioral anger management approaches and borrows from these interventions. The treatment of dysregulated anger responses is therefore seen as a useful and often necessary component of intervention, but not as a sufficient intervention in and of itself. Careful assessment of the nature and extent of anger problems for each individual helps focus the choice of treatment strategies. With that in mind, the following material provides guidance on the assessment of anger and hostility, including the definition of relevant constructs and the psychometric adequacy of available assessment instruments and methods.

Historically, hostility has been regarded as an attitudinal construct. The standard definition of hostility is often credited to Buss (1961), who regarded the construct as an attitude that involves the dislike and negative evaluation of others. Similarly, Berkowitz (1993) defined hostility as "a negative attitude toward one or more people that is reflected in a decidedly unfavorable judgment of the target" (p. 21), and Spielberger (1988) stated that it is "a complex set of feelings and attitudes that motivate aggressive and often vindictive behavior" (p. 6). In a review of research examining psychosocial risk factors for cardiovascular diseases, Smith (1994) defined hostility as a cognitive trait that indicates "a devaluation of the worth and motives of others, an expectation that others are likely sources of wrong-doing, a relational view of being in opposition toward others, and a desire to inflict harm or see others harmed" (p. 26). Thus, the central features distinctive to the hostility construct involve the cognitive variables of cynicism (believing that others are selfishly motivated), mistrust (an overgeneralization that others will be hurtful and intentionally provoking), and denigration (evaluating others as dishonest, ugly, mean, and nonsocial) (Miller,

Smith, Turner, Guijarro, & Hallet, 1996). While one would expect an individual who maintains this attitudinal set to experience frequent episodes of anger, the angry affect appears to be a consequence of the prior hostile cognitions. By implication, intervention would need to alter the hostile cognitive style to reduce the concomitant anger reaction and resultant aggressive behaviors.

Anger has typically been defined according to its subjective, phenomenological qualities. For example, Spielberger and colleagues defined anger as "an emotional state that consists of feelings that vary in intensity, from mild irritation or annoyance to intense fury and rage" (Spielberger, Jacobs, Russell, & Crane, 1983, p. 16). However, while this definition makes clear the nature of how subjective labeling can clarify negative arousal states, it does not sufficiently address the constellation of events that occur during the experience of anger. Thus, we must also consider the full range of anger-related events that occur congruently with the individual's subjective label of "anger." Current definitions therefore regard anger as a multidimensional construct consisting of *physiological* (sympathetic arousal, hormone/neurotransmitter function), *cognitive* (irrational beliefs, automatic thoughts, inflammatory imagery), *phenomenological* (subjective awareness and labeling of angry feelings), and *behavioral* (facial expressions, verbal/behavioral anger expression strategies) variables (Berkowitz, 1993; Deffenbacher, 1994; Eckhardt & Deffenbacher, 1995; Kassinove & Sukhodolsky, 1995).

A critical issue to consider at the outset is whether the assessment format allows for the complete and accurate measurement of a given theoretical construct. Thus, assessment of a multidimensional construct such as anger would involve a thorough battery of measurements regarding subjective feeling states, cognitive processes, physiological reactions, and expressive behaviors. For example, while assessing anger via questionnaire can provide a direct assessment of subjective feeling states, it can only provide an indirect assessment of other response domains. Nevertheless, the assessment of anger and hostility is dominated by paper-and-pencil endorsement methods.

## Self-Report Hostility Questionnaires

As a group, most paper-and-pencil measures of hostility suffer from inadequate construct validity and a host of psychometric problems. For example, the most frequently used measure of hostility, the Buss–Durkee Hostility Inventory (BDHI; Buss & Durkee, 1957), is a 75-item logically derived, true–false scale comprising eight subscales: Assault, Indirect Hostility, Verbal Hostility, Irritability, Negativism, Resentment, Suspicion, and Guilt. However, numerous reviews of the BDHI have indicated that it contains numerous psychometric problems, inconsistent factor structure, and a lack of clarity about the construct(s) being assessed. Similar criticisms have also been directed toward other commonly used hostility measures (Eckhardt & Norlander, in press), such as the Cook–Medley Hostility Scale (Cook & Medley, 1954) and the Hostility and Direction of Hostility Questionnaire (HDHQ; Caine, Foulds, & Hope, 1967).

The most promising hostility scale is an updated version of the BDHI, the Aggression Questionnaire (AQ; Buss & Perry, 1992). The AQ consists of four scales that assess Anger, Hostility, Verbal Aggression, and Physical Aggression. Data by the scale developers and other researchers indicate that the four scales of the AQ have moderate to high internal consistency estimates, and excellent stability coefficients over a seven-month period (Harris, 1997). However, confirmatory factor analyses indicated that the hypothesized four-factor model did not fit the data in an offender population. A two-factor model showed a stronger fit, which consisted of a physical aggression–anger factor plus a second verbal aggression–hostility factor (Williams, Boyd, Cascardi, & Poythress, 1996). High correlations were also reported between the AQ and other measures of anger, aggression, and hostility (Harris, 1997; Williams et al., 1996). An eight-item short form of the AQ has also been developed (Gidron, Davidson, & Ilia, 2001) comprising the two items from each AQ scale having the highest item–subscale total correlation. The resulting brief subscales correlated strongly with the full length AQ and were significantly correlated with Cook-Medley Hostility Scale scores, reckless driving, and coronary artery disease severity. In summary, the AQ is a very promising scale in terms of psychometric adequacy, conceptual clarity, and practical utility, although the distinction between hostility as a cognitive style and other aspects of aggressive responding remains in some question.

## Self-Report Anger Questionnaires

As was the case with hostility assessment, self-report endorsement methods also dominate the assessment of anger (for a more general review, see Eckhardt et al., 2004). Ideally, an anger inventory could take one of two forms. First, the scale could be designed to measure the multiple dimensions of the anger construct, with items assessing anger-related cognitive content, self-reported physiological changes, anger coping behaviors, and the subjective labeling of internal arousal states. A second option would be to design the scale so that it specifically targets a particular dimension of the anger construct. Most currently used scales are of the multidimensional variety, with three measures showing particular promise.

The recently revised Novaco Anger Scale (NAS) (Novaco, 1994) is a 73-item, two-part instrument (parts A and B). Part A consists of 48 items rated on three-point scales measuring the cognitive, arousal, and behavioral domains of the anger construct. Cognitive subscale items focus on suspiciousness, attention anger cues, and hostile attitudes. Items on the arousal subscale assess duration and intensity of angry feelings and feelings of tension or irritability. Behavioral subscale items focus on impulsive behavior, verbal and physical aggression, and general anger expression strategies. The 25-item Part B scale provides an index of the degree of responsiveness to a variety of anger-provoking situations across five subscales. Initial psychometric and validation data are quite promising (Novaco, 1994). The combined NAS possesses excellent internal consistency estimates (Part A alpha = .95, Part B alpha = .95, combined alpha = .98). In terms of clinical relevance, researchers have reported that the NAS is able to discriminate between samples of individuals referred for anger-management services and nonclinical comparisons with 94% accuracy (Jones, Thomas-Peter, & Trout, 1999). Part B of the NAS was used in the recent MacArthur studies on violence and mental disorders (for a review, see Monahan et al., 2001), which indicated that mentally disordered individuals scoring high on NAS-Part B were twice as likely to have engaged in violent behavior than those with low anger scores.

A second scale that is worth recommending is the State–Trait Anger Expression Inventory, now in its second edition (STAXI-2; Spielberger, 1999). The STAXI-2 is a 57-item measure of the experience and expression of anger designed to assess anger in accordance with state-trait personality theory (1) to assist in understanding the multidimensional components of anger that are distinct from the constructs of hostility and aggression, (2) specifically to differentiate between state and trait anger, and (3) to distinguish the experience of anger from the expression of anger. The STAXI-2 comprises the following scales: the 15-item State Anger Scale (respondents' current emotional state); the 10-item Trait Anger Scale (TAS; frequency of state anger over time and situation); the 8-item Anger Expression/Anger In (the tendency to suppress angry feelings); the 8-item Anger Expression/Anger Out (tendency to express anger outwardly toward individuals or objects through physically or verbally aggressive behavior); and two 8-item Anger Expression/Anger Control scales, with one assessing Anger Control-Out (how a person controls the outward expression of anger) and the other assessing Anger Control-In (how frequently a person lowers anger by trying to calm down or cool off). The STAXI-2 is based on a solid conceptual model and possesses strong psychometric properties across a wide variety of normative groups, thus making it an excellent choice for researchers and clinicians (for reviews see Deffenbacher et al., 1996; Spielberger, 1999).

Finally, the MMPI-2 Anger Scale (ANG; Butcher, Graham, Williams, & Ben-Porath, 1989) consists of 16 content-grouped MMPI-2 items. Estimates of the ANG scale's stability range from .82 to .85 (Butcher et al.,

1989). The ANG scale correlates more strongly with the TAS (Spielberger et al., 1983) than measures of depression and anxiety and appears to assess the outward expression of anger as opposed to anger internalization (Clark, 1994). Additionally, Munley, Bains, Bloem, and Busby (1995) found that individuals with PTSD, who have been suggested to present with notable elevations in anger experience and impaired anger expression (e.g., Chemtob, Novaco, Hamada, & Gross, 1997), scored significantly higher on the ANG than non-PTSD participants. The ANG would appear to be a very useful scale and is in need of further research using diverse participant samples.

## Assessing Anger in the Clinical Setting

As discussed above, assessment of an individual's anger is best done when the individual feels angry, and such a strategy may also be applied within a treatment session with at least some angry clients. This suggests that, in addition to using self-report instruments, some type of idiographic role-play technique (the clinician taking on the role of anger instigator) or anger memory induction (having the client think of and realistically re-experience his or her angriest memory) can provide the appropriate context during which a more thorough and context-relevant assessment of anger can be conducted. The point here is not deliberately to provoke and attack an angry client, for indeed such a strategy could be potentially counter-therapeutic if not dangerous for all involved. Rather, the key in this context is sufficiently to activate memory structures, attitudes, beliefs, and feelings involved in the anger experience so that the client may report more realistic triggers and maintenance factors that can be incorporated into treatment. Such factors may seem more real to clients and may prove more clinically useful than those elicited during a relatively cold and sterile questionnaire assessment of anger and hostility.

## COMPONENTS OF A COMPREHENSIVE INITIAL ASSESSMENT FOR PARTNER-ABUSIVE CLIENTS

Table 5.2 lists a number of target areas for an initial assessment of partner-abusive clients. These include a detailed analysis of the abusive behavior, problems with anger and generalized violence, the broader relationship context, psychological disorders and symptoms that are common among abuse perpetrators, attitudes about violence and gender, trauma history, and organic/physiological factors that may influence impulse control. A good, logical approach is to assess the presenting problem with abuse, closely related problems with generalized violence and anger, and the rela-

**TABLE 5.2. Target Areas for a Comprehensive Assessment of Partner-Abusive Individuals**

I. Violent and abusive behavior

    A. Types of abuse and violence
- Physical assault
- Psychological/emotional abuse
- Sexual coercion and violence
- Abuse of children
- Generalized violence outside the family

    B. Dimension of Abuse
- Frequency
- Severity
- Injuries
- Contextual cues
- Interpersonal consequences

    C. Dangerousness
- Access to weapons
- Threats of homicide or suicide
- Violent fantasies
- Stability and change in clinical state
- Separation/relationship status

    D. Sources of data
- Client self-report
- Reports from collateral partner(s)
- Official reports (arrest report or charging documents; criminal history)

II. Relationship quality and distress

    A. Global relationship adjustment

    B. Problem areas in the relationship

    C. Dyadic commitment

    D. Communication skills
- Listening skills
- Expressive skills
- Assertiveness skills
- Negotiation and compromise
- Problem solving

III. Contributing factors

    A. Anger problems
- Trait/general anger
- Anger control skills and strategies
- Angry cognitions

    B. Use and abuse of alcohol and other drugs
- Quantity/frequency of consumption
- Co-occurrence with anger and abuse
- Abuse/dependence symptoms

*(continued)*

**TABLE 5.2.** *(continued)*

---

   C. Psychological disorders associated with affect dysregulation and violence
- Antisocial personality disorder
- Borderline personality disorder
- Bipolar disorder
- Psychotic symptoms

   D. Attitudes and beliefs
- Justifications for partner abuse
- Perceived acceptability of violence
- Gender-role attitudes

   E. Organic/psychophysiological factors
- Head injury
- Seizure disorders
- Lead paint exposure

IV. Other clinical issues

   A. Trauma history
- Witnessed abuse in childhood
- Childhood experiences of abuse or neglect
- Other traumatic exposures (e.g., violent victimization, combat)

   B. Personality traits
- Obsessive–compulsive personality features
- Narcissism
- Need and desire for control

   C. Anxiety symptoms
- Panic attacks
- Social anxiety
- Generalized anxiety

   D. Jealousy and attachment insecurity

   E. Depression and suicidal ideation

---

tionship context in considerable detail for all cases. Screening instruments and strategies can be used for associated problems and issues and followed up with more extensive assessments using a fairly low screening threshold. For example, if both the client and collateral partner report that the client does not drink or use drugs, then it is pointless to administer a set of instruments assessing the negative consequences of substance use, dependence symptoms, and so on. Conversely, clients who occasionally binge drink or use illegal drugs should have a more detailed assessment of these issues to determine whether they are associated with the presenting problem of partner abuse or with other relationship or life difficulties. If the client reports no suicidal thoughts and no recent periods of depressed mood or loss of interest and pleasure in normally desirable activities, then it is probably not necessary to administer a lengthy assessment of depressive symptoms.

At a minimum, we recommend that all clients complete a comprehensive clinical interview focused on the presenting problems and other client concerns, along with pencil-and-paper measures of physical, emotional, and sexual abuse; anger and hostility; questions about generalized violence outside the family; screening questions for alcohol and drug use; screening questions for mood and psychotic disorders; some questions about childhood experiences with abuse and witnessed violence; a global measure of relationship adjustment such as the Dyadic Adjustment Scale (e.g., Spanier, 1976); and a checklist of relationship problems (e.g., Riggs, 1993).

Some example screening instruments that we have found useful in working with partner-abusive clients include the AUDIT (Bohn et al., 1995) and screening questions from the Structured Clinical Interview for DSM-IV (SCID-IV; First, Spitzer, Gibbon, & Williams, 1996) pertaining to alcohol problems, drug problems, psychotic symptoms, bipolar disorder, major depressive disorder, and various anxiety conditions. The Millon Clinical Multiaxial Inventory (MCMI-III; Millon, 1994) is a commonly used instrument with partner-abusive clients (Hamberger & Hastings, 1991; Murphy et al., 1993). Although there is no single profile that characterizes abusive clients, the MCMI can be helpful in screening for personality disorder characteristics and symptoms of psychotic, mood, and anxiety disorders and may be useful in detecting subgroups of abusive clients (Hamberger et al., 1996; White & Gondolf, 2000).

Attitudes toward wife beating can be assessed using a measure developed by Dan Saunders and colleagues (1987). This inventory contains five subscales assessing the idea that wife beating is justified, wives get things out of being beaten, help should be given to battered women, the offender should be punished, and the offender is responsible. Many of the items tap into especially pernicious attitudes that can seriously impede treatment engagement, such as the belief that women want to be beaten. Although there is no widely used measure of attitudes toward aggression and violence, the acceptance of partner violence has been shown to correlate with actual perpetration of partner violence (Riggs & O'Leary, 1996; see Eckhardt & Dye, 2000, for a review). Most researchers who have studied this issue have used brief questionnaires that ask the extent to which partner aggression is ever justified and whether it is ever effective (Riggs & O'Leary, 1996; Stets & Pirog-Good, 1987).

More general attitudes toward women and gender roles are assessed by a wide array of pencil-and-paper measures (Beere, 1990). Of apparent relevance to partner-violent individuals are the Sexist Attitudes Toward Women Scale (Benson & Vincent, 1980), the Hostility Toward Women Scale (Check, 1985), the Hypermasculinity Scale (Mosher & Sirkin, 1984), and the Rape Myth Acceptance Scale (RMA; Burt, 1980). Although the RMA has not been widely used in research on intimate partner violence, two subscales seem quite relevant, namely adversarial sexual beliefs and acceptance of interpersonal violence. Interestingly, gender-role attitudes in general tend not to distinguish partner-violent men from nonviolent control groups in case-control studies (see Eckhardt & Dye, 2000, for a review). Some studies, however, indicate that subgroups of partner-violent men characterized by antisocial and/or borderline personality problems endorse more hostile attitudes toward women and stronger beliefs in the acceptability or utility of partner violence when compared to other partner-violent men (Holtzworth-Munroe et al., 2000a; Saunders, 1992).

Of considerable interest in recent years has been the assessment of readiness to change as indicated by the stages and processes of change. Two measures are currently available to assess the stages of change (Levesque, Gelles, & Velicer, 2000; Begun et al., 2003), and recent work has developed a measure of the processes of change in partner violence treatment (Eckhardt et al., 2004). These instruments are helpful in motivational interventions, as they provide clues to the client's stage and readiness for change and potential change strategies that can be explored with the client.

## RECOMMENDING AND MONITORING
## ADJUNCTIVE TREATMENT

As discussed in Chapter 3, there is a notable relationship between the existence of psychological disturbances and intimate partner violence. One possible outcome of initial assessment is the detection of significant psychological difficulties that exceed the typical scope of treatment for partner abuse. We have found it very helpful in managing such cases to distinguish between adjunctive services that are *recommended* and services that are *required* as a condition of participation in abuser treatment. The nature and extent of the client's difficulties are carefully examined in order to make a clinical judgment about whether the individual is unlikely to benefit from treatment for abusive behavior unless the other condition is also addressed. In our experience, if the client has problems such as significant alcohol or drug dependence, bipolar disorder, or psychotic symptoms, then treatment for the abusive behavior is unlikely to be productive unless these other conditions are also effectively treated. Therefore, the safest course of action is to *require* that such clients obtain appropriate adjunctive services as a condition of participation in treatment for partner abuse. For example, for a client who has bipolar I disorder, we would typically require a psychiatric evaluation and compliance with recommended treatment. Efforts would be made to provide and monitor the referral within the context of a collaborative working alliance with the client.

Conversely, some clients present with mental health or behavioral problems that, although in need of treatment, are deemed less likely to impede progress in treatment for abusive behavior. For example, we have treated clients who had social anxiety disorder, generalized anxiety disorder, combat-related PTSD, major depressive disorder, etc. In most such cases, adjunctive treatment is *recommended* (and/or offered within our clinic) but not *required* as a condition of admission into treatment for abusive behavior. Such clients are often more likely to seek treatment for these conditions after they become actively engaged in treatment for abuse and relationship difficulties. In addition, some presenting problems, most notably depression, may be interwoven with relationship difficulties such as separation and rejection. If the depression appears linked to relationship problems or recent separation, is mild to moderate in severity, and suicidal ideation is not prominent, we often wait to see if treatment for abuse and relationship difficulties can bring about improvement in depressive symptoms. For clients who have a more chronic pattern of recurrent, severe depression or significant suicidal ideation, a referral for medication evaluation, additional psychotherapy, and/or crisis sessions are typically offered at the outset, with hospitalization as an option in the most severe cases of suicidal and/or homicidal ideation. Finally, there is evidence that, at least in some cases, certain medications may benefit individuals whose primary presenting problem is impulsive aggression (e.g., Coccaro & Kavoussi, 1997; Hollander et al., 2003). Given that studies of batter typologies have consistently identified a subgroup of men who present with severe and frequent partner violence, it is likely that these men may have more generalized problems with impulsive aggression and, thus, may be good candidates for a medication evaluation referral. While this is not meant to suggest that partner abuse is itself a medical disorder requiring pharmacological intervention, it is ethically important to remain flexible to the potential benefits that other intervention strategies may provide when the client's difficulties suggest the need for different treatment approaches.

In any event, whenever adjunctive services are required rather than recommended, there is an increased risk that the client will not comply with such services and as a result will be denied treatment for abusive behavior. For this reason, we proceed cautiously in making these clinical judgments, and we often revisit recommendations for additional services as treatment for abuse progresses, recognizing that clients may become more open to seeking help over time. Recent research has indicated that help seeking by abusive clients is facilitated by supportive motivational interventions as described in Chapter 7 (Musser et al., 2005).

# / 6 /

# Case Formulation

## THE VALUE OF A GOOD CASE FORMULATION

Although there are many theoretical and technical approaches to clinical intervention, there are two primary means to devise and implement psychological treatments. The first way, which for lack of a better term we have labeled the "cookbook approach," is to devise a specific series of intervention techniques and apply these in a structured, sequential fashion to everyone who has a particular clinical problem. This one-size-fits-all approach characterizes much of the first-generation clinical research on behavioral therapies, with prototype examples such as exposure and ritual prevention therapy for obsessive–compulsive disorder (Foa & Franklin, 2001) and panic control treatment (Craske & Barlow, 2001). Not surprisingly, highly standardized interventions facilitate controlled clinical efficacy trials because the independent variable (i.e., the treatment intervention) can be precisely specified, verified, and replicated. Such interventions also allow clinical investigators to isolate the specific effects of distinct treatment components

The use of highly scripted interventions tends to be very successful when the following conditions are met: (1) the symptom pattern is carefully defined and specified, (2) the clients are motivated to change, (3) the clients do not have other serious disorders or conditions that complicate treatment, (4) previous research and clinical theory has developed a sound formulation of processes that maintain the symptom pattern, and (5) effective strategies have been devised to influence these processes. In fact, if all of these conditions are met, highly specified "cookbook" interventions may outperform more flexible treatments that rely on clinical judgment and individual case planning, particularly if clients receive a higher dose of the effective ingredients of treatment in the highly structured intervention (Schulte, Kuenzel, Pepping, & Schulte-Bahrenberg, 1992).

The second major way to devise and implement effective treatments involves the use of general principles and a set of intervention strategies that are delivered based on a formulation of the individual case being treated. This more individualized approach is very much within the spirit of behavioral and cognitive theories that emphasize that ostensibly similar problem behaviors in different individuals may be associated with unique learning histories, unique patterns of thought and emotion, and unique behavioral functions. For example, two children may act out in the classroom or engage in self-injury for very different reasons, one seeking negative attention from the teacher and the other attempting to avoid unpleasant or difficult tasks. Obviously, a competent intervention should take these behavioral functions into account. Interestingly, whereas the individualized approach characterizes the vast majority of CBT implemented in clinical practice, case formulation has proven to be quite difficult to specify in clinical research (Eifert, Schulte, Zvolensky, Lejuez,& Lau, 1997).

Only in recent years has a newer generation of CBT manuals begun to address cases with highly complex problems and interventions that are tailored to individual needs (e.g., Linehan, 1993a; Persons, 1989). As noted by Wilson (1996), an individualized approach can be implemented in several ways. All of these methods are used in the current treatment manual. The simplest approach is to specify a series of sequential intervention methods, allowing the clinician to decide how much time and effort should be devoted to each module based on client needs and progress. The treatment approach described here does this by specifying an overarching four-phase treatment framework, including strategies to enhance motivation to change in the early phases of treatment. The second approach to individualizing treatment manuals is to provide an independent set of modules that can be selected and adapted to the client's needs, with no clear sequencing. This is done in the current treatment by specifying a flexible set of cognitive and behavioral intervention techniques that can be adapted for use within the distinct phases of intervention. Finally, a third approach involves the specification of a conceptual model and treatment principles that can be implemented flexibly based on an individual case formulation. This most flexible approach characterizes the overall spirit of the current treatment, most notable in the emphasis on assessment and case formulation.

While more flexible than the highly standardized "cookbook," these individualized approaches also have a number of notable limitations. Most obvious is the prospect of "shooting from the hip" with an unsystematic or willy-nilly application of intervention techniques that fail to achieve therapeutic goals (Wilson, 1997). A related limitation is that therapists will only deliver interventions that they personally enjoy or feel comfortable administering, rather than interventions that are most likely to benefit the client. Many effective intervention methods, such as exposure treatments for anxiety and related conditions, are rather tedious to administer. As a result, some therapists might prefer, for example, to engage in exploration of the anxious client's childhood or current interpersonal relationships rather than to implement what is likely to be effective (e.g., exposure techniques). In addition, some therapists find techniques such as role playing uncomfortable. If specified by a standardized treatment manual, these interventions may be more frequently delivered than if left up to the therapist's discretion solely. This cautionary point is supported by research on phobic anxiety conditions that has revealed greater clinical benefits from standardized in vivo exposure therapy as compared to a flexible, clinician-directed intervention (Schulte et al., 1992). The apparent reason for the disparity is that exposure is highly effective for the conditions under investigation, and the clients in the flexible treatment condition received less exposure than did those in the structured "cookbook" condition.

Nevertheless, the case formulation approach can address these limitations by having clear and sound principles of treatment, a sensible strategy for identifying and prioritizing the targets of intervention for each case, a flexible, yet well-specified, set of intervention techniques that can be used to achieve treatment goals, and guidelines regarding clinical case formulation and treatment decision making. Also, it is important to point out that competent delivery of these more flexible treatments may require specialized training that includes treatment delivery with regular feedback. Despite these challenges, flexible approaches are essential for complex clinical problems (such as borderline personality disorder), for multiple, intersecting conditions, and for topographically similar behavioral problems that have distinct behavioral functions. For example, individualized interventions based on a careful functional analysis of problem behaviors have proven highly useful in the treatment of severe behavior disorders in developmentally disabled populations (Scotti, Evans, Meyer, & Walker, 1991).[1]

## COGNITIVE BEHAVIORAL CASE FORMULATION

### Conceptual Background

The approach to case conceptualization promoted here derives from three sources. The first source is the philosophy and practice of behavioral assessment as outlined in the previous chapter. The second source is the tradition of functional analysis within behavior therapies, in which hypotheses are formulated with regard to the associations among stimuli, responses, and consequences. Functional hypotheses involve an understanding of the conditions under which problem behaviors occur, the nature of the problem behaviors, and the effects or consequences that maintain them. The third and final source derives from the cognitive case conceptualization approach, most notably as described by Persons (1989). This perspective broadens the clinician's focus to include social learning and social information processing, most notably how clients interpret and appraise others' behavior, and the utility and effectiveness of aggressive versus nonaggressive response options.

Recent research in several areas of clinical psychology has revealed that the connections among thoughts, emotions, and behaviors are complex and reciprocal. In other words, simple, unidirectional conceptualizations in which thoughts cause emotions are outdated and fail to capture the complexity of behaviors such as intimate partner violence. For example, cognitive differences between nonviolent comparison samples and partner-violent men (Eckhardt et al., 1998) are most prominent when the problematic emotional state has been induced. The differences in cognitive distortions between abusive men and nonviolent controls when both groups are in a neutral, resting state are fairly minimal. Yet, after exposure to a laboratory task that invokes anger (e.g., listening to an audio recording of a woman criticizing her husband and imagining that she was their partner), these two groups of individuals display considerable differences in their level of distorted and problematic thinking (Eckhardt et al., 1998). The same pattern, in which cognitive differences are most apparent after induction of the problematic mood, has been found in comparing individuals with and without a history of clinical depression (Gemar, Segal, Sagrati, & Kennedy, 2001; Miranda, Persons, & Byers, 1990).

One implication for clinical practice is that thoughts, feelings, and behaviors form a complex, dynamic system of mutual influence. Thought patterns may be changed directly using techniques such as rational restructuring (Goldfried & Davison, 1994), but also indirectly by altering behaviors that elicit different consequences (e.g., to get a different reaction from one's relationship partner) and a subsequent reappraisal of previous assumptions. For example, an abusive client who believes that his partner simply will not engage in collaborative problem solving might be taught to implement some new strategies for eliciting and encouraging cooperative dialogue. Successful use of such strategies may stimulate a reappraisal of the initial assumption. Alternatively, the therapist might attempt to facilitate reappraisal of this assumption more directly, for example by eliciting from the client a description of situations in which the partner has engaged in cooperative problem solving, by examining evidence that the partner may be open to such efforts, or by helping the client find different explanations for the partner's behaviors (e.g., "She is angry because of the way I have treated her but may respond differently if I show her respect and understanding"). Finally, the therapist might have the client track and analyze changes in this assumption over time, noting the conditions under which he does and does not think the partner is cooperative and how the relevant situational events lead to extreme or distorted interpretations.

Together, these approaches to case conceptualization focus on the idiographic nature of the important, maintaining, and modifiable factors surrounding partner violence. While some factors may be important to consider in the context of IPV (e.g., witnessing interparental violence as a child), they may no longer be factors maintaining current abusive behavior. Similarly, we may find that economic disparities and status differentials within the relationship (e.g., a man's wife earns more and has a higher prestige occupation than he does) are factors that maintain abusive behavior, yet these are rarely modifiable conditions. Instead, the functional analysis and cognitive case conceptualization approach focuses on the contextual, cognitive, and affective dynamics that occur when vulnerable individuals (e.g., men who have witnessed interparental violence) have particular thoughts and affective reactions in particular contexts (e.g., "She probably thinks she's better than me since she has a better job, and that just pisses me off!"). It is those very reactions that are important, maintaining, and modifiable, and the clinician can focus the intervention on cognitive change, calming strategies, marital acceptance, and building better communication skills.

## Common Pitfalls in Case Formulation

A number of pitfalls and mistakes are common in formulation-based intervention. The first pitfall is when clinicians proceed with interventions in the absence of sufficient formulation of the client's difficulties. Under these conditions, treatment often meanders aimlessly. The clinician responds to an ever-shifting set of weekly concerns but has difficulty relating these issues to an underlying organizational formulation of the client's difficulties. The clinician who has a clear formulation of the client's difficulties and change process will generally feel confident and comfortable negotiating an overall agenda for treatment and weekly agendas for each session collaboratively with the client. The ideal situation is when the clinician has a clear understanding of the priorities for treatment and does not force this framework on the client but uses it to establish a collaborative alliance.

A second common pitfall is when the case formulation process is shunted by premature closure. The clinician "has the client all figured out" and inadvertently ignores important components of the assessment. Most common is when the clinician focuses exclusively on formulating the problem behavior (usually in psychopathological terms) but fails to identify the client's motivations to change, strengths, and available supports for the change effort. In the absence of a competent change plan, a thorough analysis of behavioral pathology only produces an expectation of further problems. Competent clinicians expect change while avoiding the frustration that can arise from unrealistic expectations of rapid or complete improvement. This cognitive set parallels the realization that clients are most willing to change in a therapeutic atmosphere of empathy and acceptance (Miller & Rollnick, 2002). This cautionary note is in no way intended to encourage clinicians to ignore crucial disorders, such as bipolar conditions or evidence of psychotic thought processes, but rather to support clinicians' efforts to concentrate on strengths, resources, and the process of change and not purely on client deficiencies and pathologies.

A third pitfall arises when the client does not have a sufficient awareness or appreciation of the therapist's case formulation. In such instances, it appears as if therapist and client are operating on different wavelengths, with different formulations of the relevant treatment issues. With abusive clients, this almost invariably takes on a specific form, in which the client believes that the problem belongs to other people, and the therapist believes that the problem belongs to the client. As has been noted elsewhere, angry clients are prone to externalize blame and to have limited personal insight into how they may be causing their present distress. The clinician who rushes to explain the client's problem in terms of self-defeating cognitions (rather than other people the client perceives as annoying) risks damaging the therapeutic alliance by not having a set of agreed-upon treatment goals. The art of explaining a case formulation to a client in clear, empathic, and understandable terms, in a fashion that the client is likely to accept, without appearing critical or judgmental, is among the most important talents of the highly skilled clinician.

A few insights derived from studies of communication and social influence are quite relevant to the process of sharing a case formulation. The first is that people are most likely to accept critical feedback if it is preceded by positive appraisal. Thus, when providing clients with aspects of the case formulation, it is crucial to lead off with some positive feedback, noting things such as the client's positive motivations, efforts to change, personal strengths, and social resources. To be effective, this feedback must be genuine and should never appear contrived. Maintaining a balanced appraisal of the client's strengths and weaknesses is crucial throughout the process of sharing case formulation information. A second important insight is that clients are most likely to embrace change goals or targets that derive from information they have provided or from their own words. The goal here is to promote client feelings of ownership of the change process and responsibility for accomplishing change. Often, the clinician can translate the client's verbalizations into terms that may clarify, focus, or broaden the goals of treatment. Third, clients may be more open to the therapist's formulation if their difficulties are normalized or made understandable (without excusing or rationalizing their problem behaviors). For example, some abusive clients grew up in aversive environments, such as rough neighborhoods where aggression was a highly valued survival skill. For such individuals, "being tough," "not taking any crap from anyone," and "not backing down" promoted social status, social acceptance, or even literal physical survival. Acknowledging the value of these characteristics and behaviors in the context of development often helps the client see how such attitudes and behaviors are destructive in the current life context of intimate and family relationships. Note that this style of presenting a case formulation normalizes the client's problematic tendencies without reinforcing the notion that "this is just the way I am," in which the client expects everyone else to adapt to his problematic interpersonal style.

Fourth, effective understanding of personally relevant information in the case formulation involves both intellectual and emotional processing. Realizing this, the effective clinician fully expects that clients may need to struggle with the case formulation over time, and most will not accept it unquestioningly at the outset of treatment. One therapist described this as an ongoing process of helping the client "connect the dots." This process can require considerable patience, diligence, and a gentle yet firm style of persuasion that allows the client to develop insight into the interconnected patterns of controlling behaviors and associated thoughts and feelings and how they are ultimately destructive to self and others. Even though the patterns may be altogether obvious to the therapist, this "lived experience" is typically much more complex and mysterious to the client and accompanied by all manner of self-esteem–maintaining rationalizations.

Finally, a consistent theme stated throughout this chapter that cannot be stressed enough is that clients are most likely to consider change in an atmosphere of acceptance and empathy. The tension between acceptance and change is one of the fundamental principles of dialectical behavior therapy, which has been used successfully to treat individuals with severe personality disorder (Linehan, 1993a). Following this principle, the therapist must be able to shift fluidly between demonstration of acceptance and promotion of change.

## Specific Guidelines for Case Formulation with Abusive Clients

Figure 6.1 provides guidelines for developing a case formulation that will help direct intervention efforts with abusive clients. It is important to remember that the philosophy and practice of behavioral assessment calls for ongoing formulation as treatment develops. Thus, case formulation is more a process than a specific product (i.e., it is a work in progress). Nevertheless, we have found it very helpful to conduct a case conference on each client after an initial two- to three-session assessment. At the case confer-

**FIGURE 6.1.** Case formulation guidelines.

## PART A: PROBLEM ASSESSMENT

I. Assessment of Abusive Behavior:
   1. Describe the types of physically abusive behavior that the client has engaged in during the course of the relationship, the approximate number of episodes of physical abuse in the past six months, and the nature of any recent abuse.
   2. Describe the nature of emotional/psychological abuse, including the main forms.
   3. Describe the triggers or cues for abusive behaviors—the conditions under which abuse tends to occur.
   4. Describe the short-term effects of abusive behaviors on the partner and on the client (immediate reactions).

II. Relationship Problem List

   List the main areas of conflict and difficulty in the relationship, including topics of disagreement and problematic communication patterns.

III. Other Life Problems and Issues

   List other life difficulties that the client is experiencing (not previously addressed), including work/occupational issues, legal problems, health issues, other emotional/psychological problems, educational/literacy issues, etc.

## PART B: ASSESSMENT OF COGNITIVE FACTORS

1. Identify problematic attributions, assumptions, standards, and beliefs associated with abusive and controlling behavior.
2. Identify problematic attributions, assumptions, standards, and beliefs associated with other relationship difficulties.
3. Identify problematic attributions, assumptions, standards, and beliefs associated with other life problems and issues.

*(continued)*

FIGURE 6.1. *(page 2 of 3)*

## PART C: ASSESSMENT OF STRENGTHS AND RESOURCES

I. Motivations for Change

List any potential motivations for change that the client has indicated. Identify the most important motivations from the client's perspective.

II. Previous Behavior Change Efforts and Successes

Describe any prior efforts that the client has made to change abusive behavior patterns or improve relationship functioning (even if such efforts were only temporarily or partially successful). Also describe any areas of successful behavior change that the client has accomplished in the past, such as quitting smoking, changing or ending drug or alcohol abuse patterns, altering health behaviors such as diet or exercise, changing jobs or careers, or adapting successfully to significant life changes.

III. Positive Relationship Behaviors and Features of the Relationship

Describe aspects of the client's intimate relationship(s) that have been positive or fulfilling, and list positive relationship behaviors or skills possessed by the client.

IV. Social Supports for Change

List currently available or potential sources of social support for the client's change efforts, such as relatives, friends, coworkers or bosses, ministers or faith community members, health care providers, attorneys, probation agents, social service agents, mental health or substance use treatment providers, and any other potential sources of support and assistance in the change effort.

V. Other Life Strengths

List areas of the client's life that are going well, along with personal strengths and resources such as education, employment, hobbies, personal values, personality traits, etc., that support effective functioning.

## PART D: CASE FORMULATION HYPOTHESES

1. Formulate hypotheses about the associations among the various problems identified.
2. Formulate hypotheses about the functions of abusive behavior.
3. Formulate hypotheses about the cognitive themes associated with abusive behavior and other problems.

*(continued)*

**FIGURE 6.1.** *(page 3 of 3)*

**PART E: INTERVENTION TARGET LIST**

1. Develop a list of intervention targets for cognitive change based on themes inherent in the cognitive assessment.
2. Develop a list of intervention targets for behavior change based on the problem assessment and case formulation hypotheses.

**PART F: INTERVENTION STRATEGIES**

1. Develop a list of intervention strategies that may be helpful in achieving each targeted change.
2. Formulate hypotheses about which clinical strategies and techniques are most likely to produce the desired intervention effects in light of the client's:

   a. Interpersonal style

   b. Previous change efforts

   c. Strengths and resources

ence, we review all aspects of the case formulation, identify areas for further inquiry or assessment, and outline an intervention plan. This plan is adapted and refined as treatment develops. It provides a very helpful source of focus and continuity in treatment.

The case formulation is divided into six major categories: (1) problem behaviors, (2) strengths and resources, (3) relevant cognitions, (4) hypotheses, (5) intervention targets, and (6) intervention strategies. The overall process is relatively straightforward. A detailed analysis of problem behaviors, cognitions, and strengths is used to develop hypotheses about the associations among various presenting problems, functions of abusive behavior, and relevant cognitive themes. In turn, these hypotheses guide the formulation of intervention targets and strategies for achieving treatment goals. Thus, the process of hypothesis generation and testing is central to the case formulation approach.

As in scientific inquiry, a good hypothesis is consistent with the existing data and accounts for a broad array of observations. Hypotheses are not facts; rather, they can be disconfirmed by further observation and testing. The development of hypotheses for case formulation also diverges somewhat from scientific inquiry. Whereas most scientific theories are designed to explain the causes of important phenomena, a good case formulation is not evaluated on its ability simply to explain the origin of problems, but rather on its ability to derive effective ways to reduce or eliminate problems. Thus, case formulation is a highly pragmatic endeavor, oriented more toward clinical problem solving than theoretical explanation.

To begin the process of case formulation, we recommend that the clinician systematically answer as many questions as possible from sections A, B, and C in Figure 6.1. Almost invariably, this effort reveals gaps in information and areas for further exploration. As described in detail in the previous chapter, it is crucially important to obtain information from multiple sources to get an adequate understanding of the client's problems. We typically use self-report questionnaire data from the client and a structured phone interview with the relationship partner to supplement the interview information from the client. An example for an actual client is presented in Figure 6.2.

## Clinical Hypothesis Generation

There are three types of hypothesis generation involved in the case formulation method outlined here. The first type is descriptive in nature and involves hypotheses about the connections between various relationship and/or life problems. For example, the client may present a pattern of difficulties at work and in the home involving themes of unfairness, a lack of appreciation, and resentment, which the client then uses to justify intermit-

**FIGURE 6.2.** A sample case formulation.

## PART A: PROBLEM ASSESSMENT

I. Assessment of Abusive Behavior:

1. Describe the types of physically abusive behavior that the client has engaged in during the course of the relationship, the approximate number of episodes of physical abuse in the past 6 months, and the nature of any recent abuse.

The client reports four episodes of physical abuse during the course of their seven-year marriage. Partner corroborates this level of abuse. The most severe incident involved grabbing, punching, and locking the partner in a room when she came home after a three-day drug binge. There has been one incident in the past six months. The client pushed and grabbed his partner during a heated argument.

2. Describe the nature of emotional/psychological abuse, including the main forms.

By both partners' reports, the client engages in high rates of hostile withdrawal. Also, some dominance/intimidation behaviors were reported in the recent past, including hovering over the partner during arguments, threatening to hit or throw things, and some denigrating behaviors (e.g., implied that the partner was stupid). Little or no restrictive engulfment is reported. The client also intimidated and threatened to harm a friend of the partner who he believed was providing her with drugs. The partner complains primarily that the client is unwilling to talk, disengaged from family life, and "sulky."

3. Describe the triggers or cues for abusive behaviors—the conditions under which abuse tends to occur.

By client report, all instances of his physical abuse (except the most recent one) involved attempts to control his partner in reaction to behaviors that he deemed unacceptable. All but one of these incidents occurred while the partner was actively abusing cocaine, PCP, and prescription anxiolytics. The most recent incident occurred after the partner had been in inpatient drug rehab and sober for four months. The client was completely sober during each incident reported. The worst incident of abuse occurred when the partner came home from a three-day drug binge. The client was angered by thoughts about unfairness (e.g., his having to take care of three young sons in her absence), infidelity (e.g., assuming that she had been having sexual relations with other men), money problems (e.g., her emptying their bank account to buy drugs), and frustration over his inability to stop her from using drugs. He verbally berated the partner, accusing her of being a "worthless addict" and a "whore." He slapped her, twisted her arm, threw her on down on the bed, and blocked the door to the bedroom from the outside with a large piece of furniture. She escaped out a window, went to a friend's house, and called the police.

*(continued)*

123

**FIGURE 6.2.** *(page 2 of 7)*

In the most recent incident, he reports that they were arguing about money. She followed him around the house and outside into the yard during the argument, called him worthless, stupid, a bad provider, a bad husband, and an irresponsible father. He claims to have been "shut down," not responding to her verbally. He got into the car, and when she approached, he grabbed her, pushed her away, and hit her with his car door. She injured her ankle and forehead as she fell to the ground, and required medical attention. He drove away and came back late that night.

The partner interview corresponded quite accurately in details about the abusive incidents. The partner is obviously more afraid and intimidated by the client than he realizes. He believes "she wouldn't say those things to me if she was afraid of me."

4. Describe the short-term effects of abusive behaviors on the partner and on the client (immediate reactions).

In early instances, the physical abuse had several presumed short term-effects: (1) keeping the partner from going out of the house to use drugs, (2) "punishing" the partner for her drug use and related behaviors, and (3) reducing the client's frustration and anger level (i.e., he was taking "drastic action" to address this serious problem in his family). Client reports that he was trying to control her, to stop her from "ruining the family." He reports being extremely angry and frustrated (e.g., "I didn't know any other way to handle it, even though I knew what I was doing was wrong"). His partner showed fear in response to the abuse and became more compliant with his demands at times, yet more likely to escape altogether from the house for extended periods of time.

In the most recent incident, the client's physical abuse was in the context of his escape from arguing with the partner and getting away from her physically. He reports wishing that "she would just leave me alone" and that "she would stop arguing all the time."

II. Relationship Problem List
List the main areas of conflict and difficulty in the relationship, including topics of disagreement and problematic communication patterns.

Money (he doesn't make enough to support their family, and her work is sporadic). Emotional closeness/connection (he is emotionally withdrawn and avoidant).

Major problematic communication dynamic appears to be that he feels criticized, he shuts down and withdraws, she continues trying to engage him with negative interactions for a while, then she eventually gives up and leaves him alone (e.g., goes to bed). If he feels the criticism is particularly unfair or if his stress tolerance level is low, he responds by becoming verbally abusive. Otherwise, he is nonresponsive.

III. Other Life Problems and Issues
List other life difficulties that the client is experiencing (not previously addressed), including work/occupational issues, legal problems, health issues, other emotional/psychological problems, educational/literacy issues, etc.

*(continued)*

**FIGURE 6.2.** *(page 3 of 7)*

Financial problems (collection agents, turn-off notices for utilities, threat of eviction from their apartment).

Career choice and work issues (arguments over partner not working consistently, partner complaints about client's level of income).

Arguments about childrearing (client is overly harsh and punitive; partner is overly permissive).

Arguments about extended family (partner wants to allow her sister to stay in the house; client refuses, stating that sister is a bad influence and will promote drug relapse).

## PART B: ASSESSMENT OF COGNITIVE FACTORS

Characterize any prominent cognitions (e.g., attributions, assumptions, beliefs, etc.) associated with abusive and controlling behavior.

Client appears to catastrophize his partner's anger or complaints (e.g., "I can't take this anymore"). He uses all-or-nothing thinking in blaming the partner ("Our problems are all her fault"; "If she wasn't hooked on drugs, we wouldn't have any of these problems") and mind reading ("She blames me for everything"; "She doesn't want to be married to me anymore"). He expresses hopelessness about the relationship ("It will never get any better") and helplessness about his ability to effect change (e.g., "There's nothing I can say to make her stop complaining about me").

## PART C: ASSESSMENT OF STRENGTHS AND RESOURCES

I. Motivations for Change
   List any potential motivations for change that the client has indicated. Identify the most important motivations from the client's perspective.

Client has remorse for his physical and emotional abuse and wants to change this pattern.

Client and partner are very religious and would like to work things out without divorcing if possible.

Client states that he loves his partner.

Client wants "peace and quiet" in the home.

Oldest child is beginning to display behavior problems (aggression) in school.

Client had unstable home life with alcoholic parents and doesn't want to repeat these patterns with his children.

II. Previous Behavior Change Efforts and Successes
   Describe any prior efforts that the client has made to change abusive behavior patterns or improve relationship functioning (even if such efforts were only

*(continued)*

125

**FIGURE 6.2.** *(page 4 of 7)*

temporarily or partially successful). Also describe any areas of successful behavior change that the client has accomplished in the past, such as quitting smoking, changing or ending drug or alcohol abuse patterns, altering health behaviors such as diet or exercise, changing jobs or careers, or adapting successfully to significant life changes.

Client received group counseling three years ago at a different agency for partner abuse. Feels it was not very helpful but has made some efforts to "get away and take time-outs" when they argue. Client has been trying not to engage in verbal arguments and is often successful in refraining from arguing. Is developing some self-control strategies for responding to criticism from partner (but remains highly emotionally reactive to it). Couple attended five sessions of couples counseling with their minister. Client reports this was somewhat helpful but did not give them enough help with solving problems and communicating. Client reports being able to self-initiate behavior change (e.g., interacting more with partner and making a commitment to work on the marriage) but reports difficulty in maintaining changes over time (falls back into withdrawal when he feels criticized or blamed for things).

III. Positive Relationship Behaviors and Features of the Relationship
   Describe aspects of the client's intimate relationship(s) that have been positive or fulfilling, and list positive relationship behaviors or skills possessed by the client.

Client and partner engage in church activities together and have shared interests such as fishing, going to sporting events, bowling, movies, and gardening. They have pleasant conversations approximately one to two times per week. Client reports that the partner is an involved and competent parent when she is not abusing drugs. Partner has been drug- and alcohol-free for the past six months. Client supports these efforts very strongly in principle but doesn't know how to express this support. Client feels that both partners have "strong family values" and want things to work out.

IV. Social Supports for Change
   List currently available or potential sources of social support for the client's change efforts, such as relatives, friends, coworkers or bosses, ministers or faith community members, health care providers, attorneys, probation agents, social service agents, mental health or substance use treatment providers, and any other potential sources of support and assistance in the change effort.

Client and partner are very active in their church and have received support from the church in times of financial stress. Church colleagues and their minister appear to support their efforts to change. Social services has assigned a case worker to the family as a result of the partner's drug offenses. Both spouses have relatives in the area who have provided material assistance in times of need. Client is close to his older sister and can confide in her about difficulties. He feels that she gives him good advice.

*(continued)*

**FIGURE 6.2.** *(page 5 of 7)*

V. Other Life Strengths
List areas of the client's life that are going well, along with personal strengths
and resources such as education, employment, hobbies, personal values,
personality traits, etc., that support effective functioning.

Client completed high school and two years of vocational training, has good literacy, a strong work ethic, and a stable employment history in the construction trades. Client sought out therapy voluntarily. Client seems resilient regarding money problems and is focused on constructive solutions. Client has hobbies but hasn't pursued them in recent years. Client does not drink, smoke, or use drugs and is in good physical health. He reports stress relief from unwinding, watching TV, reading detective novels, talking to his sister, and praying.

Client displays quite remarkable resilience in the face of life stress and financial difficulties. He coped with an absent, drug-abusing spouse and three young children for several years without becoming depressed or abandoning his duties. He reports a generally positive relationship with his sons, although partner feels that he is overly strict at times (but not physically abusive).

## PART D: CASE FORMULATION HYPOTHESES

1. Formulate hypotheses about the associations among the various problems identified.

Client relies on avoidant coping with relationship issues, has difficulty tolerating and addressing his partner's criticisms and complaints without becoming very defensive, and lacks skills in listening and compromise. He has not been able to forgive partner's past transgressions, despite recognizing that she is sincerely changing.

2. Formulate hypotheses about the functions of abusive behavior.

The earlier abusive behavior appears to have been an attempt to control his partner, to stop her from using drugs and engaging in behaviors that the client deemed destructive to the marriage and family. Also, he was punishing her (perhaps making himself feel better in that process) for her bad behavior and engaged in an expression of his level of anger and frustration toward her (which he reports keeping bottled up inside).

Recent incidents appear motivated by avoidance and escape from aversive conflicts with the partner. Client "just wants her to leave me alone," withdraws, and has used physical abuse in service of his escape and withdrawal. Does not feel capable of dealing with partner's criticisms and feels helpless to solve problems mutually.

3. Formulate hypotheses about the cognitive themes associated with abusive behavior and other problems.

Mindreading: "My partner blames me for everything."
Dichotomous thinking: "All she does is complain"; "She will never be happy."
Awfulizing: "Our life sucks because we don't have any money."

*(continued)*

FIGURE 6.2. *(page 6 of 7)*

Catastrophizing: "I can't stand it when my partner complains."

With respect to earlier instances of abuse, client reports themes such as "She's making a fool out of me," and "I can't let her get away with this crap."

Now, when there are disagreements, his main thought is "Just leave me alone" or "I need to get out of here."

## PART E: INTERVENTION TARGET LIST

1. Develop a list of intervention targets for cognitive change based on themes inherent in the cognitive assessment.

Targets for cognitive change:
- Stop actively blaming partner for things that happened in the past ("It's all her fault").
- Develop a collaborative mindset to invite cooperative problem solving.
- Enhance self-efficacy for communication/problem solving (e.g., "We can work on things together").
- Challenge catastrophizing thoughts ("I can't stand it when she complains").
- Increase awareness/monitoring of partner positive behaviors and efforts.

2. Develop a list of intervention targets for behavior change based on the problem assessment and case formulation hypotheses.

Targets for behavioral change:
- Shape reflective listening to partner's concerns or complaints.
- Reduce negative emotional reactivity to partner's concerns.
- Increase dialogue and communication engagement.
- Decrease withdrawal/avoidance of interaction with partner.

## PART F: INTERVENTION STRATEGIES

1. Develop a list of intervention strategies that may be helpful in achieving each targeted change.

Stress inoculation could be used to address client's emotional reactivity to criticism and complaints (e.g., role playing these events in session to promote coping skills), along with an exposure/desensitization approach to decrease escape and avoidance of partner.

Communication training could be used to promote listening and expression skills.

Problem-solving training could be used to identify specific issues and focus problem discussions with his partner.

Cognitive restructuring methods could be used to reduce irrational and angry thinking related to the partner, including:

Decatastrophizing of partner complaints and criticisms

Education on forms of irrational thinking

*(continued)*

**FIGURE 6.2.** *(page 7 of 7)*

Self-monitoring of irrational thoughts
Development of positive self-talk regarding mutual interactions and problem solving
with partner

2. Formulate hypotheses about which clinical strategies and techniques are most likely
   to produce the desired intervention effects in light of the client's:

   a. Interpersonal style

   Client appears responsive to directive influence and willing to engage in mutual,
collaborative goal and agenda setting. Client tends to illustrate concerns with lengthy
descriptions of interactions with his spouse. The hypothesis is that he will respond
better to role plays and discussion of specific response options in specific scenarios
rather than to abstract discussions such as education about forms of irrational
thinking.

   b. Previous change efforts

   The key here has been his inability to sustain change efforts in the face of
perceived criticism and complaints by his partner. He seems to initiate change with good
intentions but needs better coping strategies and more effective ways to elicit
cooperation and mutual problem solving. He needs help to maintain motivation for
change and self-efficacy for change efforts. These prior efforts suggest the hypothesis
that skills training will be most effective if it focuses on difficult situations that
normally would cause him to backslide in the change process.

   c. Strengths and resources

   Client has initiated some efforts to change his attitude and relationship behaviors,
leading to the hypothesis that self-directed change efforts are likely to occur. He has
some good coping skills that can be generalized and built upon. He has positive
supports for his change efforts from his social network.

tent aggressive outbursts (and/or passive–aggressive retaliations). The clinician would likely hypothesize a general problem with assertiveness that accounts for the problems in various life contexts. Another common example for abusive clients involves obsession with order, cleanliness, perfectionism, and control. This rigid style may be apparent in a range of life difficulties involving relationships with children, spouses, other relatives, and coworkers. It is typically accompanied by cognitive themes of superiority, excessive moralizing, and hostile criticism of others' limitations. Obsessive perfectionism may be reinforced in some work contexts (e.g., high tech engineering, surgery, or skilled craft trades), yet create serious problems at home. Another common hypothesis regarding diverse presenting problems involves impulsiveness. Individuals with globally poor impulse control often have presenting problems that involve drugs or alcohol, impulsive sexual behaviors and affairs, and rapid escalation of anger arousal. We have also treated partner-violent men who have compulsive gambling problems, binge eating and bulimic disorders, kleptomania, road rage, and many other signs of poor impulse control. One client had experienced significant injury as a result of an accident when "surfing" on a car roof at high speed. An unstable employment history is also often present for highly impulsive clients who undermine job success with angry outbursts or impulsive gratification seeking.

The second general type of hypothesis formation involves functional explanations of target behaviors (i.e., explanations for why someone engages in activities that appear to be self-defeating or to produce negative consequences in the long term). When questioned, virtually all abusive clients can provide a list of negative consequences of their own as well as others' abusive behavior. Yet, most abusive clients have greater difficulty coming up with positive functional effects or gains that may accrue from their abusive behavior. Common examples include escape or avoidance of conflict (or of negative or critical emotions from the partner), alleviation of negative affective states (a short-term release that may follow violent behavior), coerced compliance from the partner, reassurance or efforts by the partner to allay the client's insecurities (common in cases with jealousy and restrictive engulfment), and promotion or affirmation of a sense of superiority (e.g., "I showed her who's boss"). It is important to search for hypotheses that do not provide a circular explanation that is unhelpful. For example, explaining the functions of abuse based on the notion that someone is impulsive really does not add anything given that the abuse is one major way we know the client has an impulse control problem.

The literature on behavior analytic interventions for aggressive or self-destructive behavior in developmentally disabled clients provides some interesting insights into the social functions of aggression (e.g., Thompson & Iwata, 2001). Aggression in such cases is usually maintained by one of several functional consequences. These include escape from unpleasant or unwanted activities (e.g., individual gets out of doing chores), social attention (e.g., individual receives soothing talk from caregivers), or tangible reinforcers (e.g., individual is given a toy, access to some activity, or food to help calm down). Parallels are quite apparent in adult partner violence. (Obviously, we don't mean to imply that all abusive clients are developmentally disabled.) For example, partner compliance with requests or demands may be associated with tangible reinforcers (e.g., partner tries to keep client pacified by providing services such as cooking, cleaning, childcare, etc.). Increased attention or changes in the quality of attention may follow abusive acts (e.g., partner is highly attentive to signs that the client may be upset or distressed and adjusts behavior accordingly). Likewise, social attention may be increased when the abuse is accompanied by jealous recriminations or insecurities, and the partner attempts to assuage the client's concerns by proclaiming commitment or fidelity. Escape from conflictual interactions or unpleasant commitments is also a common result of abusive behaviors (e.g., avoiding requests to perform household chores, to attend family functions, to escape from or halt the partner's expressions of anger, or to ignore or avoid the partner's requests for change). A very common description of physical aggression incidents by male abusive clients is "I was just trying to get out of there, and she wouldn't let me go, so I [grabbed her; moved her out of the way; pushed her aside; etc.]."

Finally, the third general type of hypothesis formation involves cognitive factors that may be linked to the abusive behavior and other relationship problems. The first step is to identify and describe thoughts, assumptions, and underlying beliefs that: (1) justify the use of abusive behavior, and/or (2) help fuel the arousal patterns that lead up to abusive actions. This process follows the "downward arrow" technique, beginning with surface manifestations of problematic cognitions at or near the time of abusive incidents and moving toward a formulation of underlying beliefs and schemas regarding self, partner, and relationships (Beck & Weishaar, 1989). The next step is to formulate hypotheses about how various cognitive themes are linked to the abusive behavior and how they should be prioritized in treatment.

## Selection of Treatment Targets and Strategies

The client's interpersonal and cognitive style, previous change efforts, and personal strengths and resources are used to develop hypotheses about the type of interventions that are likely to be most effective and to have the greatest impact on the client. One of the key dimensions to consider in the interpersonal domain is whether the client appears reactive to directive influence strategies or open to therapist direction. Many abusive clients have a strong antiauthoritarian streak that makes it difficult for them to take direction from the therapist. These individuals may respond best to self-directed and self-paced interventions. Another key interpersonal concern has to do with the manner in which the client may distort the therapists' verbalizations.

Clients seem to differ in their cognitive preferences for abstract versus concrete material. Examples of abstract material are lists of cognitive distortions, discussion of conceptual models such as the antecedent–thought–behavior–consequence sequence, lists of the pros and cons of change, etc. Examples of more concrete materials are self-monitoring forms, discussion of specific relationship scenarios and events, and role playing. The distinction being made here is the focus on specific, lived experiences versus reflection on one's behavior and mental functions. Most clients benefit from a range of interventions that include both abstract concepts to promote insight and self-understanding and more concrete experiential work that exposes the client directly to new behaviors, thoughts, and emotions. The trick for the clinician is to start with intervention strategies that the client finds relatively comfortable and slowly expand the client's comfort zone to include a broader range of change strategies. For example, an engineer with prior experience in insight-oriented psychotherapy was very comfortable at the outset of treatment with abstract material, such as lists of cognitive distortions and discussion of the cognitive-behavioral model of change. This individual made some rapid progress in self-awareness regarding the developmental sources of his controlling and coercive relationship behaviors and their effects on family members. Yet he needed encouragement and time before he felt comfortable engaging in role plays with the therapist that were designed to stimulate "on line" access to anger and abuse-maintaining thoughts.

It is also of crucial importance to consider strengths and resources in the change process. Clients vary tremendously in their preferred coping strategies and in the extent to which they have effective coping mechanisms to handle life difficulties and relationship problems. Effective intervention finds a balance between building on existing coping and change mechanisms and facilitating alternative coping and change mechanisms. Sometimes novice clinicians assume that everything the client has been doing has not been working for them. Such an assumption is obviously too simplistic. Some client coping strategies work well in one life context while undermining effective functioning in other contexts. For example, a construction job foreman got a lot of mileage out of his tough guy approach at work. He felt that this style was important to his success, garnering loyalty from hardworking employees who know that slackers "get what they have coming." This rough and coercive style, however, evoked fear, anger, and resistance from his teenage stepdaughter and wife. Nevertheless, it was important for the therapist to make this distinction before attempting to supplant these relationship behaviors with more constructive ones, as the client might otherwise have resisted attempts to alter an interactional style deemed crucial to his life success.

Conversely, many clients have effective coping behaviors at work that they fail to use at home. For example, some clients handle criticism or complaints at work without taking things too personally and are able to maintain a problem-solving focus when difficult situations arise. Yet, at home, they are overwhelmed by the emotional content of their partner's criticisms or complaints and lose the ability to maintain a constructive focus. Obviously, different skills and strategies are required in these different contexts, yet for some clients it is very helpful to point out their existing strengths and to facilitate better coping in the relationship or family context by building on skills and behaviors already within the client's repertoire.

The final note, which cannot be stressed too much, is that case formulation is an ongoing process of hypothesis generation and testing. The therapist should not presume that a hypothesis is correct but should continually test it out. For example, Figure 6.2 presents a hypothesis that the client will respond better to more concrete, experiential interventions than to more abstract ones at the outset of therapy. This hypothesis can be tested out by trying interventions that vary along this dimension during some early sessions, eliciting the client's feedback and reactions to the interventions, and carefully observing their acceptability to the client and apparent effects. Therapists are often surprised to find that their hypotheses were not correct, particularly by clients who prefer interventions that appear to be outside their normal coping style and comfort zone. Finally, the therapist has to make many quick judgments about both the utility of the case formulation and the efficacy of specific interventions. There is considerable peril in giving up on interventions that are sound and will eventually be effective, and there is also peril in persisting with ineffective intervention strategies in the face of client resistance or apparent failure. A good case formulation should provide the therapist with some confidence and self-efficacy in maintaining a central focus for specific change efforts. Yet the hypothesis-testing framework allows the therapist to abandon formulations and intervention strategies that are not working. Finding this balance is another key "dialectic" in the cognitive-behavioral treatment of abusive clients.

## NOTE

1. It may perhaps be more accurate to consider these two approaches to treatment development as ends of a continuum, rather than as categorically different. Obviously, even the most highly structured treatments, such as desensitization,

involve the application of general principles involving extinction of fear and habituation to fear-provoking stimuli. In addition, competent delivery of such treatments requires adaptation to the specific case in the form of a unique stimulus hierarchy, the pacing of exposure tasks, and the use of encouragement and support to facilitate exposure. Similarly, more complex, individual case treatments such as dialectical behavior therapy for borderline personality disorder often include highly structured components of the intervention. In dialectical behavior therapy, for example, clients typically participate in a weekly skills training group that contains structured sequential intervention components in addition to their participation in individual treatment (Linehan, 1993b).

# / 7 /

# *Enhancing Motivation to Change and Engagement into Treatment*

$M$any treatment programs for domestic abuse perpetrators rely on direct and often intense confrontation of defensiveness and denial. These interventions may unwittingly increase, rather than decrease, the abuser's resistance to change. A supportive and collaborative working alliance between therapist and client is an essential element in effective treatment for this population. Supportive strategies, known as motivational interviewing, are available to increase motivation to change in resistant clients (Miller & Rollnick, 1991, 2002). These techniques match therapist interventions to the client's readiness for change, relying on a comprehensive model of the change process that has been widely applied in the areas of addictive behavior reduction and health behavior promotion (e.g., Prochaska, 1994; Prochaska, DiClemente, & Norcross, 1992). This model identifies 5 stages of intentional behavior change and 13 processes that are used to accomplish change. Client resistance arises when the therapist's interventions outstrip the client's readiness for change. A more effective and collaborative counseling relationship develops when the therapist's goals and intervention strategies are tailored to the client's level of readiness for change.

## CONCEPTUALIZING MOTIVATION
## TO CHANGE ABUSIVE BEHAVIOR

### Rationale for Integrating Motivational Enhancement with Cognitive-Behavioral Therapy for Abusive Clients

Although motivational enhancement therapy is a coherent overall approach to treatment in its own right (Miller, Zweben, DiClemente, & Rychtarik, 1992), this intervention method has a more circumscribed role in CBT for abusive clients. Motivational interviewing techniques are used to promote key early conditions in the therapeutic change process, namely, (1) to diffuse client hostility about being coerced into treatment (2) to establish a comfortable style of mutual interaction (rapport), (3) to facilitate client self-disclosure, (4) to enhance the client's positive expectancies about treatment, and (5) to promote a collaborative working alliance, which includes a warm and trusting bond, agreement on the goals of treatment, and agreement on the tasks needed to induce and maintain change (Bordin, 1979). These early conditions are seen as necessary for the change process to unfold, but only in rare cases are they sufficient in themselves to establish a lasting change pattern. Stated differently, the philosophy and techniques of motivational interviewing are used to promote active engagement in the change process, to enhance the client's openness to the therapist's influence, and to gauge the client's movement through the stages of change. Even if the client is highly motivated, however, poor case conceptualization and misguided intervention strategies can nevertheless impede behavior change.

## The Stages and Processes of Change

Prochaska and DiClemente (1984) developed an overarching theory to explain behavior change across different therapeutic modalities and self-directed change in nontreatment contexts. Their model identifies 5 stages of intentional behavior change and 13 common processes used to accomplish lasting change. In the first stage of change, *precontemplation*, the individual is not actively considering change. Individuals with problem behaviors, such as addictions or partner abuse, remain in the precontemplation stage for several reasons (DiClemente, 1991). Some are demoralized, having made a number of previous failed attempts to change. Others lack awareness of the problem or the risks associated with it, for example by believing that everyone has physical altercations in their relationships. Most simply blame others for their difficulties and, therefore, fail to see the need for personal growth and change. These clients present a difficult challenge for most therapists and for others in their lives who clearly see the need for them to change their ways.

In the *contemplation* stage, the individual weighs the costs of maintaining the problem behavior and the benefits of change and develops the desire to change. One characteristic feature of the contemplation phase is ambivalence, as the individual addresses the balance sheet of reasons for changing versus those for not changing. Not surprisingly, the primary change processes used during this stage are cognitive and experiential, rather than behavioral. The work involves evaluation of the problem behavior and its effects on self and others, consideration of the prospects for change, and acknowledgment of the barriers that will inhibit change efforts. It is during these two early stages of precontemplation and contemplation that motivational intervention techniques are of the most direct and clear relevance to the treatment of abusive clients, providing both a conceptual framework and a set of helpful techniques to elicit clients' intrinsic motivation to change.

In the next stage, variously labeled *preparation* or *determination*, the individual has made a personal commitment to change the problem behavior, with a specific intention to change and a plan to do so. Adequate preparation is an essential component in the overall process of intentional behavior change, but one that is all too easily disregarded in clinical practice, where the therapist may presume that a client who expresses an interest in changing will comply with therapeutic interventions. The problem with this logic is that most clients need to buy into, or "own," the change plan. In other words, the client needs to understand and embrace the goals of treatment as well as the ways in which various therapeutic activities will facilitate accomplishment of treatment goals. The easiest way to accomplish this is to involve the client fully and actively in setting the goals of treatment and devising change plans, both in terms of the general goals and approach and the weekly change plan.

After the client has made a personal commitment to change and has developed a plan to do so, the next logical stage is *action*, during which the individual implements behavior change strategies. At this stage, the therapist's skill in case conceptualization and implementation of cognitive and behavioral change strategies becomes paramount. Motivational techniques remain important, particularly when the client experiences setbacks and challenges in the change process. With partner-abusive clients, the action stage is best conceptualized as an ongoing and evolving process of addressing targets for change, refining goals, reinstilling motivation, handling setbacks, and maintaining consistent focus on the change process.

When significant change has been accomplished, the client enters the *maintenance* stage, consolidating gains and actively avoiding a return to problematic behavior patterns. In working with clients who have complex and multifaceted problems, as is the case with most of those referred for partner abuse treatment, the client often reaches the maintenance stage for certain behavioral changes while continuing in the action stage, or even earlier stages, with other behaviors. For example, the individual may have focused initial efforts on the cessation of physical aggression, developing some rudimentary alternative behaviors such as conflict avoidance and time-out, yet may continue to engage in denigrating forms of emotional abuse and hostile withdrawal. Often the maintenance of change in one area depends on successful action in other areas. For example, if this individual does not alter the use of emotionally and verbally abusive behaviors, the risk for reoffending with physical aggression will remain high as a function of escalating conflict with limited conflict resolution skills.

## Primary Therapeutic Goals for Each Stage of Change

The goals of motivational enhancement therapy are tailored to the client's initial readiness for change and evolve as the client progresses. They may involve any or all of the following: (1) to raise awareness of the risks of the problem behavior and the benefits of change, (2) to resolve ambivalence ("tip the scales") toward a decision to change, (3) to develop a change plan that addresses key aspects of the problem and that is realistic for the client to implement, (4) to enhance the client's confidence in his or her ability to carry out behavior change, (5) to provide guidance and encouragement for the client to accomplish behavior change, and (6) to help identify potential pitfalls and prevent relapse to the problem behavior.

## BASIC CONCEPTS MOTIVATIONAL INTERVIEWING

### Conceptualizing Therapeutic Resistance

In the framework of motivational interviewing (MI; Miller & Rollnick, 1991), client resistance is conceptualized as a two-person, interactional phenomenon rather than as a trait-like feature of the client. Resistance arises when the therapist's interventions outstrip the client's readiness for change. It is an issue of poor fit between the therapist's expectations and the client's stage of change. As a simple example, a therapist who launches a plan of communication skills training with a client who has yet to embrace the need for communication skills development will likely meet with passive or active resistance. An effective and collaborative therapeutic relationship develops when the therapist's interventions are tailored to the client's readiness for change, and when the client is a fully active partner in selecting the goals and strategies for change.

### Common Therapeutic Traps

Miller and Rollnick (1991, 2002) have identified a number of therapeutic traps that are extremely common in working with early-stage abusive clients. In fact, these traps are so prevalent that they often make their way into the treatment literature as recommended intervention strategies for client populations seen as resistant to change. For almost all populations thought of as "treatment resistant," some therapists will recommend confrontational strategies to break through denial. Unfortunately, for clients who lack a firm commitment to change, direct confrontation of rationalization and denial will often serve to strengthen these negative attitudes. One reason for this is the simple tendency for individuals to defend whichever side of their ambivalence that another person is attacking. The second reason involves reactance, the motivation to establish and defend personal freedoms that are perceived as threatened by others (Brehm & Brehm, 1981). For many abusive clients, the mere thought of a "shrink" who will "mess with their head" is extremely threatening and must be counteracted by whatever means necessary. For some clients, the choice between partner violence counseling and several months in jail is a very difficult one. Discussion with one such individual revealed that jail was familiar, time limited, and less threatening to his sense of personal choice and integrity. The client believed that therapists had special abilities to "mess with his head," to change him in ways that he would not want to change, or to force him to address painful aspects of his life that would be better left untouched. Despite how unbelievable it may seem to a well-intentioned mental health professional, for some individuals, jail time seems less threatening to personal freedom than therapy! Some individuals take the offer of treatment over jail because they feel they can outsmart the therapist or resist therapeutic influence, not because they see the offer of assistance with personal change as potentially beneficial.

Given this backdrop, it is easy to see why a therapist could be motivated to attack the client's apparent resistance and defensiveness head on, attempting to force realization of the need for change (and of the error of the client's ways). This often produces the therapeutic trap labeled confrontation–denial (Miller & Rollnick, 1991), in which the client rationalizes and justifies problematic behavior in response to the therapist's attempts to point out the problem and its consequences. The philosophy of motivational interviewing promotes "soft confrontation" in which clients are guided to address the negative consequences of problem behavior and the need for personal change themselves, without being chided, lectured, or otherwise coerced into seeing the error of their ways. In addition, the motivational therapist is well advised explicitly to affirm the client's freedom and choice whether and how to change, recognizing the simple truth that change lies within the client's purview and cannot be forced by others.

Another common trap involves the use of closed-ended questions and other communication behaviors to establish a dialogue that is predominately therapist-directed (Miller & Rollnick, 1991). The therapist may inadvertently lead the client to assume a passive stance in the change process, seeing the therapist as the "expert" who will ask all relevant questions and provide all relevant solutions. Once again, the client must own the change process and must be a fully active participant. This process is reinforced early in treatment in a number of ways, especially by using open-ended questions, facilitating client expression of motivations to change and elaboration of treatment goals, and helping shape and maintain the client's change efforts. The therapist should serve as an expert consultant who is fully engaged in the treatment process, has a clear understanding of how change occurs, and can contribute important ideas, change strategies, and encouragement to the client's self-directed change process.

The last therapeutic trap of particular relevance to partner-abusive clients has been labeled "premature focus" (Miller & Rollnick, 1991). Problems can arise when the therapist shunts the process of goal setting or treatment planning by focusing only on a part of the client's present concerns or prematurely closing off exploration of potential targets of change or a broad range of change strategies. This issue is particularly pressing when we encounter clients who have been engaging in problem behaviors, such as partner violence, that are dangerous to others. Obviously, the ethical therapist will want to focus on these behaviors as rapidly as possible, setting aside other issues and potential treatment goals by ignoring them explicitly or failing to assess them adequately. However, this may not mesh with the client's perspective on the change process and may inadvertently inhibit full participation in treatment. We recommend two "antidotes" to the premature focus trap. The first recommendation is to take time to identify a relatively complete range of potential client concerns and life problems that may be important in case conceptualization and treatment planning. Initial safety interventions and safety planning are essential for partner-violent clients, particularly for cases who present with immediate crises such as suicidal issues, highly volatile relationship events (e.g., recent discovery of infidelity), or frequent and severe violence. Nevertheless, the therapist must find opportunities to assess the range of potential client concerns and change goals, even if that means going back to these issues after initial crisis intervention efforts to enhance safety. The second recommendation to avoid the premature focus trap is to include the client in all phases of treatment planning and implementation.

## MOTIVATIONAL INTERVIEWING TECHNIQUES

Before reviewing the techniques of motivational interviewing (MI) it is crucially important to explain that none of these techniques are likely to work outside the context of a warm and supportive therapeutic relationship. The techniques cannot be used to "psych out," manipulate, or otherwise trick or fool the client. The techniques cannot magically persuade someone to change nor do they consistently elicit a desired reaction. Rather, the techniques are helpful strategies that can be implemented within the general principles of treatment outlined above and in light of the client's readiness to change.

## Basic Techniques

The primary technique of MI is empathic reflection. As in client-centered therapy (Rogers, 1961), empathic reflection conveys acceptance and warmth and helps create the conditions for self-exploration and growth. Unlike in traditional client-centered therapy, however, MI also involves directive therapist interventions, including advice and guidance. Reflective listening is crucial in establishing the therapeutic context for change and in allowing the therapist accurately to understand the client's view of the problem and motivations for change. In MI, reflection usually emphasizes those aspects of client communication that are of direct relevance to the client's difficulties and change process. Thus, some inherent shaping of the client's focus is expected but not in a heavy-handed or manipulative fashion.

MI specifies several different forms of reflection (Miller & Rollnick, 2002). These include simple reflection of the client's verbalizations and affect, double-sided reflection of client ambivalence, and summarizing more extended aspects of a therapeutic dialogue. An additional technique, called amplified reflection, is described below in the section on rolling with resistance. In using all of these techniques, the therapist strives for clarity and accuracy in understanding the client's experience, including the client's emotion and cognition.

## Rolling with Resistance

Although the therapist should remain mindful of the basic concept that resistance represents a mismatch between the therapist's interventions and the client's readiness for change, a number of MI techniques have been developed to address resistance in the therapist–client interaction. All are based on the premise of "rolling" with resistance and the martial arts analogy of using the energy of the opposing force to undo, rather than trying to counter or confront it head on, which usually stimulates firmer resistance. Undoubtedly, careful and consistent empathic reflection is the most effective way to handle resistance. However, therapists often reach certain points in this effort where the question "what now?" is reasonably asked, for example when the same reasons for resisting change have been explored several times or when the client presents an unexpected shift in motivation level. At these moments, it is helpful to have a range of techniques available in addition to basic reflective listening.

One strategy for handling resistance is simply to shift the focus of discussion. When productive work seems very unlikely for a specific topic of concern and the therapist has been listening effectively and has tried to explore relevant areas of motivation to change, then it may be helpful gently to move on to a different issue. It may be helpful to shift focus after a productive discussion as well, once an area of motivation or a treatment goal has been addressed in detail. Sometimes shifting focus simply involves an open-ended question to explore other dimensions of an issue or another perspective on it.

> "I understand that you are very upset about the judge's decision to send you here to our program. If I were to call your wife up and ask her, what would she say? How does she feel about your coming to see us?"

Another technique for handling resistance is agreement with a twist, in which the therapist demonstrates understanding of the client's perspective but adds something to it that changes its meaning or implications. This is often done with respect to the positive and negative consequences of problem behavior. For example:

> "So when your partner says those things to you, you feel justified in responding with a loud argument or physical aggression . . . [here's the twist] and therefore you may just have to accept the fact that the police come around to your house on a regular basis."

A third technique for handling resistance is amplified reflection, in which the therapist intentionally heightens or exaggerates some aspect of the client's verbalization or perspective. Amplified reflection involves an accurate perception of the client's communication but with the reflective statement phrased in such a way as to elicit a reaction or alternative view. To be effective, amplified reflections usually need to be stated in the same basic tone as more straightforward empathic reflections. A prior dialogue is typically necessary in which the client feels understood, so that the amplification doesn't seem manipulative.

CLIENT: Like I've been saying, I wouldn't do these things if she didn't keep calling me names and putting me down.

THERAPY: So when you look at it, she bears 100% of the responsibility for your arguments and fights.

A fourth strategy for handling resistance is looking backward. The client is asked to recount a time when things were different, usually a time before the problem behavior was present, as a means of developing motivation to change or self-efficacy for handling things more productively.

"You mentioned before how things were better between the two of you before the abuse incident when you were arrested. What was it like? How were things different then?"

Finally, the strategy of looking forward can be used in order to develop discrepancy between reality and the client's wishes. In looking forward, the client is asked to imagine what the future will be like if things do not change and/or to imagine a future in which the problem has been resolved. Two examples follow:

"So, if things keep going the way they've been going in your relationship, what do you think it will be like a couple of years from now?"

"Let's just imagine for a minute that we are some time in the future, your relationship has improved, and there is no abuse going on; what would it be like?"

## Eliciting Self-Motivational Statements

The emphasis on self-motivation to change is more of a consistent focus of MI than a specific treatment technique. Client communications regarding change can be thought of along two key dimensions—the "will," or desire to change, and the "way," or ability to change. As clients increase their desire to change, interventions increasingly focus on the "how" of change, building self-efficacy through effective planning and implementation of change strategies. However, for most abusive clients, early interventions are needed to consolidate and elaborate the desire to change.

It may be helpful to picture the motivation to change as a tree. The root system represents a core desire for social acceptance and self-improvement. The trunk involves basic motivations for adjustment, happiness, and successful living. Large branches emerging from the trunk reflect fundamental areas of life, such as work/productivity, family, and hobbies. From these emerge many smaller, interconnected branches. The task of the motivational therapist is to help the client identify key areas of motivation and then elaborate the detailed branching structure of these important concerns.

For example, a client might express some general concern about his children and the effect that marital conflict is having on them. The therapist identifies this as a major branch in potential motivation to change, reflects the client's concern, and inquires with open-ended questions about more specific aspects of these concerns. As the client elaborates on the children's difficulties, the things they have witnessed, etc., the therapist facilitates the exploration of this complex branching structure and uses it to guide the client toward defining treatment goals (areas for improvement and change).

Several major branches of motivation for partner-violent clients have emerged from group discussions regarding the pros and cons of abusive behavior. Any individual client need not accept or experience all of these to stimulate change, yet it may be helpful for the therapist to explore as many as possible in early sessions in order to consolidate the desire for change. The first major motivation for many clients involves fear of legal reprisals. It is important to elicit each client's specific perspective on these issues and not assume that clients view the law, jail time, or other punishments in the same fashion that the therapist does. Most clients are very afraid of jail, but some are not. Some believe that they are fighting against an oppressive or unjust legal system and find little positive motivation for change from these experiences. Others do not believe that punishment will befall them or have not experienced legal complications.

Another major initial motivation for many clients involves the fear of loss of the relationship, along with abandonment anxieties and related concerns. Some clients are very upset that their partner could ever consider leaving the relationship. Others are aware that their partner has put up with a great deal, yet fear (often realistically) that the partner will not continue to put up with abuse indefinitely. It is common for individuals to present for services after a major change in relationship status, typically a recent separation. Although the initial motivation for seeking treatment may be to convince the partner to return to the relationship, the therapist should try to use this as a "hook" and then help the client elaborate areas for self-improvement to promote lasting change in the relationship.

A third major area of client motivation involves negative consequences of ongoing conflicts on the relationship and partner. Common examples include mistrust, fear and stress reactions in the abused partner, disaffection, and an atmosphere of tension in the home. Some clients recognize that their partner has become very hostile or aggressive in response to abusive treatment. Many report a series of unresolved conflicts and unremitting problems in their relationships, yet may not see the connection to their problematic conflict behaviors. Still others are intent on attaining forgiveness from the partner.

A fourth major motivational issue for many clients involves embarrassment arising from others' knowledge of their abusive behavior. It is quite common for extended family members, friends, neighbors, coworkers, or members of one's religious community to be aware of the abuse and its consequences for the partner. Although some clients are very angry at the prospect of others knowing their business and wish that these issues were kept private, this discomfort can often be shaped into an important motivation to change.

A fifth major motivational issue, mentioned above, involves the negative effects of abusive behavior and relationship conflict on children. Some abusive clients express concerns about aggressive behavior in the children, deficient academic performance, or other problems. Some express concerns about abuse by self or partner of the children. Very common areas of concern involve problems managing child visitation and ongoing conflicts with ex-partners and dealing with disciplinary issues in a blended family arrangement. Most abusive clients with children show serious strain in the parenting alliance—the collaborative element of coparenting (Hoover, 2002). Although such concerns are often raised initially as complaints about others' behavior (especially the partner or ex-partner), with further exploration motivations for self-change and for the cessation of abusive behavior often emerge out of concern for the children's welfare.

Finally, the most powerful motivation to change, and one that is expressed by the vast majority of clients under the right treatment conditions, involves self-appraisals relative to abusive behavior. Once an alliance is established, most abusive clients express shame, embarrassment, and guilt at having hurt someone that they love or care about. Even those who are bitter toward the partner are usually far from proud of their behavior. These issues of self-appraisal and self-concept are often fundamental motivations for behavior change. Interestingly, however, self-appraisals can also inhibit acknowledgment of the problem when the individual blames others as a way of neutralizing negative self-evaluations (Dutton, 1986b).

## READINESS TO CHANGE:
## COMMON PATTERNS OF INITIAL CLINICAL PRESENTATION

### Empirical Perspectives

Recent studies have begun to measure stage-of-change variables among clinical partner abuse samples and to cluster these individuals into different groups with respect to change readiness (Alexander & Morris, in press; Begun et al., 2003; Eckhardt et al., in press; Levesque et al., 2000; Scott & Wolfe, 2003). These studies indicate that abusive clients possess widely varying attitudes regarding the need for personal change at the outset of treatment. The stage-of-change measures have meaningful correlations with variables such as attributions of personal responsibility, court versus self-referred status, use of change processes, time in treatment, and the tendency to minimize reports of abuse relative to collateral partner reports. One study demonstrated a significant change over time in stage-of-change variables from before to after abuser counseling (Morrel et al., 2003). However, there is very little evidence that stage of change measured during abuser program intake actually predicts postprogram violence recidivism.

Studies to date have identified between two and eight clusters of individuals on readiness-to-change variables. All have found an "early stage" cluster of individuals who deny the need for personal change and fail to identify a personal problem with abusive behavior and a more advanced cluster who are cognizant of their problem and indicate a need for personal change. Given that there is no clear consensus on the number of different stage-of-change clusters seen at program intake, we have decided to provide general clinical descriptions of early- and later-stage clients.

## Early-Stage Clients

Although every client is unique, two distinct self-presentational styles are commonly observed during the initial sessions. The first style involves a relatively firm, outward denial of a problem or need for change. Such individuals usually display high sensitivity to being perceived by the therapist in a negative light and a strong wish to be exonerated from any apparent wrongdoing. According to the transtheoretical model of change (Prochaska & DiClemente, 1984), these individuals are in the "precontemplation stage" or early "contemplation stage" of change. The therapist often experiences these clients as uncooperative or unmotivated. Such clients usually deny guilt or responsibility for engaging in abusive acts and typically minimize the severity of abuse and its consequences. They may even deny altogether that abuse occurred despite concrete evidence from police reports or partner assessments. Early-stage clients invariably experience themselves as victims of their partner, the legal system, or other external forces, such as in-laws or the activists who are helping the partner at a domestic violence agency. Many feel that they have been discriminated against because of their gender or racial and ethnic background.

Despite outward signs of denial, these individuals vary in the extent of underlying ambivalence about the need for change. Genuine acknowledgment of personal responsibility and the desire to change is very unlikely while the client presumes harsh negative judgment by the therapist. Once this assumption is refuted (by experiential evidence), some early-stage clients will articulate a desire for relationship change or personal change, indicating that they have begun using some of the experiential change processes associated with the contemplation stage. These individuals most readily acknowledge motivations to change that are external to the relationship, notably the fear of legal sanctions. Many such individuals are troubled by the belief that they have no personal control over negative outcomes such as arrest and incarceration. Some believe that change has already occurred by force of will with little or no other change efforts needed, a pattern called "unprepared action" (Levesque et al., 2000).

The therapist has a complex and personally challenging task in handling such clients. Given that they are hypersensitive to being labeled the bad guy and experience themselves as victims, they tend to latch onto any sign that the therapist disagrees with these appraisals and use this as evidence for the belief that the therapist doesn't understand them or their situation. Considerable distortion of the therapist's behavior or verbalization can be involved. The client may say "You don't know how bad my partner is"; "Nobody believes me"; "You want to blame it all on me"; or ask "What about my partner's role in all this?" The therapist often feels conflicted, recognizing the need to build rapport and empathize with the client's emotions, yet not wanting to reinforce distorted beliefs about other peoples' evil qualities and bad intentions. Furthermore, the therapist may wish to preserve some facesaving "outs" for the client later to acknowledge personal flaws and responsibility, knowing that vehement denial of wrongdoing at this point may create a seemingly insurmountable barrier to later acknowledgment of problem behaviors and the need for change. Also, it is of no small importance that these individuals often lump the therapist with others who are seen as oppressing and victimizing the client.

Recognizing that the client is in early stages of change, the therapist must adapt his or her interventions accordingly. First, the therapist must maintain a highly empathic stance, using a great deal of reflective listening to help the client establish an alternative appraisal of the therapist and therapeutic situation. This typically involves a cognitive shift for the client from "You're just like the rest of them who see me as bad and want to punish me" to "Maybe it isn't so awful to come here and talk with you" toward "Maybe I can get something positive out of this." This cognitive shift happens rapidly for some clients, within the course of a single initial session. For others, particularly those with an extensive learning history promoting distrust and defensive self-protection, it may take many sessions for this shift in attitude to take hold. Almost all will waffle between defensiveness and trust, and the therapist has to remain mindful of the need for ongoing empathy and support to maintain a working alliance. Because of this instability, confrontational intervention tactics are especially contraindicated with clients at this stage.

Second, from the beginning, the therapist needs carefully to articulate his or her role vis-à-vis external forces such as the partner, the domestic violence agency, and the court or referral system. Third, the therapist should explicitly acknowledge some basic positions on the therapeutic process. For example, it is not the therapist's job to judge or punish the client; therapy is not about assigning blame but about helping people to develop skills that can be used to improve the quality of their relationships and to resolve difficulties in life; and no one can force the client to change (i.e., decisions about how and when to change are in the client's hands). It is not enough for the therapist simply to verbalize these positions; he or she must truly believe them to be effective with resistant clients.

The final point about working with early-stage clients is that the therapist's demeanor, including the phrasing of questions, advice, and empathic statements, is very important. The therapist must convey respect for the client, openness to the client's perspective, and empathy for the client's distress. The therapist should strive to phrase reflective statements and questions in a fashion that elicits greater description of problematic situations, problem behaviors, the client's beliefs that promote and support problem behaviors, and distressing experiences that may motivate change. The therapist should avoid asking questions or making reflective comments that force an alternative interpretation of the client's experience without first carefully illustrating an understanding of the client's emotions and perspective. This can be a difficult undertaking for the therapist given that abusive clients often express generalized sexist, racist, or proviolence sentiments.

As a simple example, after a client describes some apparent offense or negative behavior by the partner, the therapist might respond by asking, "What was your role in this argument or conflict?" This question may be interpreted by the client as accusatory (even if not intended that way), leading to increased client defensiveness and resistance. Alternatively, therapists often ask questions such as "Why do you think your partner did that?" or "What do you think was going through your partner's mind when that happened?" Here, the therapist assumes that such questions will somehow alter the client's negative appraisal of the partner's behavior or produce an acknowledgment of the client's role in the problematic interaction. Yet, more often, such questions simply elicit from the client a more elaborate negative appraisal of the partner's intentions and blameworthiness. A third alternative is to empathize with the client's distress and then attempt to elicit additional description that may lead to problem identification. For example, the therapist can state, "I can see that you were very upset (angry, hurt, etc.) by that. How did you react?" The key elements of the elicitation process are (1) to show empathy and understanding of the client's perspective and experience and (2) to elicit details and information in a way that the client perceives as nonthreatening. Obviously, clients who are further along in the change process can usually tolerate a broader range of therapist responses that are potentially challenging to the client's view.

Throughout this process, the therapist must remember that the music and words are equally important. Simply stating helpful phrases without really feeling their meaning is unlikely to elicit self-motivational statements or problem descriptions from the client. Also, these recommendations should not be taken to mean that the therapist should never directly challenge the client's problematic thoughts and behaviors, but we again caution strongly against the use of challenging or confrontational interventions early in treatment, before a strong working alliance is established and with clients who are not yet engaged in active change efforts, as such interventions are likely to invoke resistance rather than self-motivation to change.

As the initial phase of therapy progresses, a stronger therapeutic alliance begins to form. At this point, the therapist may want to take these simple strategies one step further, for example by asking the client to describe some apparently negative situation or event involving the partner in an entirely blame-free fashion (i.e., to provide details and descriptions of what happened and who did what without any reference to right or wrong and blameworthiness). As a general rule, clients are utterly unable to perform this task, and their difficulty in doing so can be used to highlight how concerns about blame get in the way of a more objective appraisal of the need for change.

To summarize, several key principles guide these therapeutic interactions with clients in the very early stages of change:

1. Use a high level of empathy and reflective listening.
2. Clarify your roles vis-à-vis the referral source and partner.
3. Let the client "own" the change process.
4. Elicit a detailed description of the client's relationship experiences and problematic behaviors in a blame-free fashion.
5. Pay attention to any potential signs of client motivation to change and facilitate client verbalization and elaboration of these motivations.

Further suggestions and techniques for handling resistance are described and illustrated later in the chapter.

## Later-Stage Clients

The second common presentation style for partner-abusive clients involves more explicit initial acknowledgment of a problem and a desire for change. Such individuals are generally in the "preparation stage" or "action stage" of change. The therapist typically experiences these clients as cooperative and motivated for change. Such clients admit wrongdoing and convey guilt or responsibility for engaging in abusive acts. Many will readily admit to a host of personal problems in addition to those relating to abusiveness. Some either fear that the partner will leave them or wish to reunite with the partner after a recent separation. The degree to which they have shifted toward active behavior change varies, however, and depends on two key factors: (1) the extent to which the client has resolved ambivalence about the need for personal change and (2) the dynamics of the relationship, including the nature and types of aversive behavior (real and/or perceived) that the partner engages in and patterns of separation and reunification.

Because these clients describe a variety of problems and present with some apparent motivations for change, therapists are often puzzled and frustrated by their ambivalence. Many of these individuals waffle in their motivation to change, periodically rescinding or qualifying the need for personal change by blaming others. As abusive clients move through the contemplation stage and into preparation and action, they often present rapid cognitive shifts entrained to a complex set of emotional reactions regarding personal responsibility. Typically, acknowledgment of responsibility for harm to the partner is rapidly avoided through appeal to external causes, usually either the partner's negative behavior or perceived unfair treatment by the criminal justice system. At an emotional level, feelings of shame and guilt may be suppressed by feelings of anger, abandonment, or betrayal. This process can be conceptualized as an "avoidance–avoidance" conflict, as both sides of the emotional equation are unpleasant. Most clients have a difficult time experiencing shame long enough to process this emotion through cognitive integration with meaningful plans for change.

The therapist can inadvertently shunt this resolution process by premature movement to action strategies or inattention to ambivalence. The first goal is to help the client resolve ambivalence about change, primarily through reflective listening and elicitation of self-motivational statements. The second goal is to help the client develop a "cognitive map" of the change process that includes the targets of desired change and the general methods available to promote and facilitate change. This is akin to a "change plan" in the language of motivational enhancement therapy that recognizes the client's need to understand and embrace the key elements of the change process. The initial goals and strategies for change must be explored and developed collaboratively with the client and then further elaborated as treatment progresses.

Throughout treatment, but particularly at its outset, the therapist must remain mindful of the "way out" of the client's dilemma, gently guiding the client toward this realization. If the client remains in the stance of blaming others, then the only apparent resolution is to leave or avoid the offending individuals. Although this may be a necessary step for some clients to take, it is not usually viable as a long-term change strategy because it keeps the client in the victim stance of blaming others for his or her problems. Novice therapists are often drawn into this logic only to realize later that much therapeutic effort was wasted on solutions that emphasize the problems and limitations of others, rather than the client's need for growth and change. On the other hand, many clients find it difficult to remain in a posture of self-blame for any length of time. It is much easier and less painful to blame others for one's problems and distress. It is also possible to become immobilized by guilt at the realization of harm and pain caused by past abusive behavior.

The therapist's task is to guide the client, with considerable support and empathy, toward an alternative resolution to the dilemma of shame versus blame, one that helps the client to tolerate and eventually resolve feelings of shame and guilt through appropriate healing strategies and behavior change. In this model, comfortable self-acceptance is not seen as a prior condition to the change process, but as predicated on a coherent plan for growth and change and positive movement toward treatment goals. The client must gradually learn to tolerate feelings of remorse, which are reality-based given the pain and distress that the client has caused to loved ones. This process, if facilitated through the therapist's supportive efforts to help the client make contact with feelings of shame and guilt, gradually exposes the client to these emotions in the treatment setting while encouraging the development of distress-tolerance skills. At the same time, the client must develop alternative cognitive and behavioral patterns that will obviate the need for further shame and guilt arising from past abusive actions. In addition, the therapist should help the client reduce expectations that the partner will provide absolution for past abuse, instead helping the client to understand and accept the partner's distress, pain, and distrust. Clients often become stuck in the desire to move forward and forget the past when acknowledgment of the pain they have caused would better facilitate the healing process.

To summarize the recommendations for establishing and maintaining a working relationship with clients who are in the later contemplation or preparation stages of change:

1. Pay attention to signs of ambivalence and help the client resolve it through careful reflection, reviewing barriers to change, and eliciting self-motivational statements.
2. Avoid conceptualizations and treatment goals that focus on others' problems, either directly or indirectly (e.g., simply avoiding others as the solution).
3. Help the client work through shame and guilt by acknowledging these feelings and their basis in reality, developing a coherent change plan, and working toward clear treatment goals.
4. Help the client transcend the desire for immediate absolution, focusing instead on the long-term healing and change process.

In the subsequent section, we review the use of specific MI techniques. This effort is undertaken with considerable caution, as we have consistently found that the use of these specific techniques is not successful unless delivered within the proper therapeutic context—in other words, the conceptual model of motivation to change and creation of the proper therapeutic atmosphere are much more important than the use of specific motivational techniques. Almost never do clients suddenly realize the error of their ways as a result of motivational interventions, a situation that can produce considerable frustration among clinicians who feel they have instituted the techniques according to plan.

In light of full disclosure regarding (1) the fact that MI techniques in and of themselves do not produce magical immediate reactions from clients and (2) the reality that readiness to change develops over a period of days, weeks, or even months for most clients, the following are examples of typical MI techniques and typical client reactions. These examples are drawn from actual interviews conducted during the first two intake sessions with a predominantly court-mandated population of partner-abusive men as part of a study comparing MI to a standard intake control condition prior to assignment to cognitive-behavioral group treatment (Musser et al., 2005). The study found that individuals who received the motivational intake procedures acted differently during the early group treatment sessions. Based on coding of early session videotapes, those who received the motivational intake verbalized more personal responsibility and less blame of others for their abusive actions and saw treatment as having more potential value to them. They also complied more with assigned homework tasks during group treatment, and were rated by their therapists as having a better working alliance (i.e., greater agreement on the goals and tasks of therapy and a better relationship with the therapist). Although the eventual abusive behavior outcomes during the six months after treatment were not significantly different for the two intake conditions, factors affected by the motivational interviewing, namely homework compliance and the working alliance, significantly predicted lower posttreatment abusive behavior in the sample as a whole (Taft et al., 2003). Thus, the findings indicate that motivational techniques can lower resistance to therapy and enhance engagement into treatment, factors that, in turn, predict positive treatment outcomes.

## CASE EXAMPLE OF AN OPENING SESSION WITH AN EARLY-STAGE CLIENT

The following passage reflects a fairly typical first session with a client in the precontemplation or early contemplation stage of change. The client is angry about being referred to treatment and blames his partner and the criminal justice system for his predicament. The therapist does an excellent job of maintaining an empathic and nonjudgmental stance. Early in the session, the therapist relies almost exclusively on open-ended questions and simple reflection. As the interview progresses, amplified reflections and double-sided reflections are used in an attempt to elicit self-motivational statements from the client. These strategies are not uniformly effective in eliciting self-motivational statements, but the therapist manages to diffuse the client's anger at being ordered to treatment, and eventually the client moves toward a more accepting attitude regarding treatment, presenting a glimmer of motivation to change. Perhaps most notably, the therapist deftly avoids several common therapeutic pitfalls with early-stage clients, including the confrontation–denial trap, question–answer trap, and premature closure on targets and goals for change.

THERAPIST: So, what brought you here today? [open-ended question]

CLIENT: Uh, the court. *(Laughs.)*

THERAPIST: Mm-hmm. So . . .

CLIENT: The court, you know, made me come here to stay out of jail.

THERAPIST: Mm-hmm.

CLIENT: Um. That's what brought me here. I mean, do I think I need help? No, not really.

THERAPIST: No, you don't need help. [simple reflection]

CLIENT: Well, I mean not, you know, not in this sense. Not that I realize.

THERAPY: Mm-hmm. So, the court sent you here, but you're not feeling like you really need to be here. [simple reflection]

CLIENT: No, I don't.

THERAPIST: Mm-hmm.

CLIENT: I really don't. [The client seems emphatic here, perhaps responding to subtle cues that the therapist may not share his view of the situation]

THERAPIST: Could you explain that to me? [open-ended question]

CLIENT: Well, I mean do you want me to explain the whole situation? . . . What brought me here, why I'm here?

THERAPIST: Yes.

The client proceeds to explain the specific conflict incident and ensuing arrest that brought him to treatment. The therapist listens intently, asks clarifying questions occasionally, and then begins to reflect and discuss what was said.

THERAPIST: And then when you started arguing about it, there was pushing on both sides.

CLIENT: Well, I mean, her first. I mean, her first. I mean, but you know . . .
I mean, yeah, I was furious.

THERAPIST: Mm-hmm.

CLIENT: Who wouldn't be?

THERAPIST: So, you were angry, but you really feel like she started it. [simple reflection]

CLIENT: She did. And she knows she did. . . . She's even admitted that, you know, that all of this was her fault. And that's what I was telling you before. She told me that she would pay for all of these sessions because she knows that she got me in here. . . . but the State's not gonna listen to it from that perspective. The State don't want to hear that. The State just wants to see me go to jail whether I was at fault or not. So, you know, if I'm angry at anyone, it's the State. That's pretty much it. I'm not angry at her, not at all.

THERAPIST: Okay, so she's really taking the blame for this. [simple reflection]

CLIENT: It's kind of mutual. Well, its mutual, but yet—what—I mean—you know, I would have to say eighty, ninety percent of this was her fault. And she's admitted to it. [The client begins taking some personal responsibility for his situation but waffles almost immediately.]

THERAPIST: Mm-hmm. So, you're feeling like really the majority of it is her fault, but at the same time you do have some of the blame. [double-sided reflection]

CLIENT: Yeah. The blame comes on me for actually defending myself. Pushing her away. Shoving her.

THERAPIST: Mm-hmm.

CLIENT: Um, this girl—this girl is not, you know, a nice little girl or whatever it's called. You know, she—she taunts a person. . . . You can actually try to walk away from her, and she just gets up in your face. She taunts . . . she thrives on abuse.

Here, the client again seems motivated to convince the therapist how difficult his partner is; he also begins displaying an underlying assumption ("she thrives on abuse") that can be addressed with cognitive intervention later in treatment. The client went on to describe how his girlfriend has been abused her whole life by her family, explaining why she "thrives on it." He states he would never hit a woman if it weren't for her. He reports that he doesn't know how to reach her when she is verbally or physically abusing him and feels that she provokes and taunts him into abusing her. The therapist uses reflective listening and then attempts to go a step further:

THERAPIST: So, you're really feeling like your response was perfectly normal based on what happened. [amplified reflection]

CLIENT: Yeah. [The client does not disagree here, so the therapist returns to simple reflections of the client's emotion.]

THERAPIST: You sound a little frustrated. . . . like you're taking all the heat for this. [simple reflection]

CLIENT: Yeah. Yeah, I am. I am a little frustrated.

Finally, after additional discussion and various subtle attempts to move the client toward self-motivational statements, late in the session the client slowly begins to acknowledge potential risks in not changing by discussing his referral to treatment:

CLIENT: She got in touch with the State's Attorney numerous times pleading with them to drop it, just drop it. And they say, "No, we're not." You know, its all for the money. . . .

THERAPIST: So, you don't see it as a big deal; she doesn't see it as a big deal. You really think they're just trying to get you for money. [amplified reflection]

CLIENT: What, the State?

THERAPIST: Mm hmm.

CLIENT: . . . Well, I don't know how long you been doing this, but I'm sure that, you know, you've actually seen cases that start out not that bad, but a couple years down the road maybe a woman ends up dead or in the hospital from this. That's probably how they see it. They want to catch it before something major happens. So, that's where I'm at right now.

THERAPIST: Mm-hmm.

CLIENT: They just want to make sure that I learn my lesson, you know, not to do anything like this. Not to get into a shoving match, even if it's not my fault, so that I don't even think about doing that again. I can understand that.

THERAPIST: Mm-hmm.

CLIENT: But it still, you know, upsets me.

THERAPIST: So it upsets you, but you can understand it in some ways. [double-sided reflection]

The therapist then attempts to switch focus and elicit motivation by inquiring about the beginning of the relationship, before the abuse began. This is largely unsuccessful, as the client focuses mostly on his girlfriend's negative characteristics and his desire to get away from her to stay out of trouble.

THERAPIST: It sounds like one of your goals is to stay out of trouble.

CLIENT: Yes.

THERAPIST: I'm wondering what sort of things you'll need to do to make changes. [evocative question to elicit self-motivational statements]

CLIENT: Um, for one, like I said I've been slowly phasing her out. In fact, I told her that last night. (*Describes an argument over the phone the previous night during which he told his girlfriend that their relationship was coming to an end.*)

THERAPIST: So one of the things to change is to get her out of your life. [simple reflection]

CLIENT: Right. Right . . . (*Continues discussion of how he is separating from the partner and how that is affecting her*) I can understand the state's point of view. It's just their procedure. Whether I need this or not, I have to do it. So . . .

THERAPIST: So, you're kind of not sure what you need from this or what you're gonna get from this, but you're here. [simple reflection]

CLIENT: Well, I mean, you know, I'm sure if anything comes out of this, it will probably be good, not bad.

THERAPIST: So you don't think this is going to hurt you. [Amplified reflection]

CLIENT: No. How is it going to hurt me? Yeah, you're right. Except for costing me money. You know—My time, my money.

THERAPIST: Mm-hmm.

CLIENT: So . . .

THERAPIST: OK. So, in terms of money and time you feel like you're going to lose, but I'm not understanding what part of it would help you? [Note that rather than jumping in to suggest ways to change or ways that treatment may help, the therapist "hangs back," and reflects again the costs of treatment before eliciting the client's views on potential benefits.]

CLIENT: What part of it would help me?

THERAPIST: Like what would be the good parts? So, the bad parts are the money and the time . . .

CLIENT: About coming here?

THERAPIST: Mm-hmm.

CLIENT: Um, I don't know. I guess probably learning, you know. Yeah. I mean, like I said, I mean in these situations now I walk away. I don't know, maybe I can learn a different approach . . .

THERAPIST: Mm-hmm.

THERAPIST: It also shows that you are capable of making significant changes in your l

THERAPIST: Maybe more than one new thing (*humorously*).

CLIENT: Right. Exactly. I mean if you learn one new thing each day you're a better person. Maybe by coming here, I'm sure I'll learn something. And I'm sure it's got to be pretty good, not bad.

Over the course of a 40-minute interview, the client makes some important progress toward the goals outlined at the beginning of the chapter: becoming less overtly hostile toward treatment and more open to the possibility of benefit from treatment. The therapist begins establishing rapport with the client but does not attempt to set change goals or provide advice about needed changes at this point in time.

## EXAMPLES OF MOTIVATIONAL TECHNIQUES FOR LATER-STAGE CLIENTS

As noted above, clients who are nearing the preparation stage when they present for treatment generally need help consolidating motivation to change, resolving remaining ambivalence about change, formulating goals for change, identifying barriers to change, and enhancing self-efficacy. The following material contains several brief case vignettes illustrating therapist efforts.

### Eliciting Self-Motivational Statements through Evocative Questions

In the following example, the client has left the relationship in which his abuse lead to a court referral for counseling and is involved in a new relationship that is reported to be going well. Establishing goals can be challenging for such clients, who often think that the problem was solved when the abusive relationship ended.

THERAPIST: It sounds to me like you are coming out of a really difficult relationship, and it's great that there are still things you want to work on, still things you want to improve. [affirming]

CLIENT: Yeah. I know there's things I need to work on.

THERAPIST: Like what kind of things?

CLIENT: Like giving Elaine [client's new partner] more attention, because that's something I wasn't doing in my last relationship. I just kept ignoring her more and more as time went on.

## Identifying and Affirming Client Change Goals

The following excerpt illustrates the value in focusing on explicit motivations. It occurred during a session in which the client was provided with basic feedback about responses to initial assessments.

THERAPIST: On the assessment, you circled that the most likely thing that would happen if you don't attend the program is that you would face legal sanctions.

CLIENT: That's what they're telling me.

THERAPIST: Mm-hmm.

CLIENT: So, I gotta be here.

THERAPIST: Right. So that's something that would motivate you to keep coming.

CLIENT: Actually, you know what really motivates me to keep coming back is that I want to learn something.

THERAPIST: What kinds of things do you want to learn?

In the following passage, the therapist elicits the client's ideas about changing aggressive behavior and affirms the client's perceived need for change. Notice that during this early session, the therapist does not attempt to alter or critique the client's notions about the targets of change. There will be time to shape the targets and strategies for change as the work progresses.

CLIENT: And, so now I'm back with my family. I'm kind of like "Man, I don't need this craziness," you know.

THERAPIST: Yes. So, what other kinds of things do you think that you can work on, that will make you less aggressive?

CLIENT: Aggressive? Huh . . . Being up front, being myself, basically. . . . not trying to keep anything from anybody, such as my feelings—what's inside, you know. Like, I feel pretty good discussing these things with someone other than my little circle.

THERAPIST: I'm very impressed with what you've said so far.

The following excerpt came from an initial session with a client who was struggling with his partner's decision to separate from him and experiencing considerable frustration as a result of his efforts to reunite with her. This is a common clinical challenge with partner-violent clients. The passage illustrates several basic techniques for eliciting goals and motivational statements:

THERAPIST: OK, well what do you think will happen if you don't make a change? [looking forward to anticipate risks of not changing]

CLIENT: What do I think? Well . . . I can't answer that part . . . it's hard for me to leave my life. So much frustration. I lost a lot of weight because of this.

THERAPIST: Mm-hmm.

CLIENT: I love my family. I love my kids . . . that's why I find it so frustrating [crying]

THERAPIST: Mm-hmm. (Pause) . . . . This is very hard for you . . . [empathic reflection]

CLIENT: I love my kids . . .

THERAPIST: It sounds like you have been thinking about some changes that you might make in your life. . . . What do you want to get out of this program? [evocative open-ended request to elicit goal setting]

CLIENT: What do I want to get out of it?

THERAPIST: Mm-hmm.

CLIENT: I want to see what happened to me. Something that can help me to get on with my life.

## Exploring Barriers to Change and Decisional Balance

In the following example, the therapist doesn't shy away from the fact that abusive actions can have short-term positive effects for some clients, effects that need to be understood to develop alternative behaviors.

CLIENT: It's not a matter of losing control, because I'm in control. That's what I think. . . . and when I release, it actually makes me feel good, but very remorseful for the outcome, you know. I just, you know, regret doing it, but when I do release, because I keep things inside, and it builds up to a point where when it releases, it's brutal. It's violent, you know, and I'm not that way.

THERAPIST: You said that it feels good; there's a sense of release . . .

CLIENT: I mean—um, I feel just empty, basically. I don't feel tense, you know. It's just like "Whew . . . Wow. That felt good," you know.

THERAPIST: I think that's a really good thing you are saying . . . it can be hard, you know, if you get violent, to see that there are things you get out of it. Otherwise, you know, people wouldn't do it.

CLIENT: Right, right.

THERAPIST: So, maybe that's one of the reasons you keep something like that going . . . because there is a kind of benefit to it. You feel better, you get some release from it.

CLIENT: Right.

THERAPIST: Less stress.

CLIENT: Right, but you know . . .

THERAPIST: There are some negative things that come out of it too.

CLIENT: Yeah, like court, from this incident.

## Supporting Self-Efficacy by Affirming Previous Change Efforts

Evidence of previous change efforts, regarding abusive behavior and/or other significant problem behaviors, should be used to support and enhance the client's perceived ability to accomplish behavior change.

CLIENT: I think every day after work I was drunk. . . . now I don't even think about drinking. I mean, before I needed it for something, or it was a routine, you know. But now there's so many other things I can do. You know, I love working, and I do side jobs, you know, there's so many other things. I guess mentally I was unstable, and now I'm stable. Yeah, that's it. Yeah, getting your head clear, I mean . . .

THERAPIST: It's the first step, isn't' it?

CLIENT: Yeah. Yeah, it is.

THERAPIST: It also shows that you are capable of making significant changes in your life.

# TECHNICAL COMPETENCE
# IN MOTIVATIONAL INTERVIEWING

Some general guidelines and principles for the mastery of MI skills as articulated by the developers of this approach (Miller, 2000; Miller & Rollnick, 2002) are as follows:

1. MI was originally designed to help clients resolve ambivalence about change and, therefore, is most likely to be helpful in the early stages of change.
2. The spirit of MI has much in common with the "nonspecific" elements of therapy that have been shown time and again to promote

change and growth. These include empathy, genuineness, warmth, and a respect for the client's autonomy and growth potential.
3. The main goals of MI are:
   a. To decrease client resistance.
   b. To increase client change talk.
4. According to process analyses of MI (Miller, 2000), to meet minimally competent performance the clinician should:
   a. Make more reflective listening statements than questions. (Advanced motivational interviewers use two to three times as many reflections as questions.)
   b. Use more open-ended questions than closed-ended questions.
   c. Use more complex reflections than simple reflections. Complex reflections add meaning or focus to the client's communication, reflect both sides of the client's ambivalence, and/or summarize various aspects of the client's situation, whereas simple reflections paraphrase what the client is saying with little or no added meaning.
   d. Talk less than the client.
   e. Consistently focus attention and comments on the client's statements regarding the desire to change, perceived ability to change, and commitment to change.

## RECOMMENDATIONS FOR INTEGRATING MOTIVATIONAL INTERVIEWING AND COGNITIVE-BEHAVIORAL INTERVENTIONS

Whereas the first phase of treatment involves enhancing motivational readiness to change in order to develop a collaborative working alliance, meaningful treatment goals, and a process of self-directed change, the remaining phases of the treatment outlined here involve more traditional cognitive-behavioral interventions. Traditionally, CBT treatment manuals do not provide much information about motivation to change or preconditions for successful therapy, focusing instead on specific, therapist-directed intervention techniques. Although behavioral and cognitive therapy techniques can be highly effective in promoting targeted change, they are typically fruitless in the absence of client motivation to change and a solid therapeutic alliance. One of the most significant challenges in treating abusive clients involves shifting from motivational interventions discussed in this chapter to the more directive cognitive-behavioral interventions described in subsequent chapters. These efforts also involve conducting CBT within the spirit of MI.

## Differences between Motivational Interviewing and Cognitive-Behavioral Therapy

CBT differs from MI in several ways. Most notably, CBT tends to be more explicitly directive, whereas MI is more implicitly directive. In contrast to MI, when conducting CBT the therapist is more likely to give explicit advice, suggest change goals, engage in directive session tasks such as role plays, and assign out-of-session tasks ("homework"), such as things to read, self-monitoring tasks, behavioral skills practice, and cognitive change assignments.

The first two examples (giving advice and suggesting change goals) are generally consistent with the spirit of MI but are used sparingly by highly competent practitioners of MI and only after obtaining the client's permission to provide advice or suggestions. The latter two examples (directive session tasks and directive homework assignments) are, for the most part, not consistent with the practice of MI, thereby raising concerns about the successful integration of MI and cognitive-behavioral interventions.

## Specific Principles and Strategies for Maintaining the Spirit of Motivational Interviewing in the Conduct of Cognitive-Behavioral Interventions

Despite the ostensible differences between MI and CBT approaches, highly competent practitioners of CBT typically engage in directive therapy tasks in a fashion that is consistent with the spirit of MI. Most important is the collaborative context within which treatment tasks are introduced and carried out, with the ultimate goal of having the client "become his or her own therapist." Competent cognitive-behavioral therapists respect client autonomy in determining treatment goals and implementing change strategies. They follow the clients' leads in pacing treatment, assist clients in devising change plans, and gently direct clients back to the target goals when they wander. Several principles guide this style of intervention, and several techniques can be used to promote it:

1. *Stay on pace with the client.* Remember that resistance is a two-person phenomenon that results from moving faster than the client is ready to move.

2. *Establish change goals and a change plan with the client when the time is right.* For some highly motivated clients, the development of goals and change plans can begin in the first session. For many abusive clients, a personal change plan is most productively negotiated after two to three introductory sessions of MI. For some, it may take longer than this. An

agreement should be made at the beginning of the first session to engage in the first explicit task of counseling: namely, to spend some time exploring the client's situation, reasons for seeking counseling, and feelings about counseling in order to determine whether and how further work together can be helpful. This clarifies the therapist's task during the early phase of treatment and ensures that the therapist doesn't try to move forward before the client is ready to do so (that is, until they have devised specific treatment goals and plans).

3. *Always respect the client's autonomy and freedom of choice.* The client should have the last word in decisions about treatment tasks and the menu of change options. The therapist should explictly affirm the client's autonomy and freedom of choice regarding whether or not to change, what to change, and how to do it. The therapist should be sensitive to any signs from the client that the client is not amenable to specific change ideas or strategies and should never try to "steamroll" the client into complying with the therapists' notions or plans.

4. *Negotiate treatment goals and strategies explicitly with the client.* The therapist should not work toward goals that the client doesn't endorse and should never sign on to goals that are ethically or clinically untenable. For example, if the client's main goal is to get the partner back after she has left the abusive relationship, the therapist should reflect these concerns, explore and empathize with the client's loss and pain, and work toward personal change goals that are in keeping with ethical practice and respect for the partner's safety, autonomy, and choice, such as helping the client cope with separation and loss, improving necessary communication around issues such as child visitation, exploring how the relationship went awry, and building relationship skills that will be useful whether or not the partner returns. This process of goal establishment can take time. The therapist must exercise patience, caution, sound judgment, and great sensitivity in attempting to extend or reshape the client's change goals, realizing that the client may opt to stop treatment or seek treatment elsewhere if the therapist can not sign on to the client's goals.

5. *Keep the client's treatment goals in mind throughout treatment.* The therapist should try to link new ideas or treatment tasks explicitly to the client's change goals and be prepared to check up on the goals and establish new or extended goals when necessary as treatment progresses. We recommend a monthly goal and change plan check-up with the client. An example form for this task is presented in Figure 7.1. The client is asked to note thoughts about these issues, which are then discussed with the therapist.

6. *Maintain the attitude that the client should "take what you want and leave the rest."* There is no single magic formula for successful change, and nothing works for everyone. The client is ultimately in control of deciding whether and how to change. This simple reality can be very difficult

**FIGURE 7.1.** Counseling and change check-up.

Please provide your honest answers to the following questions. ***There are no right or wrong answers***. When talking about changes or progress, you should think about any changes you have made, whether or not counseling was involved. It is perfectly fine if you can't answer a question for some reason. Your counselor may ask you to talk about your answers in the session today.

1. I have made progress or changes in the following way(s):

_____

_____

_____

2. Things that have been helpful to me in making changes are:

_____

_____

_____

3. Things that have made change difficult are:

_____

_____

_____

4. I would like to change (or work on) the following (you can include goals for counseling or hopes and plans for the future here):

_____

_____

_____

_____

to accept when our clients are abusive and dangerous, but it remains a fundamental truth of intentional behavior change. Sometimes by maintaining this attitude, the therapist can discard strategies that don't make sense to the client and identify other interventions that are more helpful (rather than assuming that any particular strategy is the only way to help).

7. *Remember that clients trust the therapist and accept influence to the extent that they feel truly and deeply understood.* Empathic resonance is the jet fuel of therapy. The main alternative is coercion, which invokes reactance, anger, and resistance, or the expert power of authority, which is explicitly or implicitly rejected by most angry clients and does not invoke client autonomy and self-directed change efforts.

8. *Obtain the client's permission before giving advice or direction.* Throughout CBT, the client needs to be fully engaged in setting the agenda for change and in choosing tasks and assignments to promote change. It takes a little extra time to get full cooperation and collaboration on all treatment tasks, but it is well worth the effort. Some example therapist efforts to obtain client permission before giving advice or embarking on a clinical technique are provided below.

EXAMPLE 1

"I have come across some strategies that other people have found helpful in handling difficult interactions around child visitation. Would you be interested in discussing them to see if any of these may be helpful in your situation?" [Note that the client may have more important issues in mind, can legitimately say "no" to this question, and is being given permission to ignore any suggestions that don't seem useful or relevant to his or her situation.]

EXAMPLE 2

"I have some suggestions for ways to listen to your partner that may be helpful in keeping your discussions at a calmer level. Would you be willing to talk them over with me? What are your thoughts about that idea?"

EXAMPLE 3

"I have a handout here that gives more information about active listening. As always, I don't assume that everything here will apply to your situation. This handout may provide some helpful hints, but that's up to you to determine. Would you be interested in taking this sheet home and reading through it before our next session?"

EXAMPLE 4

"We have talked quite a bit about active listening, and you came up with a lot of ways that it might be helpful for you. One possible next step is for us to practice using active listening right here in our session. First you could talk about something on your mind for a few minutes while I try my best to demonstrate active listening skills. Then maybe I could pretend to be someone that you want to work on listening to, like your boss or your partner, so you could try it out. The nice thing is that there's no risk here at all. If it doesn't go well, there's no harm done, and you can decide whether or not you want to use active listening outside of our sessions. How does this sound to you?"

Examples of the specific techniques for promoting behavioral and cognitive change appear in the next several chapters. Once again, these are most likely to be successful if applied within the spirit of MI, with regular client involvement in goal setting, and with the therapist affirming the client's autonomy and freedom.

# / 8 /

# *Relationship Skills Training*

## RELATIONSHIPS 101

The vast majority of abusive clients have profound gaps in their understanding of healthy intimate adult relationships. Typically, their negative views have been confirmed through bad relationship experiences and self-fulfilling prophecies. Concepts such as trust, support, give and take, cooperation, and shared decision making are foreign to many such clients. They may understand the words, but have little, if any, gut experience of what they mean. Some clients remain quite cynical about whether such things are even within the realm of human possibility. Therefore, it is essential that therapists not presume that abusive clients share their basic assumptions about the nature of relationships, the meaning of relationship events, or the goals of relationship enhancement. Such observations also highlight the tremendous healing potential inherent in a therapeutic relationship that is empathic, supportive, affirming of the potential for growth and change, and based on mutual collaboration.

In many cases, the therapist must educate the client about basic elements of healthy intimate relationships, including notions such as that every relationship has good and bad features, partners don't always agree but can still support and love one another, relationships require that individuals make adaptations to their partner without compromising their core values, you can't always have your way but should get your way sometimes, partners act on emotion at times, partners don't always do what they say they will do, etc. Over the years, we have come to label this process of exploration and education "Relationships 101." It is a crucial treatment component for many (although certainly not all) abusive clients and perhaps the most essential element of treatment in some cases.

167

A brief review of the social histories of abusive clients reveals the source of dysfunctional relationship attitudes and behaviors. Many grew up in homes plagued by partner abuse, child abuse, or both. Some were sexually exploited or abused as youths (Simoneti, Scott, & Murphy, 2000). Many have witnessed siblings, friends, and neighbors engaged in dysfunctional or violent relationships. Some grew up with absent, neglectful, or drug-addicted parents or in unstable foster care arrangements. Some grew up in contexts where being tough and violent was highly reinforced. Some spent crucial periods of development in juvenile detention, prison, or mental hospitals. Many spent a good deal of their adolescence and early adulthood abusing drugs and alcohol. Although none of these developmental factors is inexorably linked to partner violence, they help to explain the lack of adequate relationship models and the source of dysfunctional beliefs about relationships for many abusive clients.

Culture, religion, and social class also play important roles in the development of relationship beliefs and expectations and must be carefully considered in facilitating cognitive and behavioral change. For foreign-born clients, the process of acculturation and assimilation often fuels serious tensions in the home. Men who emigrated with their families from cultures that are highly male dominant often express concerns that their wives or children are "becoming too American," losing their traditions, or asserting rights and freedoms that are outside the client's frame of reference. Immigrant clients who have dated or married North American partners may be confused and distressed by the cultural differences in expectations regarding gender roles for work outside the home, housework, child care, and decision making. North American clients who have married foreign partners may be disillusioned by their partner's unwillingness to fulfill a subservient role. (We have seen several such cases in recent years where the partner was met through mail-order bride arrangements.) Differences in religion, social class, racial and ethnic background, education, occupational status, income, and age also often create a need for clarification of values, education about acceptance of differences, and work on communication skills to discuss and negotiate relationship expectations.

The "Relationships 101" component of treatment typically involves education, advice, exploration, discussion, and values clarification. This process may be used to promote cognitive change, including acceptance of differences between partners and adjustment of unrealistic relationship expectations. The therapist needs to explore the client's concerns and beliefs, provide relevant information, impart hope regarding the possibility of healthier relating, and facilitate client motivation to enhance relationship functioning. The fundamental goal is to help clients see that they can exert a positive influence on their relationships by enhancing their understanding of how relationships work, increasing their acceptance of the partner, acknowledging and accepting differences, developing relationship skills, and letting go of the desire to control.

It is also important to note here that the goal of relationship skills training need not only be to improve and maintain an existing relationship. When abuse has occurred, one or both of the partners may be moving toward separation, which is often a very reasonable decision that may promote safety and stability. In fact, some abusive clients wish to reunite with a partner who has moved on, and treatment needs to focus on the assumptions and beliefs that make it impossible for the client to accept the partner's decision to end the relationship. Relationship skills training can also be very helpful for clients who would like to start another relationship in the future and who lack basic communication and conflict resolution skills. Many abusive clients move very quickly from one relationship to the next, so it is common for them to experience separation from the former relationship and initiation of a new one during the typical course of treatment. It is also common that clients will reunite with a partner during treatment. Therefore, we recommend that therapists in general assume that partner-abusive clients are never far away from being in a relationship in which they could profitably use communication skills.

We also recommend that the therapist assume an agnostic stance about separations, reunifications, and initiation of new relationships, within the general framework of promoting safety. If the therapist takes a stance in favor of ending or maintaining a specific relationship, the client may leave treatment when a decision is made that is counter to the therapist's advice. The alternative stance is to advocate for healthy relationships and the use of nonabusive relationship skills in all contexts, no matter who the partner is.

## THE CONCEPTUAL MODEL AND EMPIRICAL RATIONALE FOR SOCIAL SKILLS TRAINING IN PARTNER-VIOLENT CLIENTS

### Social Learning Theory

Social learning theory (Bandura, 1986; O'Leary, 1988) provides the basic conceptual foundation for cognitive and behavioral interventions with partner-violent men. Modern social learning theory is inherently cognitive and encompasses traditional behavioral concepts of classical and operant conditioning in a framework that also includes intervening cognitive variables such as the appraisal of one's ability to enact behaviors within a specific social and situational context (i.e., efficacy expectations) and the likely effects and results of such behaviors (i.e., outcome expectations). Social learning theory distinguishes between *acquisition* of a behavior (i.e., initial learning) and *performance* of the behavior under specific conditions (i.e., enactment). These conditions include emotional and interpersonal contexts that may limit the range of available behavioral alternatives.

Thus, there are two general types of behavioral deficiency of relevance to skills interventions with abusive clients: one in which the behavior is simply not within the client's repertoire and one in which the client is unable or unwilling to perform a previously acquired behavior under specific emotional or situational conditions. These are typically labeled skills deficits and performance deficits. One common skill deficit is the client's limited ability to provide reflective, empathic, and supportive responses to the partner's concerns (Holtzworth-Munroe & Smutzler, 1996; Holtzworth-Munroe, Stuart, Sandin, Smutzler, & McLaughlin, 1997). Another common deficit involves the delivery of positive verbal reinforcement to partners or other family members. Example skill components include paying attention to the partner's positive and helpful behaviors, describing these actions in positive terms (without criticism), and thanking the partner or otherwise acknowledging the partner's efforts. Many clients have a very limited behavioral repertoire in this area, having never sufficiently developed and practiced these skills.

Some clients have the relevant behavioral skills but are unable or unwilling to use them because of their overriding negative emotions toward the partner. One common performance deficit is the inability to express hurt feelings under conditions of anger arousal for an individual who can do so under other conditions. In fact, high arousal states related to anger and connected emotions (e.g., resentment, jealousy), along with highly generalized negative cognitions about the partner, form the major barrier to effective relationship skill performance for the vast majority of abusive clients.

## The Social Information-Processing Model

In application to partner violence, and to aggressive behavioral problems more generally, a very useful variant of social learning theory is the social information processing model (McFall, 1982). The model breaks down competent performance of social skills into several sequential components. The first step involves the *decoding* or interpretation of incoming social stimuli. The second step involves the *selection* of a response from a set of available options within the individual's repertoire of social behaviors (also called the decision-making stage). The third step involves the *enactment* of the behavior, wherein a selected problem-solving behavior is put into action and its effects monitored. Difficulties can arise at any step in the process. Not surprisingly, problems in the early stages of social information processing have cascading effects on subsequent stages. For example, if the individual decodes the partner's behavior by presuming negative intentions (e.g. "She's just saying that to piss me off"), this interpretation will limit or bias the selection of a response (e.g., increasing the likelihood of a hostile retort) and may hinder attempted enactment of other response options (e.g., the individual tries to respond "nicely" but has a sarcastic or accusatory tone of voice).

In an extensive series of studies, Holtzworth-Munroe and colleagues have compared the social and relationship skills of partner-violent men to nonviolent men in distressed and happy marriages, examining each step of the social information processing model (summarized in reviews by Holtzworth-Munroe, 1992, 2000). Most of these studies use hypothetical vignettes and ask subjects to provide interpretations (decoding) for the hypothetical partner behaviors, devise or select response options (decision making), or enact (role play) responses. Their studies have revealed that relative to nonviolent men, partner-violent men interpret a wide range of partner behaviors more negatively, displaying strong evidence of a hostile attributional bias (Holtzworth-Munroe & Hutchinson, 1993). In addition, when given the opportunity to verbalize spontaneously how they would respond to hypothetical relationship events or to select from a predetermined set of response options, partner-violent men display more aggressive and less socially competent response choices (Holtzworth-Munroe & Anglin, 1991; Holtzworth-Munroe & Smutzler, 1996). With respect to the enactment of competent responses, investigations of marital interactions show that partner-violent men have deficiencies in the ability to provide social support to the partner when the partner is discussing a problem from outside the marital relationship (Holtzworth-Munroe, Stuart, Sandin, Smutzler, & McLaughlin, 1997c), and serious skill deficits manifested in aversive and defensive communication behaviors when discussing relationship problems (e.g., Cordova et al., 1993; Margolin et al., 1988). Thus, both supportive behaviors and constructive problem solving are typically deficient in their communication.

These and related investigations provide very extensive and solid empirical support for the need for social skills intervention with partner-violent clients. The evidence indicates difficulties at each step of social information processing, although, as noted above, it remains possible that the primary decoding problems negatively bias subsequent stages of social information processing. It is also important to note that social information processing does not occur in a vacuum but involves complex feedback loops based on the influence of the client's past behaviors on the partner and vice versa. Hostile interpretation of others' behavior leads to problematic responses, which in turn can create a social context in which others are not only thought to have negative intentions, but actually display more negative interpersonal behaviors toward the aggressive individual. This self-fulfilling prophesy creates considerable challenges in intervention for partner-violent clients, many of whom have developed a longstanding pattern of hostile thinking and behavior in their relationships and come to treatment with many objective examples of mistreatment by the partner or others in their lives.

## The Challenge of Teaching Relationship Skills with Only One Partner Present

One of the more daunting challenges of behavior skills training for abusive clients involves the fact that only one member of the couple or family system is present in the treatment sessions. The standard wisdom in marriage and family therapy circles is that multiperson interventions are more powerful and more beneficial than single-person interventions. This wisdom is supported by research on "individual" conditions such as depression and addictions that shows added benefits from partner involvement in treatment (O'Leary & Beach, 1990; Jacobson, Holtzworth-Munroe, & Schmaling, 1989; O'Farrell, Cutter, & Choquette, 1992; Fals-Stewart et al., 1996).

To date, however, three studies have examined conjoint couples treatment versus gender-specific treatment for couples experiencing husband-to-wife marital violence, and none showed a significant advantage for conjoint treatment in reducing abusive behavior (Brannen & Rubin, 1996; Dunford, 2000; O'Leary et al., 1999). All of these studies were conducted using the group treatment format, so it is not clear whether the findings would generalize to working with specific couples or individuals. In addition, it should be noted that none of these studies have shown any significant dangers from conjoint treatment as compared to gender-specific treatment.

Practical concerns make it difficult or impossible to conduct conjoint treatment in many cases of partner violence. First, some partners are unwilling to participate in conjoint treatment, and it may be unethical, imprudent, and even illegal to consider mandating victims of crimes such as partner violence to participate in conjoint sessions (O'Farrell & Murphy, 2002). In addition, most advocates of conjoint treatment believe that a necessary condition for embarking on a course of couples' treatment is that both partners make some commitment to stay together to work on the relationship while in therapy (e.g., O'Farrell, 1993). Roughly half of the men seeking treatment for partner violence in a community agency are separated from their partners when they begin services, and, although some reunite during treatment, others break up. Finally, in order to promote safety, the more dangerous and potentially injurious cases are typically screened out from consideration for conjoint treatment (Bograd & Mederos, 1999; O'Leary et al., 1999).

Some of these practical concerns regarding couples intervention are illustrated by the results of the San Diego Navy experiment (Dunford, 2000). For abusive men who were randomized to a conjoint group treatment condition in that study, the average ratio for attending group sessions by female partners was 2:5, so for every five abusive men attending the "conjoint" treatment group, only two partners, on average, were in attendance. Further research and treatment development efforts are clearly warranted in this area, particularly given the tremendous success of couples' interventions with a range of other emotional and behavioral problems such as alcoholism (O'Farrell et al., 1985, 1992), drug abuse (Fals-Stewart et al., 1996) and depression (O'Leary & Beach, 1990). Yet practical concerns necessitate the use of interventions focused on the abusive individual in many cases, and the available studies to date have not shown a significant advantage of conjoint treatment for partner abuse.

Nevertheless, substantial practical problems arise in the effort to enhance relationship skills by working with only one member of a dyad. Often, the first obstacle is the client's belief that the partner needs to change (e.g., "She's the one with the problem") or related concerns about fairness (e.g., "Why am I the only one who has to change?") or efficacy (e.g., "I can change, but it won't have any effect on her, so why bother?"). Gentle persuasion, education, and various cognitive restructuring techniques discussed in the subsequent chapter are often essential in overcoming these barriers. Some clients can be convinced to work on becoming the best relationship partner they can be, shifting focus away from the partner and onto the self. Many clients come to embrace the notion that they can only control themselves, not others around them. Many eventually accept the idea that positive influence strategies are more effective and more ethical than coercive influence strategies. Some change their efficacy expectations when they enact a different relationship behavior and get a different reaction from the partner. Others benefit from reappraisal of their own responsibility in creating negative emotions and behaviors in the partner or in understanding that the process of healing from abuse requires great patience and a long-term commitment to change.

A second obstacle is the uncertainty created by not having the partner present. Thus, the therapist cannot predict with any certainty how the partner or other family members will respond to the client's change attempts. Relationship and family systems are inherently complex, and change is often nonlinear. The therapist may need to help reduce the client's expectations of favorable immediate effects on the partner from personal behavior change and to remobilize the client's motivation when things don't turn out as planned. For example, as the client learns to listen more effectively, the partner may begin expressing hurt and betrayal that resulted from the abuse. Levels of emotional communication and distress within the relationship may initially increase. At first, such expressions may seem overwhelming to the client who has used various strategies to suppress and avoid dealing with the partner's reactions to abuse.

A third obstacle imposed by the individual treatment format is the challenge of shaping skilled performance of relationship behaviors for use in the client's world, working within the artificial context of the therapy relationship (i.e., in the absence of the operative social stimuli in the client's daily life). The skillful therapist often becomes adept at portraying the client and partner in role plays in order to simulate real world experience. Focus on client behaviors in the therapeutic relationship can also provide an *in vivo* context for insight and behavior change. The artificial nature of individual treatment for relationship change is counterbalanced against the fact that it is a relatively safe environment for practicing new ways of interacting and communicating. Mistakes have little untoward consequence in this context, and the therapist can be patient and encouraging through repetitive efforts to learn communication skills. However, the generalization of relationship behaviors to life outside of treatment sessions requires careful planning and thought, which is especially the case in the development of meaningful and safe task assignments (homework). As a general rule, a client should not be encouraged to use a new communication behavior with the partner until the therapist has witnessed a reasonably skilled performance of the behavior in the treatment session. On the other hand, even a relatively inadequate performance of a behavior such as active listening may be a considerable improvement over typical communication behavior in the client's world, and, therefore, risk and benefit should be weighed with respect to the likelihood of stimulating conflict that could escalate to verbal or physical abuse. The skilled therapist will take note of many examples and opportunities for the client's use of new relationship behaviors that arise spontaneously in the therapeutic dialogue and that can be brought up at an appropriate time in efforts to shape and generalize relationship skills.

## Partner Involvement in Treatment of Abusive Clients

We have found it helpful to go beyond the dichotomy between conjoint and individual treatment in our thinking about partner involvement in the treatment of abusive clients. First, it is essential to realize that the partner (as well as other important people in the client's life such as children, extended family members, coworkers, and friends) is there in the client's daily life, whether or not such individuals are here in the treatment sessions. Therefore, concerns about safety are present no matter what the treatment format and are not unique to inviting partners to attend treatment sessions. Second, it is helpful to conceptualize partner involvement along a continuum. At one end of the continuum, the therapist has no contact with the partner whatsoever and conducts assessment and treatment by relying solely on the information provided by the client. In this arrangement, all information and knowledge regarding the partner is mediated by the client's communications and the therapists' interpretations thereof. At the other end of the continuum is a thoroughly conjoint form of treatment in which the therapist has absolutely no contact with either member of the couple individually, always meeting with both partners conjointly in conducting assessment and treatment. In this format, the individuals would have no opportunity to express concerns to the therapist, such as fears about safety or infidelity, in a way that was confidential from the spouse. It is our sincere belief that neither of these extremes on the continuum is sound clinically, and, therefore, that all therapists must make judgments about the extent to which the individual versus dyadic contact is useful and the extent to which partners should be involved in the assessment and treatment of abusive clients.

There are a number of ways to involve partners in assessment and treatment beyond traditional conjoint therapy. The first is to involve the partner in the assessment of abusive behavior, safety issues, and relationship functioning. This can be done only once (at intake) or can be an ongoing feature of treatment. In our individual treatment protocol for abusive clients, the therapist is strongly encouraged to contact the partner by phone roughly once a month. The goal of these conversations is to check in and obtain the partner's perspective on therapeutic progress and the goals for ongoing work. Therapists usually find this to be very helpful, as the partner may: (1) confirm the client's perceptions of events and change (helping the therapist to proceed confidently on the basis of the client's perspective), (2) provide a different perspective on events, progress, and change targets, such as different priorities for client behavior change or different interpretations of the meaning and success of the client's change attempts, or (3) invalidate the client's perspective in serious and substantial ways, for example by reporting on abusive or violent incidents that the client did not reveal, giving evidence of alcohol or drug abuse, affairs, or other serious relationship problems that the client has neglected to report or outwardly denied. These latter cases present a very significant therapeutic challenge, often revealing a serious rift in the collaborative alliance, significant unaddressed clinical issues, or psychopathic personality disturbance.

A second form of partner involvement is the provision of education or information to the partner about the treatment of the abusive client. It can be very helpful to ensure that the partner is informed of the client's efforts to implement strategies such as time-out during conflicts. Partners may not understand the goals of treatment or may disagree with the goals and strategies for change (e.g., "He is just using time-out as a control tactic to avoid addressing my concerns"). Partners differ in their desire to be informed about treatment. Some want extensive information from the therapist, whereas others may express a more general wish for the therapist to "fix him." Some partners presume that the client can never change, so it doesn't really matter what is done in treatment. Nevertheless, regular contact with the therapist usually helps the partner appreciate the benefits of the client's treatment or, in some cases, confront the risk of remaining in a relationship with a client who is not actively benefiting from treatment. Most partners feel empowered by the therapist's showing concern for their opinions about the client's behavior and goals for change, and some decide to seek counseling for themselves to address the negative effects of abuse. Obviously, the therapist should never be pushy (overtly or covertly) in involving partners and should show the utmost respect and concern for the partner's feelings and perceptions and the potential power imbalance between therapist and partner.

A third form of partner involvement falls into the general category of "partner-assisted" treatment. Although the treatment focus remains squarely on the abusive client, the partner may be enlisted to cooperate in some change efforts. Quite often, partners express the desire to be more involved in the treatment of the abusive client. There may be ways to do this without resorting to conjoint treatment. One example would be to bring partners in for some group discussion and information sessions in which the therapist can provide some general guidance and advice to promote safety and well-being and to enhance relationship change efforts. A second example would be to invite the partner to attend treatment sessions on occasion in order to facilitate the client's communication skills training—a sort of *in vivo* exercise in the safety of the therapist's office. Obviously, such intervention only makes sense if the partner is planning to stay in the relationship, is willing to be involved in this way, and feels comfortable doing so. Therapists must be very conscious that their position of authority might inadvertently pressure or coerce an unwilling partner to be involved in this manner, and, therefore, we recommend such intervention strategies only in cases where the partner has expressed a desire to be involved in the client's treatment.

Finally, a fourth form of partner involvement calls for an individual treatment stage followed by a conjoint treatment stage. A number of practical and ethical issues arise in the effort to add a conjoint component to individual treatment or switch to a conjoint format. For example, the client (and the partner) may have come to trust the therapist and may sincerely wish that the therapist would conduct conjoint sessions. Yet the therapist has inherent issues in allegiance with the partner or equity in the conjoint treatment, given that the partner does not share the same depth of treatment history that the client has with the therapist. Conversely, given that the client has been identified as the abusive partner, the therapist may have a tendency to form an unproductive alliance with the partner in a dyadic treatment context, rather than expecting both partners to work at change. On the other hand, referral to an unbiased practitioner for couples' therapy may mean sending the couple to a therapist who has more limited experience with partner abuse issues. We advise therapists to think through these issues carefully and consult with peers or supervisors in making decisions about conjoint treatment for an individual client.

Another concern involves the conditions under which conjoint treatment should be considered. When in the evolution of individual treatment is couples' therapy most likely to be safe and effective? Should it be an adjunct to individual treatment or a replacement for individual work? At present, there are no empirically based guidelines to answer these questions, and, therefore, clinical judgment and appraisal of safety issues must be used to make these determinations. Our recommendation is that couples' work be considered subsequent to individual abuser treatment only if several conditions are met, specifically: (1) the therapist and partner have noticed considerable improvement in the client's behavior as a function of individual treatment; (2) the partner feels a subjective sense of safety and has experienced no physical assault for at least 6–12 months; (3) both partners plan to stay in the relationship and are not doing so as a condition of conjoint treatment; and (4) the partner expresses an interest in being involved in conjoint treatment with no evidence of coercion.

## SKILLS TRAINING STRATEGIES

### Five Basic Steps in the Process of Skills Training

The therapist needs to develop a basic set of strategies for imparting relationship skills to abusive clients. The process of skills training has been broken down here into five steps. Clients may differ in their need for and responsiveness to each step. The steps are not always done in exact sequence, although the earlier steps involving learning and motivation must logically precede the later steps of practice and generalization. In essence, training is designed to help the client understand what the skill is, when to use it, and how it is done. The principles of training rely on information provision, observational learning, successive approximation of skilled performance (shaping), and generalization to current life contexts.

The first training step involves the provision of *information* about the skill(s) under consideration. Information is typically imparted in a straightforward, somewhat didactic fashion. The therapist must be careful to use terms, concepts, and examples that make sense to the client. As with any learning process, multiple modes of information provision, with some redundancy, tend to be more effective than a single mode of information. Common informational strategies include description of the skill and its utility, discussion of the skill with the client, provision of written material about it, and demonstration of the skill. Sometimes, demonstrations of ineffective or problematic relationship behaviors (negative modeling) can also help stimulate understanding and motivation. Whenever possible, therapists should provide information in a lively, interactive fashion. For example, in teaching active listening, the therapist might start by asking the client what makes a good listener, how one knows that someone is listening, which listening skills the client possesses and performs well, and which aspects need improvement. The therapist might then provide a brief written summary of listening skills (asking the client to review it in detail between sessions) and demonstrate in a brief role play some good and bad examples of active listening, soliciting the client's appraisal of the ingredients of good and bad listening examples. The goal here is to help the client understand what the relationship skill is and how it looks in practice.

In Step 2, the therapist works to *enhance the cognitive framework* for the use of the skill. Effective implementation of relationship behaviors is much more likely if the individual has a mindset that is consistent with the use of this skill. The goal here is to impart attitudes and beliefs that facilitate effective skill performance. Often, the mere adoption of a more constructive mindset will convey effort and intention to the relationship partner, which can help compensate for inadequate skill implementation. As a classic example, there is no simple way to characterize effective listening, and it is difficult (perhaps impossible) to identify precise components of active listening that are invariably effective. Competent listening requires interest and concern. The effective listener is focused on the other person, relatively free from distraction, and motivated to understand what the other person thinks, feels, and wants. Efforts to break this process down into techniques such as paraphrasing often fall short of the mark, because an individual can reflect or parrot what the other person is saying without conveying genuine interest and concern. Conversely, an objectively poor example of paraphrasing may be experienced as supportive by the partner if it is provided in a context of genuine interest and concern.

The client needs to have a clear sense of the intention and purpose behind the use of a particular relationship skill. This is particularly true for abusive clients who may be predisposed to see a relationship skill as a new method of controlling the partner. Following the active listening example, the therapist must help the client see that active listening involves an intention to learn more about what the other person thinks and feels and understand how and why the other person has these thoughts and feelings without judging or trying to change the partner's feelings. Although this goal may never be fully realized, the effort to understand the partner without judging can have a profound effect on the flow of communication.

In Step 3, the therapist reviews events and *situations for skill use*. Often, this involves scenarios from the client's life that have been previously discussed in treatment. The therapist and client can explore times when it might have been very helpful to use a specific communication or relationship skill and imagine how events might have progressed differently with the use of these skills. Even more important is a discussion and review of the times and places when specific skills are most likely to be helpful in the future. For example, when teaching a client how to negotiate and compromise, it is often helpful to review topics that are not likely to be negotiable (e.g., fundamental religious beliefs, basic relationship expectations regarding sexual fidelity, etc.) versus topics that are normally open for negotiation (e.g., how to spend vacations and holidays, major household purchases, etc.). Abusive clients sometimes act as if all issues are nonnegotiable and require either forcing one's will on the partner or acceding completely to the partner's will. In addition to the topics of compromise, the timing of such discussions and strategies for approaching them are crucial as well. Some clients inadvertently come to believe that relationships are endless drudgery, requiring constant discussion of every issue or feeling. Other clients believe (or wish) that they can avoid all discussions with the partner and somehow maintain a good relationship through the magic of love.

Step 4 involves shaping of the behavior through *role-playing exercises*. Most therapists use a combination approach where they play the client in reverse role plays for some of the time and play the partner (or some other person) most of the time. Role plays are facilitated by supportive feedback offered with the intention of shaping the behavioral skill(s). Feedback should be phrased positively and should neither be critical nor overly laden with evaluative content. The use of audio and/or video recording is extremely helpful in shaping relationship skills, as clients learn a great deal from hearing or watching themselves enact the behavior. Skill acquisition tends to be much more efficient with the use of these teaching aids. In a classic implementation, the therapist would set up a realistic scenario with the client that is derived from the client's experiences, audio tape a role play (from one to several minutes in duration), and then review the recording with the client. In some cases, the client may wish to repeat the role play a second time before reviewing the recording. When reviewing a role play, the therapist should refrain from immediate evaluation, relying, whenever possible, on the client's self-evaluation to shape skilled performance. Typically, the client is asked what he or she liked about their performance and what he or she would like to do differently the next time. It is absolutely crucial for the therapist to avoid using a critical tone when shaping communication skills and to focus on successive approximation to skilled performance. After several repetitions, improvements are typically seen in complex skills such as active listening, emotional expression, and respectful self-assertion.

Finally, Step 5 involves *generalization* of the skill to real life situations through task or homework assignments. Several key principles should guide the clinician in this effort. The first is to involve the client fully in making decisions about homework assignments. Clients need a sense of ownership over these tasks and are often quite capable of devising ways to use the skills outside of sessions. The second principle is not to push too hard. Clients tend to know when they are ready to try out a newly developed skill, and their reticence may offer an opportunity for cognitive restructuring or skill refinement. Third, the client should be given permission not to follow through with a task assignment if it is not feasible or seems like a bad idea at the time. This not only facilitates a sense of ownership, but also may help prevent a scenario in which the client is concerned about letting the therapist down. Some clients may even avoid treatment sessions altogether after several perceived homework failures. Obviously, the therapist must exercise caution in encouraging generalization of skills, particularly when the client retains a controlling attitude or has not shown sufficient skill mastery to facilitate constructive interactions.

## Suggested Guidelines for Role Plays

Given that role plays are the core strategy for shaping of relationship skills, the following guidelines provide additional recommendations to make the role plays as helpful as possible.

1. *Make the role-play situations as relevant as possible to the client's situation and life experience.* Take the time to find out some details, such as where and when a discussion or argument would happen, how it would begin, and how it would develop. Listen carefully to the client's descriptions of the partner's behavior and take them into account in the role play. One of the best ways to depict the partner is to let the client reverse role play to see how the client portrays the partner. There is an important therapeutic potential in portraying the partner accurately, as this conveys empathy and understanding for what the client has to cope with while also portraying confidence that it is possible for the client to respond constructively.

2. *Don't be afraid to overact or be negative.* As an extension of the first principle, it is better to err on the side of exaggeration than understatement. It is better that the client comes away from a role play thinking "My

partner wouldn't act that bad" than thinking "You don't really understand how bad my partner can act." It is important to remember that you are trying to help the client to cope with difficult relationship situations, so it is reasonable to portray difficult partner behaviors.

3. *Always rely on the principles of shaping.* Reinforce successive approximations of desirable relationship behaviors. When responding to a client, remember how negative he or she can be and how challenging it is to develop new communication skills. There is no room for perfectionism, only improvement. Finally, shaping relies on positive reinforcement, not punishment.

4. *Allow opportunities for repetition of skills, both within and across sessions.* Practice is particularly helpful in shaping communication skills. Usually, two to three or even more repetitions of the same scenario provide continuous improvement in skill performance. It is also crucial to revisit skills over time for continued enhancement or "tune ups."

5. *Facilitate client self-evaluation of communication skills.* Help clients to develop an "inner compass" to evaluate their relationship skills. Given that the goal is not to need treatment forever, clients must develop their own ability to evaluate and self-correct. Most abusive clients are somewhat resistant to being directed and told what to do. This reactance can be used to the advantage of therapy by promoting full and active engagement and self-directed effort in developing and practicing relationship skills.

6. *Use multiple methods to shape skills and impart relevant information.* Remember the normal sequence is: discuss, describe, demonstrate, practice, and generalize. Skilled practice is typically promoted when clients understand the skill, know when it can be used, develop motivation to use it, and witness examples of it. Observational learning is a key facet of this process.

7. *Downplay expectations for partner responses.* There are certainly cases where clients see significant positive short-term effects on the partner's behavior as a result of changing their own communication behaviors. However, communication skill development should be seen as a long term effort. Clients sometimes claim that certain techniques didn't work. When this happens it is very important for the therapist to explore what is meant by "working," and to help the client develop reasonable expectations for the partner's reactions. Consistent with point 5 (above), this type of reaction can be used to help focus the client's evaluation more on his or her own effective relationship behaviors, promoting a general philosophy of evaluating the relationship based on what the client is able to give rather than what he or she gets in return. Being a good relationship partner (or a good parent, good friend, etc.) pays dividends in the long run and provides a basis for positive self-evaluation.

## BASIC RELATIONSHIP SKILLS
## FOR PARTNER-VIOLENT CLIENTS

### Active Listening

*Description of Active Listening Skills and Common Targets
for Intervention*

In a recent study of an intensive prevention program for teen dating violence, a teen's listening skills, as rated by group facilitators, were the most powerful protective factor in predicting partner aggression outcomes (Wolfe et al., 2003). This finding squares with our clinical experience. Simply put, a great deal of partner abuse can be prevented if abusive clients learn to listen effectively while modulating emotional reactivity.

Marriage therapists often break communication down into two separate roles, the speaker role and the listener role (e.g., Jacobson & Margolin, 1979). Although good communication is experienced more holistically by participants, as a give and take, nevertheless a distinct set of skills is needed to speak and listen effectively. For almost everyone, the most efficient way to improve communication is to work on listening skills. Interestingly, however, when most clients describe communication problems, they focus on the need to express themselves better so that the partner will understand them, rather than ways better to understand the partner.

It is very difficult to define active listening objectively through a set of observable behaviors because so much of the concept has to do with the effect on the felt experience of the partner in being heard or understood. Thus, instead of trying to define exactly what makes up active listening, the therapist should try to foster a constructive attitude and a set of behaviors that usually facilitate understanding.

Nonverbal cues are the most important listening skill targets of intervention for most abusive clients. During role plays, clients will often display nonverbal reactions that convey disagreement or disdain or signs of an impulsive need to respond. Examples include eye rolling, toe or finger tapping, moving forward in one's seat, shifting visual attention away from the partner, zoning out or tuning out, and interrupting. On the flip side, nonverbal behaviors that convey active listening include turning to face the speaker, making eye contact, and displaying facial expressions consistent with interest and concern. Most abusive clients need explicit instruction to mute the television, turn off the radio, turn away from the computer, put down the newspaper, and otherwise stop engaging in distracting activities when the partner is speaking to them. They need encouragement to sit down and focus attention on the partner (some need help being able to stay in the same room or house!). Often, these behaviors can be addressed with humor in the session. Despite the comic features, such behaviors often convey a crucially important signal to the partner: "What you have to say is not as important as these other distractions."

Clients often catastrophize about nonverbal listening cues (e.g., "How come she always wants to talk to me when the game is on?"). They may need to discuss the value being placed on the partner, the message being sent by ignoring the partner, and the typical impact of effective listening. In most relationships, a moderate amount of effective listening goes a long way and usually prevents the need for lengthy complaint sessions. In our experience, improvement in basic nonverbal listening behaviors, along with exploration and change in the attitudes and beliefs that prevent effective listening, typically provides the most significant clinical improvements in this area.

In addition to nonverbal listening cues, verbal responses are often necessary to convey understanding. Techniques such as paraphrasing tend to be helpful in illustrating active listening but are not widely adopted in actual communication. One of the most important goals in teaching paraphrasing is to edit out the evaluative and critical tone of voice and commentary. Clients often use paraphrasing in an attempt to prove the partner wrong, dispute something the partner has said, or change the partner's opinion. Once again, the client's intentions and attitude tend to be more important than the specific behavioral technique to convey acceptance of the partner's thoughts and feelings. Paraphrasing is a very helpful exercise in teaching listening skills because the client's limitations and difficulties tend to be readily revealed in attempts at paraphrasing during role-play scenarios.

Validating is a step beyond paraphrasing. It involves not only a reflection of what the partner has said, but conveys understanding of why the partner has certain thoughts or feelings. Validation tends to be facilitated in treatment by inquiring and exploring the reasons for the partner's thoughts and feelings in a supportive atmosphere. Many abusive clients have trouble understanding why the partner can't simply forget about the past, move forward, and forgive them for their abusive acts. They fail to comprehend the extent of negative impact their abusive behaviors may have had on the family, particularly in terms of trust and safety concerns. As a result, the client may appear motivated to avoid or ignore the partner's negative communications or may make the partner out to be crazy, irrational, overly emotional, and so forth. These views must be effectively addressed in treatment and often emerge during role plays in which the client is instructed not only to paraphrase, but to reflect an understanding of how and why the "partner" (i.e., the therapist) has certain thoughts and feelings.

At basis, most listening skills boil down to acceptance of the partner's thoughts and feelings. Active listening is promoted by beliefs and attitudes indicating that the partner is a person of value, worthy of love and attention, understandable, possessing meaningful opinions, and capable of praiseworthy acts. This valuing of the basic person can be used to overcome barriers to understanding and other impasses in communication, including obvious shortcomings and flaws. Without such cognitive groundwork, however, effective listening is often precluded by the idea that the partner is blameworthy and should be punished, has bad intentions, or is deficient in ways that preclude the need or ability to understand her.

### Facilitating the Mind-Set for Active Listening

In addition to fundamental, core appraisals regarding the partner that can promote or inhibit understanding in communication, some common beliefs also often inhibit abusive clients' motivation for developing better listening skills. Perhaps the most common one is that they already listen to their partner, maybe even too much (e.g., "I just sit there and listen while my partner puts me down for hours"). The accuracy of such claims notwithstanding, the partner in these situations typically feels ignored or misunderstood. The client may be confused about the difference between hearing what the partner says and actively trying to understand the partner's feelings and wishes. In these cases, the client usually lacks sufficient skill to convey understanding to the partner and may be highly critical of what the partner thinks and feels. "I just wish she would shut up" is not usually a good automatic thought for effective listening. Other people know when we are actively trying to understand them, when we are just hearing them out in order to get our turn to speak, and when we are tuning them out or discounting what they have to say. Thus, the development of empathy usually goes hand in hand with the development of listening skills.

Another common belief is that listening means losing the argument, allowing the partner to control the discussion, or giving in. Clients with such beliefs need education about the differences among listening, agreeing, and decision making. Active listening means understanding the partner's feelings, opinions, and desires. It does not imply agreeing with the partner or acceding to the partner's wishes. These are separate issues. Interestingly, however, there is a grain of truth in this belief, given that active listening often opens up new possibilities for the client to identify areas of agreement and to fulfill the partner's requests. Usually, such developments can be reframed as relationship enhancing, rather than self-defeating. This latter point often relates to a more extensive set of assumptions regarding relationships as a zero-sum game, with winners and losers and adversarial needs. Such deeply held beliefs require exploration and reappraisal to facilitate communication skill development.

Perhaps the most efficient way to facilitate better attitudes about listening is for the therapist to role play some examples where he or she is a good listener with the client, reviewing the elements that went into effective listening as well as the therapist's thoughts and intentions when enacting this role.

> "What I was trying to do in this last role play was *really to understand* what you were saying, to put myself in your shoes and ask myself questions like 'How does he truly feel?' and 'Why does he feel this way?' without judging or second guessing you. A couple of times I had the impulse to say that you should think about it differently or to disagree with something you said, but I told myself to be patient and focus on understanding you first."

## Emotional Expression

### Description of Emotional Expression Skills and Common Targets for Intervention

Many abusive clients are quite rightly surprised by the idea that they may need help expressing their emotions. Typically, they are in treatment because they have overexpressed the emotions of anger, frustration, and rage through aggressive behavior. Interestingly, with respect to emotional expression styles, abusive clients typically characterize themselves in one of two extreme ways, corresponding to the distinction between overcontrolled and undercontrolled aggression (Hershorn & Rosenbaum, 1991). One group claims to be generally unemotional, usually stating "I never get angry." For these individuals, angry and violent outbursts are experienced as overwhelming, surprising, and out of character. They typically have significant deficits in emotional tracking skills (i.e., the awareness and labeling of emotions). Clinically, this tendency to suppress and avoid emotional awareness has been labeled alexithymia, and abusive clients in general have been found to show elevations on measures of this construct (Yelsma, 1996).

The other group of clients typically characterize themselves as "having a hot temper," and they may claim to be emotionally sensitive and/or frequently angry. Jealousy, envy, emotional dependency, and low self-esteem often accompany this highly arousable pattern. For these individuals, who fit an undercontrolled hostility profile, angry outbursts and high levels of experienced negative affect are regular features of their interpersonal transactions. Such individuals lack emotional self-regulation skills and may also have problems tracking and labeling emotions other than anger and rage. Abusive clients, as a group, show elevations on measures of emotional vulnerability and negative affectivity (Murphy et al., 1994).

Thus, the behavioral skill targets for effective expression are complex and vary depending on the specific style and features of each individual abusive client. In brief, the skill requires (1) awareness, tracking, and labeling of one's emotional experiences (including not only classic emotions such as fear and sadness, but also thoughts and wishes or desires) and (2) expression of feelings and wishes in a clear, and nonthreatening fashion. Self-expression of feelings and desires is most successful in the context of active listening, which tends to facilitate receptivity in the other person to one's communications.

Among individuals with high and chronic levels of anger and negative emotions, the motivation for developing expressive skills is usually to find more productive ways to express oneself. The training usually involves editing out nonverbal anger cues and hostile (or condescending) voice tone. It may also involve relabeling of "soft" emotions, such as hurt, disappointment, fear, and sadness, which tend to be covered by the "hard" emotions related to anger and dominance.

Among individuals with suppressed emotionality, the motivation for developing expression skills usually involves greater accuracy in communication and the potential for greater fulfillment in relating to others. Many such individuals show a generalized fear and avoidance of emotions, which may reflect an overlearned coping strategy or, in some cases, a response to traumatic experiences. A process of exposure to internal emotional cues is typically part of the treatment, which usually requires structured self-monitoring and work on labeling emotions, as well as guidance in expression.

As with active listening, our success with highly technical training strategies, such as the use of "I" statements, has been quite limited. These recommendations fail to capture the essence of good communication, although they can provide helpful practice tools for in-session activities.

## Facilitating the Mind-Set for Emotional Expression

As with all the relationship skills presented here, the first impulse for clients who have serious problems with control will be to use these expressive behaviors as an alternative means to control or manipulate the partner. Therefore, the first order of business regarding education is to explore the reasons for expressing one's wishes and feelings and to help adjust expectations for the effects of such expressions on others, for example the expectation that partners or children should always comply with one's requests. One key distinction that we teach is the difference between *requests* and *demands*. Requests are made in a positive or neutral tone and stated in such as way as to provide the partner with freedom of choice whether or not to fulfill them. Demands are made in a negative or critical tone and accompanied by a real or implied threat of negative consequences for noncompliance. It is impoitant for the therapist to be sensitive to the context and history of abusive relationships when discussing and shaping these behaviors, as any hint of demand may be experienced as coercive or threatening by an abused partner. This work is often accompanied by cognitive restructuring around themes of control, entitlement, and perceived victimization.

Another key point stressed in the education about emotional expression is responsibility for one's own feelings and reactions. This usually involves identifying and editing out blame, both in content and in tone of voice, from the expression of feelings and desires. The therapist should model appropriate assumption of personal responsibility for feelings and reactions throughout treatment, as well as a nonblaming, forward-looking perspective on change. Through role-play exercises, the therapist can demonstrate ways of stating feelings or desires that carry a blaming, critical, or judgmental tone and ways that do not. For many clients, seeing clear of the "blame game" that has become a central component of their relationship is very liberating and opens up many possibilities for new ways of interacting. However, transcending the tendency to blame the partner also means taking responsibility for the negative effects of one's own actions, including long-term negative effects of abusive behavior or other betrayals on the partner and relationship.

The painful nature of assuming personal responsibility for very negative effects of one's behavior puts many abusive clients into a trap involving shame and blame. If they take responsibility and honestly appraise the negative effects of their abuse, they become rapidly and deeply ashamed, guilty, and embarrassed. These negative self-evaluative emotions are acutely painful and present a difficult coping task. One way out is to control and shunt the feelings of shame and guilt through the cognitive shift of blaming—making it someone else's fault. This process can be likened to the dynamic concept of projection, but without appealing to unconscious motivations or object relations. The blaming process creates a negative feedback cycle that increases the likelihood of further abuse and relationship disruption. By blaming the partner for one's own bad acts, the individual justifies the use of abusive and coercive behaviors, reduces the motivation to use more constructive, less aversive behaviors in the future, and fails to enact conciliatory behaviors that can repair some of the damage of bad actions. In addition to this "intrapsychic" process, there is also an interpersonal version of the shame–blame spiral that is stimulated by the client's desire for forgiveness or wish to avoid responsibility for past actions, along with the recognition that the partner harbors ill feelings about past abuse or continues to experience negative effects of the abuse. The client is then motivated to avoid or suppress any negative reactions by the partner or cues that remind the abuser of past misdeeds.

The process of expressing conciliatory and apologetic feelings and intentions to change is an interesting and complex one that has received a good deal of attention in the clinical literature on partner violence and bears further exploration here, particularly given that effective and honest self-expression by abusive clients usually involves these emotions. In her classic work on the cycle of violence, Walker (1979) indicated that there is a reconciliation phase of the cycle, wherein the abuser attempts to make up, apologizes, says it will never happen again, buys flowers, etc. We have certainly seen some extreme and compelling examples of this in clinical practice, including things such as buying the partner new appliances or jewelry after a violent incident. Nevertheless, the majority of abusive clients actually do not engage in conciliatory behaviors after violent incidents. They remain entrenched in a blaming and hostile stance that justifies their abusive actions. When asked about a set of conciliatory behaviors after abuse, such as buying flowers or taking the partner out to dinner, a sizeable percentage of men in treatment for partner violence, as well as their partners, did not report engaging in conciliatory behaviors (Remington & Murphy, 2001). In itself, this finding does not directly contradict Walker's observations, as she claimed that conciliatory behaviors may decrease over time as the pattern of partner violence becomes repetitive and entrenched. Interestingly, however, in the study by Remington and Murphy, the tendency to engage in conciliatory behaviors was significantly correlated with borderline personality features, suggesting that the subgroup of partner-violent men who have intense fear of abandonment is more likely than others to engage in these behaviors. Thus, cycles involving escalation of tension and hostilities, violent outbursts, and reconciliation may not only vary over time for a specific abusive client, but also across individuals as a function of personality, relationship, and situational factors.

It is important to help clients see distinctions that may characterize their prior attempts to reconcile after abuse. One is the nature of their intentions. Were they expressing genuine remorse, or attempting to manipulate the partner into making up or reuniting after a separation? Another distinction has to do with the difference between stating an intention not to be abusive again and actively working on self-change in an attempt to accomplish this goal. Clients fully comprehend the distinction between words and deeds but often have difficulty accepting the fact that the partner is listening to the deeds, rather than the words, in determining whether the abusive client "really means it" when he says he will change. If clients can understand this distinction, they can usually see the need for patience and persistence in the healing process, as well as ways to express genuine assumption of personal responsibility for the effects of prior abuse. One

final important note regarding reconciliation is that effective problem resolution and apologies have been found to exert a strong soothing effect on
child witnesses to interadult conflict (Davies & Cummings, 1994). Given
that even in the healthiest of relationships, partners sometimes disagree,
exchange negative words or comments, are short with one another, etc., the
ability to apologize and take responsibility for one's actions is a communication skill worthy of sincere clinical attention.

## Assertiveness (Demonstrating Respect for Self and Partner)

### Description of Assertiveness Skills and Common Targets for Intervention

Assertiveness training has a lengthy history in clinical practice, originally
emerging from the personal growth movement of the 1960s and 1970s
and from feminist perspectives on women's difficulty with self-assertive
behavior as a result of traditional gender-role expectations (Alberti &
Emmons, 1970, 2001; Bloom, Coburn, & Pearlman, 1975). There is an
undeniable irony in conceptualizing the problems of abusive, coercive,
and controlling clients in terms of assertiveness deficits. After all, aren't
these individuals already demonstrating too much assertion of their will
on others?

Surprisingly, however, the vast majority of abusive clients lack the
interpersonal skills of appropriate assertiveness, including the social problem-
solving abilities required for assertive behavior. Given hypothetical or
actual personal scenarios, abusive clients can readily generate passive and
aggressive response options. In fact, most of them see these two extremes as
the only available choices. Thus, with regard to disagreements or decisions
in their relationships, most abusive clients see the options of either giving in
to the partner's demands or forcing one's own demands on the partner.
Despite objective evidence that many abusive clients exert considerable
control in their relationships, most feel that they chronically concede to the
partner's wishes.

The passive–aggressive spiral is deeply ingrained for many abusive clients. They feel "bossed around," "nagged," or "controlled" by the partner
or otherwise believe that they are conceding excessively to the partner's
wishes. (Note that these feelings and assumptions may or may not represent an exaggeration of reality for different individual cases.) As a result,
strong feelings of resentment arise, accompanied by automatic thoughts
about unfairness or victimization. Eventually, resentment builds to the
point where the individual "can't take this anymore," lashing out in anger
and aggression.

*Facilitating the Mind-Set for Assertiveness*

In this formulation, both aggressive and passive responses reflect a lack of assertiveness skills. Assertiveness is the middle ground between passive and aggressive behaviors. The simplest way to conceptualize assertiveness for most clients is a response that is both respectful of one's own and the other person's rights and feelings. In this formulation, passive and submissive behavior is not sufficiently respectful of one's own rights and feelings, whereas aggressive behavior steps over the line to be disrespectful of the other person's rights and feelings. The client is then challenged to find the assertive option(s) that respects both self and partner, first as a hypothetical response option and then in role plays designed to shape these skills.

Obviously, some abusive clients need education and values clarification regarding the rights of self and others (Pence & Paymar, 1993). Therapists cannot assume that abusive clients share their assumptions about equal rights, mutual respect, equal roles in decision making, and self-determination. Some clients may assert the belief that they have rights and freedoms not shared by their partners, usually as a function of their gender ideology, which may be linked to religious and cultural values. With such clients, we have found it very helpful to review a set of basic rights and freedoms in order to elicit their perspective. These typically include the right to be treated with respect (and how respect is communicated to the partner), the right to be involved in important family decisions (e.g., financial decisions, purchases, living arrangements, child bearing and child rearing practices, time together, leisure activities, time with in-laws and extended family, etc.), and the right to make various requests of the partner (e.g., to engage in household tasks, child rearing tasks, sexual requests or demands, etc.). With respect to these various rights and freedoms, it is important to evaluate both the client's view and the client's understanding of the partner's view or, if not in a current relationship, the client's understanding of the views of other people with whom the client is likely to have relationships in the future. The cognitive challenges are often pragmatic and based on the realization that others, including one's relationship partner, may not share the client's assumptions about differential rights, roles, and freedoms. In fact, clients may be operating under the common assumption that the attitudes or beliefs of close friends are more similar to one's own than is actually the case (Fiske & Taylor, 1991).

Assertiveness skill training is relatively culturebound to American middle-class values of self-expression, personal rights, and fairness. Cultures that place a higher emphasis on collectivity and belonging to a family or social unit often have a very different conception of the need for assertiveness and the range of reasonable assertive options. Behaviors promoted by assertiveness manuals may appear brash, selfish, or aggressive in some cultural and social contexts. Certain life decisions or areas of family activity may be experienced as nonnegotiable and off-limits to assertiveness, for example, caring for elders or inviting extended family members to live in the home. Relationship partners from different cultural and social backgrounds need strong communication skills in order to understand and negotiate differences that arise from basic assumptions about personal rights, appropriate family relationships, displays of respect, and gender roles. Therapists must be very sensitive to the client's perspective on assertiveness while promoting the fundamental concept of behavior that is respectful of self and partner.

## Negotiation and Compromise

### Description of Skills for Negotiation and Compromise and Common Targets for Intervention

Negotiation and compromise represent the process whereby partners devise and evaluate alternative solutions or decisions, attempting to find solutions that provide maximum benefit for all involved. Effective negotiation and compromise is greatly facilitated by understanding one's own and one's partner's priorities, avoiding critical generalizations, and focusing more on what one is willing to give than what one expects to get in return. This process draws upon a mature understanding of relationships as involving give and take, reciprocity, mutual respect, and the recognition that one cannot always get one's way nor should one rarely or never get one's way.

   Negotiation is seen here as the process of working out differences or disagreements to arrive at possible solutions. Therefore, it relies primarily on the communication skills previously covered, especially active listening and effective self-expression of feelings and desires. The ability to compromise is a unique skill that involves creative problem solving to consider a range of options that will promote both partners' interests.

   Typically, in work with abusive clients, we define compromise as giving something to get something. Compromise need not be "50/50," or equal in a mathematical sense, as such outcomes are often not possible for family or relationship concerns. Take, for example, a scenario in which the couple needs to decide where to go on vacation. One partner wants to go to the beach; the other wants to go to the mountains. A 50/50 solution would be half of the vacation in each location or separate vacations, both of which are likely to be impractical or undesirable due to cost, time together, or time spent traveling. Therefore, compromise may involve a third alternative that is neither person's first choice but acceptable to both, for example, going to a lake near the mountains. Alternatively, compromise could result from offering to accept the partner's choice this time in return for getting to choose next time (e.g., beach this year, mountains next year). Compromise may mean adapting one partner's choice to help meet the other partner's wishes (e.g., go to the beach but spend some of the time hiking and fishing nearby). Sometimes compromise means "trading" decisions or different aspects of decisions based on what is most important to each person. This can be very productive when each partner has different aspects of decisions or activities that are most important or most desirable (e.g., "I'll wash the dishes if you cook dinner"; "I'll mow the yard if you do the gardening"; "How about if we visit your mother on Saturday so I can watch the game on Sunday?").

The process of skills training for negotiation and compromise often involves some of the steps of traditional problem solving, especially brainstorming alternatives. For example, the therapist might begin by posing a hypothetical example of a relationship decision that the client can relate to but one that is not taken directly from the client's experience. The client might be asked to generate and write down a list of possible alternative solutions or decisions, for example, using the vacation decision described above. The therapist could prompt for examples of different types of compromise in this situation. Next, the therapist would usually try to find an example from the client's life experiences in which compromise could be helpful, often an example where the client and partner have different areas of priority, and go through a similar process of devising a range of possible options. In this example, the client can be asked to identify which aspects of a decision or issue are most important to him or her and which are least important as a means of identifying areas for compromise. Clients should be given the opportunity to engage in negotiation and compromise role plays, as they often have difficulty phrasing and expressing their ideas in a way that is likely to elicit a constructive response. For example, clients may have a critical or condescending tone when they suggest a compromise solution.

### Facilitating the Mind-Set for Negotiation and Compromise

Several common beliefs inhibit effective problem solving in relationships. The first involves the concept of winning and losing, or getting one's way versus giving in. Most clients believe, quite strongly, that relationships involve a struggle for power and control. When problems or disagreements arise, one person has to win, and the other has to lose. One person gets his or her way, and the other does not. Many clients possess a generalized version of these beliefs in which men and women are inherently adversarial (Burt, 1980). Another common belief is that someone must be right, and someone must be wrong. Many abusive clients confuse matters of fact with matters of preference, presuming that there are "right" and "wrong" preferences and tastes.

In fact, in most disagreements, it is possible for both people to win or for both to lose. Clients may be able to recall times when they got their way through manipulation or coercion, feeling bad about this Pyrrhic victory. Conversely, clients may be able to recall times when they gave in to the partner but later realized that this "defeat" had unexpected benefits. There are cases in which both people are "right," neither person is "right," there is no "right" or "wrong" answer, or there are many "right" answers. Many relationship disagreements involve a combination of facts (e.g., how much money the family makes) and opinions or preferences (e.g., how the money should be spent). Negotiations proceed much more smoothly if people get the facts reasonably straight and then treat the other issues as honest differences with no easy "right" or "wrong" answer. Most issues regarding finances, housekeeping, child rearing, etc. have many possible solutions and no one right way.

Therefore, the mind-set for effective compromise usually involves acceptance of differences, willingness to separate fact from opinion and preference, and recognition of possibilities for win–win solutions. The bottom line is that compromise involves giving something to get something. Rather than trying to make things perfectly fair, it is more a goal to make everyone reasonably happy. Clients will be most effective if they focus on what they are willing to give (without resentment), rather than what they are trying to get. It is also very helpful for the client to work on developing an openness to alternative solutions and perspectives, to find the positive value in the partner's suggestions, and to avoid rigid fixation on particular outcomes (e.g., "It has to be this way"; "My way is the only right way"; "My partner must give in here"; etc.).

## INTEGRATING RELATIONSHIP SKILLS TRAINING WITH COGNITIVE RESTRUCTURING

In practice, the distinction between cognitive and behavioral change strategies is often arbitrary or meaningless. As with recent developments in the treatment of social anxiety disorder (Turk et al., 2001), the treatment of abusive clients often involves simultaneous focus on behavioral skills and cognitive restructuring. In the context of a role play, for example, the therapist may go over with the client some of the irrational thoughts that are likely to arise and ways to counteract them. Problems in the performance of skills that have been adequately acquired usually reveal negative relationship assumptions that form the basis for further cognitive work. Conversely, when abusive clients change a pattern of thinking, this often reveals a serious gap in relationship skills that have not been developed due to the negative assumptions. The next chapter provides a set of ideas and intervention skills to accomplish cognitive restructuring with partner-abusive clients and further discusses the synergy created by effective dovetailing of cognitive and behavioral interventions.

# / 9 /

# *Cognitive Intervention Strategies*

$A$s reviewed in Chapter 3, a number of cognitive factors are commonly associated with partner-abusive behavior. An individualized assessment and case formulation should identify the key cognitive features for each treatment case. These can encompass underlying relationship beliefs and standards, hostile biases in information processing, and beliefs about the utility and appropriateness of aggression as an interpersonal problem-solving strategy. Increased awareness of cognitive distortions, insight into one's emotional reaction patterns, more adequate coping strategies to self-regulate emotional reactivity, and the development of rational problem-solving skills provide the main alternatives to abusive thinking patterns. A number of cognitive therapy techniques can be used to disentangle the confusing array of thoughts and feelings experienced by abusers in their relationships and to alter the beliefs and information-processing styles that lead to aggressive and controlling behaviors.

## COGNITIVE CONTENTS: THEMES AND VARIATIONS IN ABUSIVE THINKING

Table 9.1 contains a list of common themes in abusive thinking. The list was culled from clinical experience with abusive clients and was informed by a growing set of empirical studies examining common beliefs, cognitive distortions, and attributional styles in partner-violent individuals (for reviews, see Eckhardt & Dye, 2000; Holtzworth-Munroe, 2000). The list begins with some of the more extreme rationalizations used to justify perni-

**TABLE 9.1. Themes and variations in Abusive Thinking**

*Theme:* "She made me do it."

*Variations:*   "She knows how to piss me off."
"It's all her fault."
"She likes to push my buttons."
"She provokes me."
"She started it."
"I'm not the one who needs to change."

*Theme:* "She wants abuse."

*Variations:*   "Some women just like being abused."
"Everyone she's ever known has abused her."
"She thrives on it."
"She expects me to abuse her."
"When I treated her nicely she . . . [left me; cheated on me; played me for a fool; etc.].

*Theme:* "She gets something out of it."

*Variations:*   "She likes to feel like a victim."
"She wants to make me look like a fool."
"When I get mad, she gets all smug and superior."
"She starts it, then I look like the bad guy."
"I'm always the one who has to apologize and give in."
"Now she can just call the police and get me . . . [tossed out of my house; locked up; in trouble; etc.]."

*Theme:* "What's the big deal?"

*Variations:*   "It's not like I . . . [abuse her every day; sent her to the hospital; beat her senseless; etc.]."
"Everybody loses their temper once in a while."
"Why can't she just let it go and stop bringing it up?"
"Why does she have to keep throwing it in my face?"
"That's all in the past."
"I'm not like that anymore."

*Theme:* "She's just crazy."

*Variations:*   "She's irrational."
"She's too emotional."
"I'll never understand her."
"All she does is rant and rave."
"Even . . . [her family, her friends, her doctor, her therapist; etc.] say she's out of her mind."
"It's just that time of the month."

*Theme:* "She's inadequate."

*Variations:*   "She can't do anything without me."
"If it wasn't for me she . . . [would be living in the street; would have no clue what to wear; couldn't get up in the morning, etc.]."
"She's . . . [fat, ugly, stupid, mean, nasty, crude, worthless, etc.]."
"She's from the wrong side of the tracks."
"Her family is a bunch of losers."

*(continued)*

TABLE 9.1. *(continued)*

*Theme:* "This is just the way I am."

*Variations:* "She knew that I was like this, but she married me anyway."
"I've always been like this."
"People need to accept me the way I am."
"I just have a bad temper."
"I can't change."

*Theme:* "It's my way or the highway."

*Variations:* "The man is head of his household."
"A woman should know her place."
"What I say goes."
"I am in charge."
"I make the decisions."
"If she doesn't like it, then she can . . . [just leave; find someone else; go #$%& herself, etc.]."

*Theme:* "Might makes right."

*Variations:* "I showed her she can't get away with that crap."
"Now she knows who's boss."
"She won't try that again."
"She had to learn her lesson."
"If she starts it, then I'm going to finish it."

*Theme:* "She just wants to control me."

*Variations:* "She won't let me go anywhere or do anything."
"She doesn't want me to have any friends."
"As long as she gets her way, everything is fine."
"She's just a spoiled brat who has to get her way."
"She just wants to bust my balls."
"She expects me to act like I'm. . . . [an old man; boring; married; etc.]."

*Theme:* "I'm not appreciated."

*Variations:* "She acts like I never do anything around here."
"No matter what I do, it's never enough."
"All I hear is "honey do this, honey do that."
"To her, I'm just . . . [cheap labor; a paycheck; a meal ticket; etc.]."
"It's always nag, nag, nag."
"I bust my ass all day and then have to deal with this crap when I get home."
"She doesn't know how good she has it."

*Theme:* "She's disrespecting me."

*Variations:* "I'm not taking any crap off [any woman; anybody]."
"She plays me for a fool."
"Women only respect a firm hand."
"It's a sign of disrespect whenever she . . . [disagrees with me; gets mad at me; does something I don't like; looks at another man; says something about my family; etc.]."

*(continued)*

**TABLE 9.1.** *(continued)*

*Theme:* "Never show weakness."

*Variations:*    "Never give in."
"If I tell her how I feel, she'll just use it against me."
"Even though I know she's right, I would never say so."
"If I give in, she'll treat me like a chump."
"I can't give her the satisfaction of knowing she hurt me."
"I have no feelings; I can't be hurt."

*Theme:* "I can't live without her."

*Variations:*    "I can't stand it when she's not around."
"I can't take care of things myself."
"I've never been alone before."
"If she leaves me, it means . . . [she never loved me; I'm a loser; no one will ever want me; etc.]."
"We were meant to be together."
"If I can't have her, no one else will."

*Theme:* "She can't live without me."

*Variations:*    "She wouldn't know what to do without me."
"She'd be lost without me."
"As soon as the kids start fighting, she'll be begging me to come back."
"When she sees me with another woman, she'll be on her knees; you'll see."
"Divorce is a sin; God will punish her for leaving me."

*Theme:* "I can't tolerate it when my partner gets mad at me."

*Variations:*    "She has no reason to get mad."
"I didn't do anything, and here she is giving me a load of crap."
"She's always accusing me of something."
"When she starts in, I just have to get out of there."
"I tried everything, but she wouldn't . . . [shut up; leave me alone; get off my case; forgive me; etc.]."

*Other example themes:*

"My partner should be perfect."
"All women lie."
"All women cheat."
"She deserves to be punished for her evil deeds."
"I keep choosing the wrong partners."
"If I'm upset or unhappy, it must be her fault."
"I'm really the victim here."

cious acts of abuse (e.g., "My partner wants to be abused"; "My partner gets something out of it"). At the other end of the continuum are problematic thought patterns that are common targets in cognitive-behavioral couples' therapy for general relationship distress (Baucom & Epstein, 1990).

Individuals who perpetrate severe partner violence may have distorted thinking that differs both in *degree* and *kind* from the thought patterns common to unhappy, but not physically abusive, relationships. That is, abusive individuals tend to display the same negative cognitions observed in distressed nonviolent relationships, often to an exaggerated degree. Thus, virtually all of the generalizations that can be made regarding the role of negative cognition in establishing and maintaining marital distress apply to partner-violent clients as well (Baucom & Epstein, 1990; Bradbury & Fincham, 1990; Fincham, 1994; Fincham, Bradbury, & Beach, 1990). In addition, abusive clients often display unique cognitions that provide justification for abusive and violent behaviors. Given that safety is the first order of treatment, beliefs that make abuse seem justified, necessary, or otherwise "OK" receive top priority. Examples include the idea that the partner wants to be abused, gets something out of it, asks for it, or deserves it and the notion that abuse is not a big deal, is normal, is the only option, or has few negative consequences. It is important to realize that many abusive clients do not come right out and endorse such beliefs explicitly (although some do); rather, these underlying assumptions emerge as clients discuss and describe their relationship problems and abusive situations. The sensitive clinician infers these assumptions and presents them to the client through reflective listening, drawing parallels across situations or events or providing a descriptive formulation of why and how abuse occurs.

Even though the link to abuse and violence is less direct, beliefs that promote and maintain relationship distress are also very important, as they often set the stage for conflict escalation. Clients typically endorse these beliefs more overtly, as there is less social stigma attached to having a bad relationship or a bad partner than to the idea that abuse is justified or necessary. Common examples include the notion that all disagreement must be avoided, that relationships are inherently conflictual or unfulfilling, and that the partner is controlling, crazy, out of control, unappreciative, disrespectful, immoral, or deficient. These latter beliefs, overgeneralized negative assumptions about the partner's personality or character, are highly pervasive in abusive clients and have many forms and variations. It is also important to note that although problematic relationship beliefs are delineated separately here, they form a complex and interconnected network for the individual client.

Although efforts are made throughout this book to maintain gender-neutral language, in recognition of the fact that both women and men can perpetrate partner abuse (in both heterosexual and same-sex relationships), many elements in Table 9.1 use gender-laden phrasing. This was done for two reasons. One involves the recognition that most of the available research and clinical wisdom is based on studying and treating men who have abused women. Research and clinical practice with abusive heterosexual women, gay men, and lesbians, are relatively new and emerging areas of investigation, and it is difficult to determine as yet which generalizations derived from heterosexual abusive men will hold up in application to these clients or whether new or different clinical concepts will be needed. Second, some patterns of abusive thinking possess a uniquely gendered form. For example, one variation under the theme "it's my way or the highway" involves beliefs about men's right to be in control of the family or household and the "proper" place or role for women. Religious and cultural ideologies are sometimes used to support these beliefs, as noted by a long tradition of feminist scholarship on woman abuse (e.g., Dobash & Dobash, 1979; Martin, 1976; Schecter, 1982).

## COGNITIVE PROCESSES
## ASSOCIATED WITH PARTNER ABUSE

### Sentiment Override

Humans in general display a remarkable ability to interpret events and evidence in line with existing beliefs and predominant emotions. In the context of marital distress, Weiss (1980) has labeled this process "sentiment override." The underlying emotional disposition toward the intimate partner exerts a powerful influence on the processing of social information. A classic example is when one partner in a distressed relationship does something nice for the other person, who interprets this gesture as "trying to manipulate me," "trying to get something from me," or "doing it just because the therapist said to." The dominant negative sentiment channels information processing toward a hostile and suspicious set of interpretive options in which the positive act must be discounted as "manipulative," "out of character," "temporary," "not genuine," etc. The negative emotional disposition toward the partner overrides any potentially favorable interpretation of the partner's behavior.

The entrenched and global nature of these cognitive operating principles can present a daunting challenge to clinicians working with abusive clients. Many of the beliefs listed in Table 9.1 represent highly generalized negative attitudes toward the partner, for example, "She's just crazy" or "She wants to control me." These global negative appraisals are highly interwoven with predominant negative affect toward the partner. Aversive behavioral responses provide the third point in a reciprocal causal dynamic that establishes a self-fulfilling prophecy. The abusive client can enter the cycle at any point and start it spinning like a rotary engine. For example, the client may observe some action by the partner and filter it through the interpretive lens "She's acting crazy again," which produces frustration and anger, leading to a critical comment, which in turn stimulates a negative partner reaction that supports the initial appraisal. Conversely, the client could begin the vicious cycle with an aversive behavior or with a negative sentiment.

## Hostile Attributional Processes

As noted in Chapter 3, one of the most salient cognitive processes for partner-violent clients involves the tendency to interpret partner behaviors in a negative light. This process is so powerful, pervasive, and automatic that not only are clients convinced of the reality of their negative attributions, but clinicians are sometimes persuaded that the partner has negative intentions as well. The attributional process as applied to close relationships can be broken down into two major dimensions: causal attributions and responsibility attributions (Bradbury & Fincham, 1990). *Causal* attributions concern the explanation of events (i.e., why they occurred in the first place). *Responsibility* attributions contain an evaluative dimension, focusing on blameworthiness for negative events and credit for positive events.

Two pervasive social-cognitive phenomena conspire to promote distressed relationship cognition. The first is the fundamental attribution error (Ross, 1977), the tendency to explain others' behavior (in this case the partner's) as a function of internal trait characteristics that are global and stable while explaining one's own behavior as a function of state (situational) characteristics that are specific and transient. Thus, abusive clients, like most people, are prone to assume that the causes of a given behavior directly correspond to the internal traits of the actor, a tendency known as the "correspondence bias" (Gilbert & Malone, 1995). However, the consequences of this bias become magnified given the second social-cognitive phenomenon, which is a greater tendency to invoke attributional processes in response to negative relationship events than in response to positive relationship events (Holtzworth-Munroe & Jacobson, 1985). Together, these processes promote the common phenomenon of partner blaming. Blame results as a function of (1) the tendency to spend time and energy thinking about the causes of, and responsibility for, negative relationship events while ignoring positive events, and (2) the tendency to explain these negative events as a function of the partner's global and stable traits while dismissing one's own contribution as a function of unique and temporary situational factors.

A series of logical steps must be traversed in order to arrive at an assignment of blame for bad events or bad outcomes in a relationship (Bradbury & Fincham, 1990). In order for the partner to be held maximally blameworthy, first the event or outcome must be appraised as negative, and then the partner must be seen as having caused it to happen, with awareness (foreknowledge) of the outcome or consequences, having done it in an intentional fashion, and with the express purpose of bringing about the negative effect. "She did that in order to piss me off" is a classic automatic thought that encapsulates these steps, implying cause, awareness, and intentionality. In addition, a variety of attributions may mitigate against partner blameworthiness, such as adopting a causal focus on external events, other people, or oneself (e.g., "I started the argument in the first place"), considering that the partner was unaware of the potential negative effects (e.g., "She didn't know I would react this way") or that the partner did not intend for the negative effect to occur (e.g., "She didn't mean it").

Often, the statements made by clients about negative relationship events demonstrate that they are trying to shore up the weak links in the process of partner blaming. For example, clients often say:

"She *should have known* what would happen" or "She *should have known* how I would react" (implying that the partner may not have foreseen the negative outcome).

"It *seems like* she does these things on purpose" or "She says she didn't mean it, but she keeps on doing the same thing" (implying uncertainty about the partner's intentions or that negative intentions are only apparent in looking at a broad pattern of events rather than at a specific event).

In most instances, the attributional processes described above occur rapidly and with relatively little conscious effort (Gilbert, Pelham, & Krull, 1988). Therefore, one of the major clinical tasks is to slow down and "deautomatize" the process in order to help the client examine the logical steps used to blame the partner. The process can be likened to looking for "chinks in the armor," places to begin questioning assumptions about the partner's behavior and intentions. As noted in the previous chapter, reattribution training often proceeds hand in hand with communication skills training, as the client needs skills to gather more accurate information from the partner about thoughts, feelings, and intentions in order to arrive at more accurate appraisals. The powerful process of sentiment override is a major impediment to cognitive restructuring of hostile attributions, as negative global assumptions about the partner, accompanied by negative emotions, motivate the logical assignment of blame, even in the presence of contrary evidence or plausible alternative explanations. Linked to this is the cognitive tendency to catastrophize or awfulize relationship events, making them out to be more negative than necessary and, therefore, heightening the need to assign blame.

## Outcome Expectancies: The Correctness and Value of Aggressive Solutions

Another common cognitive process linked to abusive behavior is the tendency to overvalue aggressive solutions to interpersonal problems. Whereas attributional processes are used to promote feeling wronged and assigning blame, additional assumptions are necessary to support an aggressive response to the blameworthy party. Two predominant logical assumptions promote both the generation of aggressive solutions and the tendency to favor aggressive response options over nonviolent alternatives. One of these assumptions involves the moral correctness of aggression and violence. The other involves the functional utility, or practical value, of aggression and violence in bringing about desired interpersonal outcomes. In short, aggressive responses are appraised as "right" and "effective." These cognitive biases often operate in the short-term, immediate context of aggression and may be inconsistent with long term evaluations of the costs or immorality of aggression.

This aggressive shift in thinking usually involves the just-world belief that blameworthy people should "get what is coming to them." Thus, it is morally correct that the blameworthy individual should be punished or harmed. Violence under these conditions is not only justified, but praiseworthy. This thought process is linked to sentiments such as righteous indignation and is a pervasive backdrop for political violence and war (Beck, 1999), as well as a myriad of media depictions in which the bad guy "gets what is coming to him." As indicated in Chapter 3, empirical research has found that partner-violent individuals tend to endorse the belief that relationship aggression is acceptable or necessary under some circumstances (Bethke & DeJoy, 1993; Roscoe, 1985; Sugarman & Frankel, 1996). Clinically, we often see abusive clients justify the moral correctness of their actions through appeal to the partner's misdeeds, such as the partner's abuse of drugs or alcohol, affairs, deception, disrespect, etc. In fact, many abusive clients demonstrate a generalized version of this thought process outside of the family, engaging in road rage incidents, stranger assaults, and other violent and dangerous acts as a function of their positive appraisal of aggression.

This perception of moral rectitude is perhaps most intensely observed in beliefs about the physical punishment of children. Some abusive clients assert that the physical punishment of children, in and of itself, inherently imparts moral values. This thinking takes on almost magical proportions as

it ignores virtually all other considerations in the complex process of raising and educating children. For many abusive clients, these beliefs are confounded by their own histories of harsh discipline or childhood abuse. "I
was raised this way, and I turned out OK" is a common refrain and one
that needs to be explored carefully and sensitively as treatment evolves, as
the client is often suppressing or avoiding negative emotions about childhood experiences and ignoring or denying negative effects of physical punishment or abuse of his or her own children.

As evident in the beliefs about physical punishment of children, the
appraisal of violence as morally correct usually works in concert with the
belief that violence will have desirable effects. "She won't do that again,"
"I guess I showed her," and "That will teach her a lesson" are examples of
generic positive appraisals of the outcomes of abusive behavior. As indicated in the material on case formulation, beliefs about the effects of abusive behavior are often specific to particular situations and interpersonal
goals. For example, abuse may be seen as a way of getting the partner to
shut up, to stop nagging, to understand how angry or upset the client is, to
comply with certain demands, etc. The objective functions of aggression
may or may not map onto these subjective appraisals of its utility, but in
either event, the client will tend to continue using aggression if it is subjectively appraised to be correct and functional. It is also important to note
that it is possible to perform a behavior because it is judged to be effective,
even if it is seen as incorrect or immoral ("I know it was wrong to hit her,
but how else could I get her to stop yelling and nagging?"). Typically, as
with sentiment override in the attributional process, the predominant negative emotions of anger, pain, or hurt fuel the process of justifying aggression
as morally correct and create a biased appraisal of likely positive benefits
from aggressive acts.

## COGNITIVE RESTRUCTURING

### Classic Cognitive Distortions

The classic works of Aaron Beck (1976, 1999) and Albert Ellis (1994) have
provided an extensive list of cognitive distortions that can be usefully
adapted to clinical work with partner violence, as displayed in Table 9.2.

### Formulation of Therapeutic Change

Altering highly ingrained thought patterns is a challenging endeavor. Clinical experience reveals that both insight and behavioral practice are typically
needed to produce cognitive change in abusive clients. "Insight" here refers
to "a ha" experiences in which the individual has a realization regarding

**TABLE 9.2. Common Cognitive Distortions with Examples**

| Cognitive distortion | Description | Example(s) |
|---|---|---|
| Arbitrary inference/ causal thinking | Conclusion is drawn in the absence of evidence or counter to available evidence. Often involves an illogical leap that certain events are caused by others' misdeeds or hostile intentions. | "My partner is wearing a new perfume, so she must be having an affair." |
| Dichotomous thinking | Categorizing events, experiences, or people into one of two extremes. | "If she won't take me back, it means she never loved me." |
| | | "She's just evil, that's all there is to it." |
| Selective abstraction | A detail is taken out of context and other relevant information is ignored. | "I'll tell you how irresponsible she is. It was past one o'clock, and the children hadn't even had lunch yet!" |
| Overgeneralization | A general rule is made from a single incident or small number of incidents and then applied broadly. | "I'll never trust a woman again. They all cheat on you as soon as they get the chance." |
| Personalization | Attributing external events to oneself in the absence of a causal connection. | "I was responsible for my parents' divorce because I couldn't stop my father from hitting my mother." |
| Minimization | Viewing something as far less important than it is. | "I don't know why she can't just get over it. It's not like I sent her to the hospital." |
| Magnification | Viewing something as far more important than it is. | "I can't stand it when she talks about her favorite movie star. I know she's in love with him." |
| Catastrophizing | Expecting the worst possible outcomes of events and assuming these outcomes are inevitable. | "If my partner doesn't get tough on those kids, they'll end up on drugs and working the streets." |

*(continued)*

**TABLE 9.2.** *(continued)*

| Cognitive distortion | Description | Example(s) |
|---|---|---|
| Low frustration tolerance | Claiming that events are more horrible or unbearable than they truly are and that one is unable to tolerate such circumstances. | "I can't take it anymore." "I can't let her get away with this." |
| Demandingness | Harshly evaluating others' actions against unrealistic standards of conduct. | "When I come home from work, the house should be clean. There shouldn't be toys on the floor. What is she doing all day, anyway?" |
| Self/other rating | Evaluations of the total value or worth of a human being on the basis of a specific behavior or attribute. | "She's a lazy slob." "She's a spoiled brat." "Everyone said she was no good from the start." |

the irrational or dysfunctional nature of a specific thought, assumption, or belief. "Practice" refers to disciplined focus over time—a repetitive, self-directed effort to reconceptualize important aspects of experience. Sometimes, cognitive change appears to occur rapidly or instantaneously, following the logic of phase shifts in complex dynamical systems (Hayes & Strauss, 1998). These rapid shifts are typically preceded by instability. A previous system of thought is shaken up and thrown into flux before a new pattern emerges. Thus, "a ha" experiences aren't always spontaneous, in a strict sense, because they usually arise only after the foundation for cognitive change has been established. This groundwork involves awareness of the connections among thoughts, feelings, and actions and recognition of discomfort or difficulties associated with existing thought patterns. With or without rapid shifts of insight, lasting change almost invariably requires longer-term efforts to consolidate more rational and functional ways of thinking. The client must recognize problematic thoughts and beliefs in real life situations. Generalization may also result from this process, as the client comes to notice and counter dysfunctional thinking in various areas of life, such as work and parenting, in addition to spousal relations.

Following the pioneering work of Beck and colleagues, the main procedures of cognitive therapy arise from the principles of *guided discovery* and *collaborative empiricism* (Beck et al., 1979). "Guided discovery" refers to the ways in which the therapist helps the client unravel experiences, events, and personal history in order to discover themes running through the client's beliefs and misperceptions. This process follows the "downward arrow" technique of uncovering ever deeper layers of problematic thinking, beginning with conscious, momentary thoughts (e.g., "I can't let her get away with this"), moving toward automatic thoughts that hover at the edge of conscious awareness (e.g., "She's always taking advantage of me"), then toward underlying assumptions and beliefs (e.g., "She doesn't love me"), and finally to basic schemas regarding the self, world, and others (e.g., "No one will ever love me"; "People are never there for you when you need them"). These core schemas are presumed to have roots in childhood experiences, most notably in attachment relationships (Guidano & Liotti, 1983; McGinn & Young, 1996), yet they may also be altered through ongoing life experiences, including intimate relationships. Core schemas are invoked under specific emotional conditions that prompt a shift toward more primitive and less elaborate forms of thought, a style Beck (1999) has labeled "primal thinking." Basic themes of trust, acceptance/abandonment, freedom, respect, worthiness, and lovability pervade self and other schemas at these core levels of organization. If sufficiently entrenched and dysfunctional, these beliefs form the basis for a diagnosis of personality disorder, exerting a pervasive negative effect on interpersonal functioning (Beck, Freeman, Davis, & Associates 2004).

Collaborative empiricism refers to the process of working with the client to gather evidence and test hypotheses derived from the client's operating assumptions, beliefs, and schemas. As hostile automatic thoughts are exposed and identified, problematic underlying assumptions and beliefs that promote hostile thinking can be clarified and objectified. Next, various cognitive restructuring techniques are used to evaluate and appraise the accuracy, utility, and need for these assumptions and beliefs. Alternative perspectives are usually explored and evaluated as well. Finally, the client is encouraged to develop more realistic and functional ways of thinking, using strategies learned through the therapy process to detect problematic thinking and counteract its effects in life situations.

As noted in the previous chapter, in application to partner-violent clients, the cognitive therapy model is most helpful when integrated with behavior change methods. Successful cognitive and behavioral changes tend to feed off one another in a positive spiral. Conversely, problems in one area tend to impede change in the other. Attempts to change dysfunctional thinking often reveal the need for new behavioral skills, and attempts to change behavior often reveal the need for new ways of thinking.

For example, when the therapist begins working on listening skills with an abusive client, cognitive resistance often emerges. The therapist who inquires about difficulties in listening will hear clients state things such as:

"I know I'm right, so why should I listen to her?"
"If I listen to her, then I will have to give in to her."
"I'm never going to get a chance to say my piece."
"If I give her the chance, she'll just rant and rave for hours."

Skill training uncovers these dysfunctional assumptions, which, when addressed with cognitive interventions, create further opportunities for behavior change. Quite often, inadequate skill development, inadequate skill use, or noncompliance with skill task assignments can be traced directly to underlying cognitions.

Change in cognition likewise often reveals behavioral deficits. As the client arrives at a new perspective on the relationship or partner, the need for alternative behaviors may present a significant new challenge. For example, one client stated, "Now I see that she's not just trying to piss me off. I understand that she is upset about something, but I don't know how to approach her without making it worse or starting a fight."

The CBT model is learning based, forward looking, and optimistic. The working hypothesis is that even deeply held beliefs and assumptions about the self and relationship partners can be altered therapeutically. The client is a fully active partner in treatment, involved in establishing the overall goals of therapy, setting the agenda (priorities) for each treatment session, self-monitoring situations, thoughts, and behaviors, and challenging and altering dysfunctional patterns of thought and action. Abusive clients often respond quite positively to the empowering message inherent in the cognitive-behavioral model: namely that they can exert a positive influence on their emotional state by examining and altering their thoughts and actions. Many clients come to understand that efforts to control the partner are often misguided efforts to regulate one's own emotions.

## Cognitive Assessment

Assessment of dysfunctional thinking in abusive clients focuses on the idiosyncratic content of distorted thinking for the individual client and general themes that are common to this clinical population. Two important considerations in the assessment of cognitive distortions bear mentioning. First, the distortions outlined in the previous section of this chapter are typically tacit cognitive constructs that are not accessible to the client in the absence of particular internal or external cues. Thus, one should not assume that abusive clients have ready access to a "file" called "My Abuse-Promoting Thoughts" that can be opened simply because they're working with a CBT-oriented therapist. The therapist makes inferences about underlying assumptions and beliefs from the client's verbalizations and descriptions of situations. However, the therapist should not make unnecessary leaps of logic that are not clearly supported by the clinical material, nor is it necessary to press the client to accept the therapist's hypotheses about underlying assumptions and beliefs.

The second, related, consideration is that abuse-promoting cognitions will be most readily accessible for assessment and restructuring when activated by relevant internal or external cues. While the attentive therapist will find many examples of problematic thinking in abusive clients, at times it may be useful to have the client take a moment and remember the last time a particular argument occurred or the last time he was angry or enraged and so on. This simple retrieval technique often activates associated images, emotions, automatic thoughts, and underlying beliefs and assumptions. The core cognitive-assessment technique remains clinical interviewing in which the therapist is attuned to evidence of dysfunctional beliefs. Open-ended questions, empathic listening, focused probing, and detailed review of events and situations facilitate cognitive assessment.

Below are five cognitive-assessment techniques to help uncover irrational beliefs, as outlined by DiGiuseppe (1991a)

## Inductive Awareness

Inductive awareness involves simply asking clients to report what they are telling themselves when they feel upset. This is the most basic assessment strategy that is useful in teaching the general cognitive model to clients, as they are repeatedly exposed to therapist queries about underlying thoughts, beliefs, self-statements, etc. that accompany dysfunctional emotions and behaviors.

## Inductive Interpretation

Inductive interpretation is a related technique that involves tying together the common elements of beliefs uncovered during inductive awareness questions. Thus, the therapist will have gathered a variety of inferences from the abusive client after several sessions, for example:

> "When I come home from work, she should have the house clean."
> "She should know when to keep her mouth shut."
> "This is just the way I am, and she knows it."

The therapist reviews these inferences, searching for a common theme (e.g., "My partner should do what I expect her to do at all times; if she doesn't, then I have a right to punish her"). This can be done socratically, soliciting the client's assistance in seeing common threads, or it can be done in a more deductive fashion, with the therapist offering the interpretation as a higher-order inference to be explored and disputed.

While inductive awareness and inductive interpretation techniques are often very useful, they are directed toward client inferences rather than deeper, underlying schemas. Such core beliefs can often be uncovered by using two additional assessment techniques (DiGiuseppe, 1991a; Ellis, 1994).

### Inference Chaining

In inference chaining, the therapist asks the client to assume that a given inference is true in order to facilitate discovery of underlying assumptions or beliefs or to expose an interconnected set of dysfunctional ideas. Example prompts in inference chaining include phrases such as "Assuming that is true, then . . . . , " "What would it mean if . . . . ?" etc.

### Conjunctive Phrasing

In this strategy, the therapist responds to client inferences with a conjunction or conjunctive phrase, such as "and therefore . . . ," "and that would mean . . . ," "and that means that I would be . . . " Sometimes a series of inference chaining prompts and conjunctive phrases can be used to elaborate interconnected assumptions and underlying beliefs.

Obviously, inference chaining and conjunctive phrasing must be done cautiously and in the context of a collaborative therapeutic alliance. If this strategy is too hastily applied, the client may be put off by the unusual and intrusive form of questioning and by the long pauses that sometimes occur as clients try to put their thoughts into words. Because the inference chaining process involves some degree of self-discovery, it is important to relay rapidly the results of these self-explorations as described in the next section.

### Deductive Interpretation

In this technique, the therapist offers an interpretation about an underlying irrational belief or set of beliefs. Such interpretations are carefully presented, often using hypothetical phrasing:

> "We've talked about a number of situations that were difficult for you, where you became very upset or angry with your partner, and I'm starting to get a picture of what may be going through your mind at these

times. Based on what you've told me it sounds like you might be thinking something like 'I can't let her control me.' . . . What do you think about my guess here?"

The client may welcome this hypothesis. If the therapist is off the mark, however, or if the client is not yet ready to address the relevant beliefs, the client may reject it outright. More often, the hypothesis is only an approximation of the client's thinking and will need to be refined and reshaped. This process may go through several iterations before the client and therapist agree on the core belief, which in turn becomes a central treatment target (DiGiuseppe, 1991a).

It is worth restating that these assessment techniques are most effective if the therapist imparts a genuinely inquisitive tone, rather than a judgmental one. It is not recommended here as a "Socratic dialogue" to refute the client's dysfunctional thinking, but rather to uncover and elaborate the client's automatic thoughts, assumptions, and beliefs.

In addition to clinical interviewing, self-monitoring (e.g., thought records) can also provide a rich source of cognitive material for many clients (see Chapter 5). Periodic and systematic review of self-monitoring logs can reveal important themes for cognitive restructuring. It is often extremely helpful as part of this process to make a written list or schematic drawing of the client's basic irrational thoughts and beliefs, one that ties together important themes. Most clients not only find this process illuminating, but are often much more willing to begin evaluating assumptions or beliefs that have been objectified in some way. Many clients respond differently to seeing one of their core dysfunctional beliefs written out on a marker board or clipboard than to having it verbally reflected in ongoing dialogue with the therapist. Seeing it in writing provides distance that is often necessary to begin evaluating the belief or assumption, whereas a reflective comment by the therapist simply resonates with the client's ongoing, lived experience, leading the client to confirm or defend its reality. A number of the cognitive change techniques outlined in the following section capitalize on this clinical observation by objectifying thoughts or assumptions before evaluating them, most commonly by writing them down.

## Types of Cognitive Challenge

Clients persuade themselves to change a specific belief or assumption under one of several conditions. Note that the words "persuade themselves" are used, rather than "be persuaded." Even with the most cooperative clients and the most persuasive therapists, the cognitive change process is of necessity client-directed, as it requires generalization to the client's life situations. The first type of cognitive challenge occurs when the client realizes that a specific thought or belief is not logical, that it involves some type of inference or leap in logic that should not be made. The second type of cognitive challenge involves the realization that a belief or assumption is not in line with reality and, therefore, there is a more accurate way to conceptualize events. The third type of cognitive challenge involves the realization that a belief is not useful or functional (regardless of its accuracy) and that an alternative view would be more helpful in meeting one's needs or achieving personal goals. The fourth type of cognitive challenge occurs when the client realizes that a specific thought, assumption, or belief is simply not necessary in the first place. Regardless of whether the thought is logical, realistic, or accurate, it is simply not worth the time or effort to worry about it—it just doesn't matter. For simplicity, these four types of cognitive challenge are labeled "logical," "empirical," "heuristic," and "subversive" (DiGiuseppe, 1991b). Interestingly, therapists often begin with the assumption that they must convince clients that their beliefs are illogical or empirically inaccurate. In practice, however, clients are sometimes more willing to start by exploring the utility of or need for a certain style of thinking, later realizing the inherent logical or empirical inaccuracies.

The attributional example earlier in which one partner does something nice and the other interprets this as manipulation can be used to illustrate these distinct forms of self-persuasion with the following examples:

- *Logical challenge*: "It is not logical to presume that when people do something nice they always want something in return."
- *Empirical challenge*: "The facts just don't support my assumption here. My partner never asked for anything in return. She is probably trying to show that she cares, attempting to improve our relationship, or just being nice—not manipulating me."
- *Heuristic challenge*: "When I think of her as being manipulative, I get angry and say things I later regret. If I can look at her actions in a different way, then I can stay calm and react more positively."
- *Subversive challenge*: "It doesn't matter why she is doing nice things. I shouldn't waste my time trying to figure out her motives. I should just accept her kindness, show some appreciation, and move on."

Note that all of these examples focus on reappraisal of the activating event for the distressing emotional reaction. It would also be possible to challenge the beliefs and assumptions that produce distress in response to the activating event, first assuming that the partner *is* attempting to manipulate the client and then challenging the reasons that is upsetting. For example, this may involve challenging beliefs such as "My partner should never manipulate me," "My partner should always act the way that I expect her to," or "If someone manipulates me, then I am a chump or fool."

The following is an actual (verbatim) example of a client providing a subversive challenge regarding the importance of getting worked up over his partner's requests or complaints:

THERAPIST: (*reflecting what client had been saying*) Your arguments don't get to the extreme that perhaps they used to in the past.

CLIENT: And to take that a step further, then why is that? From my perspective, my responsibility is to be able to, while it's happening, to take a look at myself and be able to say "Is it really that important? Whatever the hell it is, it probably isn't, so why don't you just listen to whatever she has to say, and just deal with it, and then just move on, and chill out, and assume you'll feel better, and it won't be a big deal."

Logical and empirical challenges form the mainstay of Beck's cognitive therapy (e.g., Beck et al., 1979). The client and therapist are thought of as collaborative empiricists, seeking a more valid and accurate understanding of the client's world and experience. Depressive thinking often lends itself quite well to such challenges because the driving assumptions usually involve serious distortions about the self (e.g., "I am worthless") and are therefore accessible to exploration and change based on logical analysis, personal experience, and observations. In contrast, abusive individuals are prone to perceive relationship events as being caused by others' hostile intentions, which pose a threat to the self, leading to the experience of distress and the conclusion that the event is an unjustified violation of a strongly held personal rule (Beck, 1999). It can be very difficult to gain a foothold for realistic reappraisals because interpretive ambiguities are inherent in thinking about others' behavior. In addition, the client's perceptions and interpretations may be accurate. Sometimes a mistrusted spouse is, in fact, having an affair, or an angry spouse does intend to hurt one's feelings.

In such cases, logical and empirical challenges may hit a roadblock, particularly if they rely on the same "fuzzy" evidence used to bolster the hostile attributions, namely mind reading of the other person's intentions. Sometimes the client can learn to check out an assumption or belief by communicating more effectively with the partner (e.g., by asking for clarification or listening more effectively to what the partner is saying) or by considering a broader range of evidence (e.g., by avoiding selective abstraction or magnification of circumscribed negative events). However, the therapist may not be able to identify credible evidence that runs contrary to the client's assumptions and beliefs, especially given that the other party is not present in the treatment sessions to correct misappraisals.

Nevertheless, there are different ways to think about such relationship events and partner behaviors that can diffuse problematic reactions even in the absence of logical and empirical challenges. For example, in the case of an angry spouse who appears intent on hurting the client's feelings, the client may come to think, "My partner has some reason to be angry at me. Maybe I would be better off trying to understand why she's upset, rather than giving her back more of the same" or "Even though I don't like the way she is asking me, I can still respond to her request. I don't accomplish anything by thinking of her as a nag." Such heuristic challenges can be very helpful in shifting the client's frame of reference and reducing the reactive defensiveness to cognitive disputation. In addition, such challenges often go hand in hand with an analysis of self-fulfilling prophecies because the client's hostile attributions and responses help to create unwanted reactions and intentions in others.

Most abusive clients begin a relationship with global negative expectations (e.g., "Women are not trustworthy"), are hypervigilant regarding any possible evidence to support this belief (e.g., hanging on every word to find a contradiction or potential lie), and then act in ways to make the belief increasingly true (e.g., by giving the partner the third degree over meaningless issues, forcing the partner to omit details or facts in an attempt to avoid further conflicts). Clients can often be made aware of these self-defeating behavior patterns as a first step toward more constructive relationship beliefs. The pervasive need to find fault and blame is a cognitive style that lends itself to heuristic challenge, as clients come to realize that placing blame, regardless of its accuracy or validity, doesn't actually solve their problems.

For angry and hostile clients, subversive challenges can also be highly effective. Albert Ellis (1994) calls this "the elegant solution." Rather than quibbling about the facts of a given situation, which may involve a quagmire of "he said/she said" suppositions, one can begin by assuming the reality of the client's perspective, which often involves assuming the worst of another person or situation (e.g., "Let's assume you're right and your girlfriend may leave you for another man"). The therapist then follows this disarming acknowledgment with a question that essentially asks "What then?" (e.g., "How would you deal with that situation? What would that mean about you? What would it mean about her? How might it influence future relationships you might have?"). Clients are often hamstrung by the assumption that they cannot cope with an undesirable event or potentially painful reality (e.g., "If my partner leaves me, my life will be worthless. I can't go on without her"). One common reaction to such concerns is to reassure the client that the feared outcome is unlikely or impossible. However, such assertions are patently illogical, since the therapist, like the client, cannot foretell the future and does not know whether the partner will leave. Although the client may, in fact, be torn up over something that is highly unlikely, it is a position of greater emotional strength to believe "It would be heartbreaking, but I could cope with it and move on" than "It's an unlikely event, but it would be unbearable if it happened." Subversive challenges tend to undermine the awfulizing elements of irrational thinking and are particularly helpful in the acceptance of painful realities (e.g., "I guess it's not the end of the world if she doesn't want me back") or in diffusing the intensity of negative emotional reactions to actual or expected events (e.g., "It's not a big deal if my partner is not in the mood to have sex"). Obviously, some cognitive interventions combine elements of two or more of these change patterns.

Ineffective interventions are often mismatched to the nature of the thought being challenged or may be insufficient to overcome its grip on the individual. Effective interventions typically mesh well with the nature of presenting concerns. For example, a client may believe "My partner nags me constantly. She never stops. I can't take it anymore." Obviously, there are several irrational distortions here. One is the absolutistic, all-or-nothing nature of the idea that "she *never* stops" (overgeneralization and dichotomous thinking). It is highly unlikely that the partner nags 24 hours a day, never coming up for air or taking a break for lunch, coffee, or a phone call. Another unrealistic feature is the belief that the client cannot tolerate the partner's behavior (low frustration tolerance). The therapist could spend some time helping the client to realize the irrationality of these elements, perhaps helping the client to develop a more muted version, such as "My partner nags me quite often, and I don't like it." This version of the thought is less likely to produce violent rage, but still likely to be distress-maintaining because of the pejorative connotation regarding the partner's complaints or requests.

A next step might be to explore further the client's definitions of "nagging" and attributions about the partner's intentions for engaging in these behaviors. This process may involve relabeling the behavior as complaints and requests in an effort to reduce the highly charged, pejorative connotation of the "nagging" label. For example, the therapist might write "labels" at the top of a column on a page or whiteboard, putting the words "nag," "complaint," and "request" underneath, adding columns for feelings and behavioral reactions. The client is prompted to provide feelings and likely behavioral reactions associated with each label as a way of illustrating the value of relabeling the partner's behaviors. Alternatively, the therapist may ask the client to generate various hypotheses about why the partner engages in these behaviors. The therapist may contribute some interpretations, often extremely positive or negative ones, to the list. Example hypotheses regarding the partner's intentions for "nagging" might include "to piss me off," "to put me down," "to ruin my weekend," "to keep me from watching the football game," "to show me how much I have hurt her," "because she is frustrated that I don't keep my promises," or "because she wants the house to look good." After generating the list, the therapist can ask the client to evaluate the associated feelings and behavioral reactions that arise from these different attributions.

Subsequently, the therapist can help the client to explore underlying assumptions and beliefs that give rise to labels such as "nagging" and associated hostile attributions. For example, attention could be given to relevant gender beliefs, specifically the way that terms such as "nagging" delegitimize women's concerns and stereotype women's behavior and the extent to which the client may have internalized negative messages about "nagging wives" from various sources. Alternatively, relevant underlying beliefs about the relationship may be explored (e.g., "My partner doesn't appreciate me"; "My partner doesn't want me to be happy"; "If my partner loved me, she wouldn't complain about me"; etc.). The therapist may also explore the "demandingness" inherent in complaints about the partner's behavior ("e.g., "I shouldn't have to put up with her crap" or "She has no right to nag me day in and day out"). A series of cognitive disputes can be initiated around the underlying demand:

> "Is it logical to assume that because you want her to stop nagging you, therefore she must do so or else?" [logical]

> "Tell me about all those times when you demanded that she stop. Has her behavior forever changed and the nagging disappeared?" [empirical]

Note that in the above example, the therapist avoids quibbling with the client about *whether* the partner is, in fact, nagging. It is often useful to accept the client's perspective and assist him in realizing that, regardless of whether she nags or not, he needn't become unduly upset about her behavior.

If presented appropriately, *humorous* disputes can be used for particularly rigid and absolutistic demands ("It sounds like you have discovered the 11th commandment—Thou shall not nag thy husband!"). Humor can work quite effectively provided the therapist never makes fun of the client or otherwise creates the impression that he or she is picking on the client. The target of the humor should be the thought or behavior being disputed, not the client. Such interventions should be used only within the context of a strong working alliance, with careful attention paid to the client's reactions.

Alternative behavioral strategies also need to be considered, including ways to display consideration for the partner's complaints and requests, active listening, how to respond to the partner's requests in a fashion that is both respectful and assertive, and ways to negotiate and compromise in response to the partner's requests. In this example, the treatment process involves cognitive restructuring through the use of logical, empirical, heuristic, and subversive challenges, proceeding from outward manifestations of problematic thinking toward underlying assumptions and beliefs (using the "downward arrow" principle), and resulting in behavioral skills training. This example demonstrates the integration of cognitive and behavioral interventions and the need for flexible interventions that address a coherent set of concerns and themes. Throughout this effort, the therapist must walk a fine line, validating the client's frustrations and difficulties in coping with the partner's complaints while holding a firm expectation that the client can and should alter assumptions about the partner's behavior and find more functional and supportive ways to react.

## COGNITIVE RESTRUCTURING TECHNIQUES

There are a number of distinct approaches to cognitive therapy, with a range of available intervention techniques. The descriptions here are extracted from several sources, including McMullin's (2000) excellent compendium of cognitive therapy techniques, treatment protocols for depression, anxiety, and anger problems (Beck et al., 1979; Ellis, 1994; Turk, Heimberg, & Hope, 2001; Walen, DiGiuseppe, & Dryden, 1992), cognitive therapy strategies for couple intervention (Baucom & Epstein, 1990), previous work on cognitive interventions for partner-abusive individuals (e.g., Russell, 1995; Sonkin & Durphy, 1997), and our clinical experience. Before providing detailed suggestions for technique, it is important to mention that these strategies are most effective in the context of a collaborative alliance, with sufficient client motivation to change and a sound case formulation. Techniques cannot be applied willy-nilly and cannot take the place of careful conceptualization of the key factors in need of change for each individual case. On the other hand, a solid therapeutic relationship and sound clinical case formulation are not sufficient in the absence of effective intervention techniques. Thus, intervention techniques and case conceptualization combine synergistically to create a treatment approach that is much greater than the sum of its parts.

### Reattribution

As indicated earlier in this chapter, aggressive behavior is highly associated with hostile cognitive distortions at the encoding stage of social information processing. Thus, abusive clients display a strong tendency to attribute negative intention to their partners, to feel victimized by the partner, and to place blame. Causal and responsibility attributions form a common intervention target for these individuals. Several specific intervention techniques can be helpful in analyzing and altering hostile attributions. The first step involves education and exploration regarding the links between angry emotions and angry cognitions. Clients are provided with information about how being in an angry or irritable mood or in a high-stress state of mind alters thinking about others' behavior and intentions. Next, they are asked to apply these principles to their own experiences, exploring how thoughts and feelings are interconnected and how thinking becomes distorted under conditions of anger arousal. Self-monitoring greatly facilitates this awareness for many clients. Third, clients are asked to identify common attributions that they have regarding the partner's behavior, and the therapist helps the client to isolate the logical steps involved in arriving at an attribution of blame. (This step need not be specific to the relationship partner, as many clients engage in similar hostile thinking toward children, other family members, coworkers, and others.)

Following these efforts to identify problematic attributions and the relevant logical steps in assigning blame to the partner, the client is then asked to generate alternative attributions regarding the partner's behavior. The therapist should leave this process up to the client as much as possible in order to facilitate learning and to avoid a "yes, but" dialogue in which the client rejects the therapist's reattributions of the partner's behavior. Early in the treatment process, however, it is often necessary for the therapist to suggest alternative interpretations directly because the client's thinking is rigid and entrenched. Client resistance is least likely if the therapist does this in a "thought experiment" fashion, stating, "Let's just imagine for a minute that there is a different reason for her to do these things than the one you have come up with," "Let's just imagine that you thought about it this alternative way," or "You know we talked about how different things bother different people because they think about them differently. What if someone else was in your situation and he thought about it this other way?" It is typically most helpful to come up with several attributions. Commonly, the therapist might suggest an extremely positive attribution (if the client has an extremely negative one), and then one or more additional attributions that fall in-between the extremes.

After some alternative hypotheses for the partner's behavior have been generated, the client and therapist begin evaluating them. Typically, heuristic concerns are emphasized first, exploring different attributions based on the effects each would likely have on the client's emotions and behavioral reactions. The therapist asks, "If you thought about it this way, how would you feel? How would you react?" Heuristic challenges help to illustrate the potential value of reattribution and can be used to begin breaking down rigidity in thinking simply by illustrating that alternative interpretations exist and may be more functional. Realistic challenges are often used as well, evaluating various attributions based on available evidence. The therapist asks questions such as "What is the evidence in favor of this view? What is the evidence against it? Are you evaluating the evidence in a fair and impartial fashion, or are you selecting evidence that supports your attribution while ignoring evidence that refutes it?" Realistic challenges can help elaborate processes that support hostile attributions, including selective attention, negative underlying beliefs and assumptions, and behavioral reactions that promote negative self-fulfilling prophecies. Finally, subversive challenges are also quite helpful in some cases. The therapist can attempt to undermine the need for hostile attributions altogether by asking questions such as "Is it really important to know why she does this?"; "What's the difference? Why does it matter?"; "What makes it so important for you to maintain this interpretation of your partner's behavior?"; "What if no one is really to blame here?"; or "Is there any way to know the truth for certain here?" Heuristic challenges can help illustrate motivations for blaming the partner in the first place and can undermine the intense need to explain the partner's behavior in a negative light.

Figure 9.1 presents an example of a thought record for attributions regarding a partner's reactions to the client's questions about weeding the garden. The situation is rather mundane, yet provides a nice illustration of how different attributions lead to different emotions and actions.

As treatment progresses, the client is encouraged to engage in the reappraisal process between sessions, without the direct aid of the therapist. The use of a self-monitoring form that includes questions about alternative attributions is very helpful in this process. As the client begins to develop active listening skills, another helpful homework assignment involves asking the partner for more information to facilitate the evaluation of alternative attributions. The process of eliciting relevant information from the partner can be role-played in session.

## Label Shifting

Many abusive clients have automatic trait labels for others' behaviors that are highly critical and judgmental. It is quite common for individuals to find some trait or behavior in the partner attractive when first dating and then to relabel this trait or behavior as a deficiency later in the relationship. For example, a partner who was once seen as "laid back" and "fun-loving" is now seen as "lazy" and "irresponsible." This process, called "character assassination" in communication training (Gottman, Notarius, Gonso, &

**FIGURE 9.1.** Sample Thought Record

**SITUATION/EVENT**

Partner asked me to weed the garden, and snapped at me when I asked her to come outside and show me which ones were weeds and which ones were flowers.

| Attributions | Emotions | Reactions |
|---|---|---|
| She thinks I am stupid. | Anger Embarrass-ment | Swore at her, put down her garden. |
| She doesn't appreciate me. | Resentment | Told her to weed the f-ing place herself and went back inside. |

**Alternative Attributions**

| | | |
|---|---|---|
| 1. She thinks I am trying to dodge the work by playing dumb. | Hurt Frustration Humor | Tell her that I really want to help, but need a little direction. Joke about not trying to play dumb. |
| 2. She was busy doing something important, and I interrupted her. | Frustration | Apologize for interrupting her; ask her if she can show me in a little while; do something else for a while. |
| 3. She is upset because I don't take an interest in her hobbies. | Guilt Concern | Apologize for not paying attention to what she has told me about the plants. Ask her the names of the flowers and when they bloom. |

Markman, 1976), is a hallmark of distressed relationships. In the label-shifting technique, the therapist becomes attuned to the harsh words that clients use to label partners, children, coworkers, etc. At opportune times (and with sufficient empathy for the client's distress), the therapist reflects on the terms that are being used by the client, evaluating their meaning, fairness, and implications for the client's emotional and behavioral responses. Alternative labels are usually generated and similarly evaluated. Questions are considered, such as:

- Is this label a fair and complete representation of the person's trait(s)?
- What evidence is being ignored when this label is used?
- Is it fair to reduce the person to a trait description such as this?
- Does the label describe the person, when it would be more accurate to label the person's behavior?
- What emotions are felt when this label is applied?

- What behavioral reactions are suggested by the label?
- What are some alternative labels that are less harsh and critical?
- What emotions and behavioral reactions are likely in response to these alternative labels?

The ultimate goal is to formulate alternative, less pejorative labels, even potentially positive ones, through a process of rational evaluation and reframing. For example, a relationship partner can be thought of as "lazy" or as "relaxed and laid back"; an "unruly" child can be thought of as "energetic"; a "difficult" child can be thought of as "strong-willed" or "independent." "Overwhelming problems" can be relabeled as "challenges." This technique often helps clients see the crude intensity of highly charged cognitions. A helpful exercise is provided in Figure 9.2. Typically, the therapist would conduct this exercise with the client in session and then ask the client to think of other examples of negative labels for homework, along with cognitive challenges and counteracting labels.

## Exploring Different Reactions to Similar Situations

One useful technique that can be applied early in treatment involves identifying a situation in which the client engaged in problem behavior and then a similar situation in which the client did not engage in the problem behavior. The two situations are then used to uncover differences in thinking, including naturally occurring rational thoughts. These can then be explored and used to shape alternative ways to look at problematic situations. This technique can be very helpful early in treatment to help convince clients that the way they interpret situations influences their emotions and reactions.

## Decatastrophizing

This technique is very useful when clients have a tendency to exaggerate the negative features of life events and to ruminate about potentially negative outcomes. Although often recommended for anxious clients, decatastrophizing also works well with angry rumination. It can be applied to expectations of negative reactions from others (e.g., "I can't talk to my girlfriend like that. She will walk all over me"). This technique is also useful in dealing with feared rejection or with concerns that give rise to the impulse to isolate the partner and control the partner's actions or social contacts. In the "upcoming week" version of this technique, the client is asked to write down, in the session, the feared outcomes of an upcoming event or activity that is particularly troubling. The client may be asked to rate the anticipated damage (e.g., the negative effects of the anticipated outcomes), for

**FIGURE 9.2.** Negative labels and "character assassination."

When we have difficulties or disagreements in our relationships, or when our partners act in ways that we don't like, we tend to apply general negative labels to the partner. Instead of describing the partner's behavior, we label the person. For example, a partner who doesn't clean up may be labeled "sloppy," or "a pig"; a partner who doesn't finish a task may be labeled "lazy" or "irresponsible"; a partner who shows anger may be labeled as "mean," "nasty," or "cruel." If we can't understand the partner's point of view, we may label the partner as "irrational," "crazy," or "stupid." Once a negative label is applied, we look for evidence to support it, and we tend to ignore evidence that refutes it. This process is sometimes called "character assassination." The following exercise asks you to examine negative labels that you have applied to your partner.

First, think of a situation in which your partner did something that upset you, that you didn't like, or you didn't approve of.

1. What was the situation, and what did your partner do?

_____

_____

_____

_____

_____

_____

_____

2. What negative labels for your partner came to mind, or come to mind now, from this situation?

My partner is (or was)

_____     _____

_____     _____

_____     _____

3. Now look at each label, and ask yourself the following questions.

   Is this label fair?
   Is it complete? (Does my partner always act this way?)
   Is it accurate?
   What evidence am I ignoring when I use this label?
   What am I assuming when I use this label?
   Is the label based on my feelings, or on my partner's personality and judgment?

*(continued)*

**FIGURE 9.2.** *(page 2 of 2)*

4. What other negative labels have you applied to your partner?

_____

_____

_____

_____

_____

_____

_____

Again, for each label, try to come up with an honest answer to the questions posed above.

**Solutions**

1. Try to catch yourself thinking in negative-label terms.
2. Ask yourself questions like these to challenge the negative label.
3. If your partner does something that you really don't like, and you feel the need to discuss it:

   a. Describe your partner's *behavior* rather than *personality traits.*

   b. Describe your own feelings about it.

   c. Avoid distortions such as "You always," "You never," "You are just . . . . ," etc.

4. Keep positive labels in mind. Complete the following list, and add to it whenever you can.

**My Partner's Positive Traits**

I should remember that my partner is:

_____

_____

_____

_____

_____

_____

_____

_____

_____

_____

example on a scale from 0 (no problem) to 100 (totally devastating). The client is then asked to write down the best possible outcome of the situation, again rating the extent of damage on a 0 to 100 scale, and, for some situations with many possible outcomes, to formulate the most likely outcome. The therapist then asks the client to rate the likelihood of the various outcomes, for example on a scale from 0 (impossible) to 100 (100% certain to happen). Figure 9.3 contains an example log used in this process.

The therapist or client retains the catastrophic predictions. At a subsequent session, after the actual events have transpired, the therapist and client review the real and predicted outcomes. Over several successive applications of this technique, the client usually comes to see how and when catastrophic thinking is taking hold and to begin developing strategies for counteracting it. Obviously, therapeutic discretion must be used in selecting events for this technique, which is most helpful when likely outcomes are not the most negative imagined. It can be very helpful for situations in which a client may have to cope with the partner's angry feelings (e.g., dealing with pick-up and drop-off at visitation times, listening to a partner's concerns or complaints), as clients often exaggerate the level of negative impact of such events, leading them to react in unproductive ways.

In the "distant future" version of decatastrophizing, the client is asked to think through the "what ifs" of some deeply feared event or outcome that is not likely to occur in the immediate future (upcoming weeks). One common example is when a client is deeply troubled by jealous thoughts, fears of abandonment, or the desire to reunify after a relationship separation, to the point that such concerns significantly increase the risk of abusive and controlling behaviors. Such clients can be asked to write down and then discuss the feared outcomes, best possible outcomes, and most likely outcomes related to their concerns. For example, the worst outcome might be "She'll leave me for another guy and try to keep me from seeing the children," the best outcome might be "We'll stay together, work things out, and improve the relationship," and the most likely outcome might be "She'll leave me and won't be with anyone else right away, and I will see the children for regular visits" or "We'll stay together and continue to have a lot of difficulties getting along and a lot of hurt feelings about the past."

During this process, the therapist can probe for details, use rational restructuring techniques to evaluate the evidence for and against certain claims, explore potentially positive aspects of feared outcomes that the client may be ignoring, de-escalate the level of negative affect associated with these concerns, and help the client see how his or her own behavior and change efforts may influence the feared outcomes. The goal is to proceed with an "elegant solution" and to help the client shift from the perspective that a particular outcome would be devastating, unbearable, overwhelming, or warranting of extreme behavioral reactions toward the perspective

**FIGURE 9.3.** Decatastrophizing log.

## DESCRIPTION OF UPCOMING SITUATION OR EVENT:

_____
_____
_____
_____
_____
_____

| Feared outcome | Worst possible outcome (if different from feared one) | Best possible outcome | Most likely outcome (if different from others) |
|---|---|---|---|
| | | | |

### Awfulness rating

On a scale of 0 (no damage) to 100 (maximum damage), how awful is each outcome?

____    |  ____    |  ____    |  ____

### Likelihood rating

On a scale of 0 (totally impossible) to 100 (certain to happen) how likely is each outcome?

____    |  ____    |  ____    |  ____

that this outcome, although potentially troubling, is a tolerable situation that can be borne without the need for drastic responses. For example, the client may believe "If she leaves me, my life won't be worth living anymore," "If she leaves, I will make her life miserable," or "If I can't have her, no one else will." Yet many such clients have survived breakups in the past, and some have even moved on from betrayal and infidelity. The client is asked to draw upon strengths and resources in order to imagine ways to cope with the feared outcome. This intervention process is often very significant in the treatment of abusive clients who struggle desperately to control the partner in order to prevent a feared outcome such as the loss of the relationship. A great burden can be lifted if the client can get to the point of thinking "Even if my partner leaves me, I will be OK—I will make it through."

## Depathologizing

Depathologizing is a special case of relabeling and decatastrophizing that is useful for some, but not all, abusive clients. Through education, exploration, and relabeling, the goal is to alter clients' view of themselves, their partners, or other important people as sick, disturbed, crazy, etc. Such trait descriptions render change very difficult to imagine or suggest solutions like hospitalization and medication but downplay the potential role of cognitive and behavioral change. A social learning explanation can be very helpful in these endeavors as a way of normalizing the client's condition while providing an optimistic perspective on the prospect of change. Although most abusive clients attribute their difficulties to external events and causes (e.g., partner blaming), some harbor deep underlying concerns about their own sanity. In fact, as noted earlier in the book, some clients waffle between shame at the prospect of being a batterer and anger in blaming others for one's behavior. Shame and guilt are sometimes attached to generalized fears or beliefs that one is sick, disturbed, crazy, and out of control. These beliefs can be used to motivate change but often require some restructuring to facilitate self-efficacy for change.

## Objective Analysis of Beliefs

The straightforward, logical analysis of beliefs remains a mainstay of cognitive intervention. The client's belief is objectified and clarified in a relatively dispassionate way. Then supportive evidence and counterevidence are examined in a rigorous logical analysis using the disputation techniques outlined above. As in Beck and colleagues' (1979) cognitive therapy, behavioral experiments are sometimes designed to gather additional data in order to test assumptions and beliefs. With respect to angry and abusive clients, this first step of objectifying the assumption or belief is often therapeutic because it is extremely difficult to counteract angry thoughts when they occur rapidly and with great emotive force in actual life contexts.

## Objectifying a Network of Associated Beliefs

Abusive clients typically display an interconnected set of problematic assumptions and underlying beliefs about relationships. In response to specific relationship events and isolated partner behaviors, these fragmented assumptions may appear reasonable, even unassailable, to the client. It is only when viewed in light of a larger network of beliefs that their problematic nature becomes apparent. In a group session a number of years ago, Murphy went to the board and wrote down "Robert's Rules for Relationships," proceeding to list a series of implicit and explicit rules for conducting relationships that one of the group members, Robert, had verbalized at various points during the first six or seven group treatment sessions. The list included things such as "never give in," "always hurt them before they have a chance to hurt you," "don't get emotionally involved," "always keep the upper hand," and "never feel like you owe them anything." Other group members (and the therapist) had neglected to challenge each of these specific statements, in part because they came up in isolation, often provided as advice in response to another group member's situation (when more helpful advice from other group members was also available for discussion). Yet, once confronted with an extensive list of these rules, mostly based on verbatim quotes, the group members rapidly identified why Robert was having unsatisfying relationships, which he had attributed to the failures of his specific partners and the shortcomings of women in general. This insight reflects a Gestalt principle that can be used constructively in cognitive therapy, sometimes even with resistant clients, namely the tendency to construct a coherent, holistic image from a set of perceptual fragments. Once confronted with this list of rules, Robert was able to verbalize the underlying belief "you can't trust women." He began discussing the source of this belief in past betrayals, along with ways in which this belief impeded any effort to develop a healthy relationship.

## Coping Dialogues

Coping dialogues are often developed to accompany role plays. One way to do this is to have the client imagine being in a challenging situation and then prompt for things that the client could be thinking in order to cope with the situation effectively. Once the client develops some coping statements, the therapist can then role-model an internal coping dialogue, verbalizing the statements for the client. Next, the client is asked to do the same in session and then finally outside of the session in *in vivo* practice. Sometimes this process, which has been used in treating angry clients in other contexts (Novaco, 1975) is done using a hierarchy of difficult situations. We have used it productively with clients who have obsessive and controlling reactions to a range of family situations in order to shape internal dialogue that helps the client to cope with distress associated with messy rooms, household noise, children's squabbles, etc. The need for constructive internal coping dialogues is clearly illustrated by research asking abusive clients to say what they are thinking in response to audiotaped anger-producing scenarios. Abusive clients display very few anger control statements in this laboratory paradigm, indicating a significant deficit in self-talk to regulate anger arousal (Eckhardt et al., 1998). These findings suggest the importance of not only correcting distorted and biased cognitions, but also of creating a new set of cognitive skills that can be put into place during emotionally laden conflicts.

## Using Humor

Effective therapists tend to use humor, judiciously, for several purposes. Humor is an important form of social "glue" that can facilitate the establishment and maintenance of the working alliance. It also can lighten the atmosphere of therapy at times, to avoid an unnecessarily somber or depressing mood. Humor can also provide a unique form of empathy by demonstrating an understanding of the client's frame of reference. In the context of cognitive interventions, the judicious use of humor helps clients laugh at their irrationalities and see them in new light. As stated earlier in this chapter, the therapist must be very certain always to laugh with, but never at, the client. Humor is a spontaneous and natural element of interpersonal dialogue, and the absence of all humor from a treatment relationship is often a bad sign regarding the sense of shared purpose and meaning necessary to facilitate change.

## Gathering Counterevidence through Behavioral Experiments

One very useful set of techniques involves gathering evidence to test out problematic core beliefs and assumptions. This strategy is particularly helpful for beliefs that are rigidly embraced and not readily amenable to logical analysis. Often, abusive clients believe that the therapist just doesn't understand what life is like for the client, due to differences in upbringing, social class, culture, etc. One client said to Murphy, "Doc, you just don't understand how rough the women are out here nowadays." The client might imply that the therapist's perspective is out of touch with reality or is nice within the therapist's insular world. Certainly, if the therapist is too much of a Pollyanna, the client may be correct in such assertions. Also, there are many cases in which certain core beliefs have had tremendous survival value for the client in harsh life contexts such as on the street, in prison, or in illegal occupations (e.g., you have to be tough and violent, or others will take advantage of you). In such cases, after objectifying the relevant belief, the therapist must inquire how one would go about determining whether the belief is an accurate representation of reality or, conversely, what types of evidence would justify the conclusion that this is an inaccurate or false belief. For example, perhaps the client believes "You can't count on other people. They are all just in it for themselves." The therapist would ask about the types of evidence that would force the client to reconsider this assumption. Finally, the client and therapist can devise strategies together for gathering relevant evidence, for example through homework tasks that seem meaningful to the client. Again, however, the therapist is encouraged not to become overly consumed with whether the client's perspective is fully in line with reality, as this type of conclusion is not easy to agree upon and rarely fruitful therapeutically. The idea is to impart a useful set of information-processing tools that may aid the client in constructing a some-what more objectively accurate reality.

## Countering Techniques

"Counters" are thoughts, images, or actions designed to work against an irrational or problematic belief. Clients generally need both initial insight into the problematic or irrational nature of specific thought patterns and strategies to "take on the road" in order to address and alter these ways of thinking. Thus, countering techniques are used by the client to alter his or her problematic thinking over time in real-life contexts. Many counters are created spontaneously by clients during the process of change. The therapist can facilitate this process by exploring the client's counters, helping to generalize and further shape effective strategies to alter problematic cognitions.

To be effective, counters must not simply "replace" irrational beliefs but must be sufficient to counteract the forceful power of these beliefs (McMullin, 1986). Most counters reflect alternative forms of self-talk, but imagery and various action-oriented strategies are also used by some clients. Altering the effects of negative assumptions and beliefs on ongoing emotions and behaviors is a lengthy, repetitive process.

Counters take on many forms. Some are simple words or phrases, such as "that's a dumb idea," sentences (e.g., "It won't kill me to hear her out"), or more abstract philosophical beliefs ("To have deep and meaningful relationships with other people, I have to take risks and tell them how I feel"). These deeper, more philosophical "counters" often carry greater weight.

Clinical observations indicate that these deeper beliefs are more effective in clearing out irrational thoughts (McMullin, 1986). In general, counters that are personally meaningful to the client, rooted in the client's own experiences and philosophy, are more effective than vague catch phrases or affirmations. Counters that are deeply personal have intuitive truth value for the client, whereas externally provided ones may lack power or credibility within the client's frame of reference.

Some therapists recommend that the client generate as many counters as possible to address a specific irrational belief. Alternatively, it may be helpful to have the client develop a core or central counter that can then be elaborated through experience and practice. A very common example in treatment of abusers is "I can't control my partner. I can only control myself." This is a very helpful way of thinking, but it is likely to have a lasting effect on the client's behavior to the extent that it is linked to deep personal values and philosophy and is elaborated meaningfully in relevant situations and life contexts. Examples of the former include beliefs about the importance of individual freedom, the idea that love or attention that is freely given is much more valuable than anything that can result from control or coercion, or the importance of accepting those we love, imperfections and all. These examples are innumerable, arising from many aspects of couple relationships and family life.

Effective counters should be realistic and sensible. For example, a counter like "My relationship will improve a little every day" is not sound or sensible. Moods, stressors, and other factors make it such that bad days will happen, and one cannot reasonably expect linear growth in relationship adjustment or happiness. Thus, this counter will be undermined by life experiences. Another consideration is that effective counters tend to include the same cognitive modality as the problematic idea. For example, if the client has a concern about the partner's fidelity that is associated with powerful imagery (e.g., imagining the partner in bed with someone else), counters should usually include imagery as well as self-talk (e.g., create an image of what the partner is most likely doing at the present time). In general, thoughts involving compassion, concern, and caring for others provide the most powerful antidote to thoughts involving hostility, aggression, and violence (Stosny, 1995).

## LIMITATIONS AND CHALLENGES

Many partner-abusive clients have personal characteristics and problems that impede progress with the traditional cognitive-behavioral interventions outlined above. Most notable are rigid resistance to direction or advice, serious difficulties in forming a collaborative alliance, and personality problems involving antisocial, borderline, and/or narcissistic features. Significant dependent, avoidant, and/or obsessive–compulsive personality problems are also commonly observed in abusive clients. In our experience, individuals who have severe difficulty benefiting from traditional cognitive-behavioral interventions typically possess deeply entrenched and maladaptive self-schemas associated with abusive or neglectful childhood experiences. In recent years, the practice of cognitive therapy has evolved to begin addressing these deeper underlying assumptions about the self and others under the general rubric of "schema therapy" (Young, Klosko, & Weishaar, 2003), which developed as a response to treatment-resistant patients and those with significant personality disorders. Given the emphasis on early maladaptive schemas, aspects of this emerging perspective are covered in the subsequent chapter on trauma recovery.

# / 10 /

# *Trauma Recovery*

Trauma recovery is an important phase of treatment for many partner-abusive clients. Many of these individuals display long-term effects of having witnessed or experienced abuse in childhood. If not addressed, the lasting effects of childhood trauma may inhibit successful treatment outcome for these individuals, many of whom demonstrate a muted response to traditional cognitive and behavior change strategies outlined in the preceding chapters. This chapter provides some background on the rates and forms of childhood trauma exposure in clinical samples of partner-abusive individuals and common emotional and cognitive consequences of childhood trauma exposure in this treatment population. We describe basic cognitive and behavioral strategies to promote the emotional processing of traumatic memories, to alter underlying maladaptive self-schemas, and to reduce negative effects of trauma in the relationship functioning of partner-abusive clients.

## RATIONALE FOR THE TREATMENT OF TRAUMA IN PARTNER-ABUSIVE CLIENTS

Although estimates vary from study to study, on average about 60% of partner-assaultive men recruited from clinical settings report exposure to family violence during childhood (Delsol & Margolin, 2004). When broken down by type of family violence exposure, roughly one-third of clinical sample abusive men, on average, report witnessing interparental violence and roughly one-third report being the victim of child abuse (Delsol &

Margolin, 2004). These rates of family violence exposure are roughly three times higher than the corresponding rates observed in nonviolent control group men. Level of family violence exposure also correlates with the level of partner violence in clinically abusive samples (Murphy et al., 1993). In addition, childhood family violence exposure is a significant risk factor for adult partner abuse in nonclinical samples (Ehrensaft, Cohen, & Brown, 2003; Schafer, Caetano, & Cunradi, 2004; Whitfield, Anda, & Dube, 2003).

Several prominent theories have been used to account for the role of childhood trauma in intimate partner abuse. These theories can be divided into two broad categories: traumatic stress approaches and social learning approaches. Traumatic stress approaches emphasize the effects of trauma on emotion regulation and personality development. The most prominent example of this approach is Dutton's theory of the abusive personality (Dutton, 1995a, 1998). Dutton draws from the clinical literature on borderline personality disorder, Walker's (1984) cycle of violence theory, and aspects of object relations theory to explain the emotional and behavioral characteristics of the abusive individual. In this model, adverse childhood experiences involving abuse, neglect, and/or parental rejection are associated with attachment insecurity. Individuals with insecure attachment develop problems in self-regulation and emotional instability and rely on coercive interpersonal behaviors to meet attachment needs. Individuals with these developmental histories have great difficulty regulating the intense emotions brought on by intimate relationships. This emotional dysregulation is expressed through intermittent cycles of abusive behavior (Dutton, 1998). Dutton's model is designed to explain why individuals with abusive personalities waffle between intimate rage (with controlling and abusive behavior) and desperate fear of abandonment (with conciliatory behavior) and how adverse childhood experiences contribute to the cyclical pattern of abuse. Stosny (1995) has developed a clinical approach emphasizing compassion for self and others that is based on similar theoretical ideas in attachment theory.

Social learning theories (e.g., Bandura, 1986; O'Leary, 1988) maintain that growing up in a violent family can increase risk for adult partner abuse through both direct and indirect means. The direct effects involve shaping of aggressive responses to interpersonal difficulties as a result of being raised in a family characterized by high rates of aversive and coercive behaviors. Caregivers and other family members both model aggressive behavior and reinforce aggression by the child (Patterson, 1982). In such homes, children learn via basic processes of positive and negative reinforcement that aversive behaviors "work" to bring about desired short-term effects on others' behavior, such as compliance with demands or cessation of unpleasant interactions. In a longitudinal study, Capaldi and Clark

(1998) reported a direct link between coercive and inconsistent parenting and childhood antisocial behavior, which in turn uniquely predicted IPV when these boys entered young adulthood. From a cognitive perspective, exposure to family violence instills generalized beliefs about the appropriateness of aggression as a means to resolve interpersonal conflicts and promotes hostile biases in the processing of social information, key cognitive change targets discussed in Chapter 9. These cognitive shifts influence both the encoding of incoming social information and the selection of aggressive response options. Such beliefs widen the range of social situations in which aggression in seen as necessary, override social inhibitions against the use of aggression, and promote positive expectancies about the effects of aggression.

Trauma and social learning theories are not mutually exclusive. They focus on distinct aspects of childhood violence exposure and subsequent functioning. In fact, each of these models has considerable research support. A number of negative clinical factors have been shown to correlate, or cluster together, with childhood violence exposure in samples of partner-abusive men. These include trauma-linked problems such as dysregulation of negative emotions, borderline personality features, and substance abuse, as well as social learning influences such as generalized problems with aggression (within and outside the home) and more frequent and severe perpetration of partner violence (Saunders, 1992; Murphy et al., 1993; Holtzworth-Munroe et al., 2000a).

Available evidence, although limited, indicates that some abusive clients suffer from posttraumatic syndromes that negatively influence their relationship functioning. Dutton (1995b) found elevated trauma symptoms in a sample of abusive men relative to a control sample of men from the community. Among the abusive men, the level of trauma symptoms was positively correlated with the extent of physical abuse perpetration, emotional abuse perpetration, and general anger. In addition, the average clinical profile for abusive men on the MCMI-II (a widely used clinical assessment tool for personality disturbance and psychopathology) resembled that found in populations affected by posttraumatic stress disorder (PTSD), with elevations on the negative, avoidant, and borderline personality scales. Relative to PTSD sample norms, the abusive men showed somewhat lower scores on general anxiety and somewhat higher scores on personality disorder scales, which might be expected from long-term effects of childhood trauma as compared to more acute effects of adult traumatic exposure.

In addition to general trauma symptoms, some abusive men display severe expressions of traumatic stress in the form of dissociative experiences and symptoms, which correlate with childhood exposure to physical abuse, sexual abuse, or interparental violence (Simoneti et al., 2000). As in

Dutton's (1995b) study of trauma symptoms, dissociative symptoms were also correlated with the level of partner abuse perpetration. In addition, 5–10% of abusive men reported dissociation-type experiences during their perpetration of partner violence, such as flashbacks, depersonalization (feeling as if it were someone else abusing the partner), blacking out, or being unable to recall perpetration episodes. Experiences related to alcohol and drug use were explicitly ruled out in the interview questions used to assess dissociative violence. Although some individuals may deny recalling violent incidents in order to imply that they were never abusive, some state that they do not question the veracity of the partner's report of events, even though they cannot recall the incident or key parts of it themselves.

In summary, posttraumatic symptoms may be present in a sizeable proportion of partner-violent clients, and a small proportion may have clinically significant dissociative symptoms that are linked to their perpetration of abuse. Childhood trauma exposure appears to be an important source of emotional, cognitive, and behavioral problems associated with partner violence. Abusive clients with significant trauma histories, when compared to abusive clients who lack such histories, are more emotionally volatile, more frequently and severely violent, more likely to have substance-abuse problems, and display greater average levels of personality disorder symptoms. These factors complicate the treatment process and highlight the need to address posttraumatic reactions in the treatment of partner-abusive clients.

## PRIOR EFFORTS TO ADDRESS TRAUMA HISTORIES AMONG ABUSIVE CLIENTS

To date, very little controlled research is available on the treatment of trauma symptoms in partner-abusive clients. The one notable exception is work by Dan Saunders (1996), who reported on a group process–psychodynamic treatment program (Browne et al., 1997). During the first several sessions of this 20-week program, group members drafted autobiographies that focused on childhood experiences and shared these with the group. Many reported on serious trauma exposures. In subsequent sessions, structured group exercises and unstructured process discussions addressed common results of childhood trauma, including trust issues, forgiveness, substance abuse, poor relationship boundaries, and problems with intimacy. This treatment was equally effective in ending partner-violent behavior when compared to group CBT conducted from a feminist perspective, and the process–psychodynamic condition produced significantly lower dropout from treatment. This approach contrasts somewhat with the treatments that are most commonly validated in contemporary research on trauma therapy, as these interventions focus on repeated and systematic exposure to traumatic memories, enhancement of coping skills, and cognitive restructuring of trauma-related assumptions and beliefs (e.g., Foa et al., 1999; Resick, Nishith, & Weaver, 2002). Although a number of clinical scholars have written about the importance of childhood trauma in the etiology and treatment of partner abuse, there are as yet no controlled investigations of empirically supported trauma therapies for this population. The initial results reported by Saunders (1996) provide support for continued efforts in this area.

## CLINICAL CONSIDERATIONS

The adaptation of trauma therapies to partner-violent clients presents a number of challenging questions. When in the course of treatment should trauma work be introduced? Which techniques are most useful (e.g., prolonged exposure, coping skills, cognitive processing therapy)? Are special adaptations to existing protocols needed for this population? Are these techniques relevant only if the individual is displaying obvious trauma symptoms, or can they be used to address relationship concerns and abusive behavior more generally? What type of agreement or consent should be secured from the client before embarking on a course of trauma reprocessing (e.g., can this be done routinely with court-mandated clients)? What are the associated risks for emotional and behavioral stability? Is special training or experience needed for therapists to administer these interventions?

Although some suggestions and guidelines are available from clinical experience and related research, there is as yet no clear empirical foundation for answering these questions. With respect to the timing of trauma reprocessing, our recommendation is always to address safety concerns first and, whenever possible, to address life instabilities and salient aspects of relationship functioning prior to initiating trauma recovery work. The main exception to these recommendations is for cases in which the client is not currently involved in an intimate relationship, has no ongoing aversive contact with an ex-partner, and presents for treatment with a clear request to address a troublesome personal history. With respect to informed consent, although it is necessary to secure such agreement before embarking on any psychotherapeutic or psychoeducational intervention, full disclosure appears to be particularly important when the intervention involves the recall of painful memories. We recommend that such work be pursued only with the explicit agreement of the client after full disclosure of the treatment plans and methods. In court-mandated cases, this would imply that other treatment options and approaches be made readily available so that trauma treatment is a voluntarily chosen element of such intervention.

The primary risk of trauma reprocessing appears to be the personal discomfort invoked by revisiting traumatic experiences. Nevertheless, the clinician cannot rule out the possibility that irritability and anger could accompany the exposure tasks in trauma reprocessing, perhaps carrying over into the relationship sphere and increasing the risk for aversive or abusive behavior. The clinician must be attuned to these potential reactions and should check in with the relationship partner regularly during this phase of treatment. As noted elsewhere, we recommend periodic phone contacts with relationship partners throughout treatment as a source of information on intervention goals and effects.

In our experience, although many abusive clients have symptoms and interpersonal difficulties related to trauma exposure, relatively few fit the classic diagnostic profile of PTSD. Given that the predominant trauma therapies focus on alleviating symptoms such as anxious arousal, avoidance, and re-experiencing of traumatic memories, some adaptations are necessary to address the long-term effects of childhood abuse exposure in this population. Although some partner-abusive clients suffer from significant PTSD symptoms and may benefit from all aspects of current trauma treatments, for most the main focus is on how traumatic exposures have influenced their interpersonal functioning and close relationships. This includes understanding the effects of trauma on relationship schemas, interpersonal problem solving, and emotional functioning in close relationships. Primary targets for such exploration include things such as partner selection, regulation of closeness and distance conflicts, intimate anger, the perception of self as victim in relationships, ruminative obsession with order and perfection, and the desire to have control over partners and children. Many individuals with family violence histories conduct their relationships according to victim–perpetrator scripts. They have internalized both these roles, take on either role when it is to their benefit, and use the sense of victimization to justify their abusive actions. Clients who are recovering from substance-abuse problems often identify ways in which they have been self-medicating painful emotions associated with traumatic memories.

## THE SCHEMA THERAPY PERSPECTIVE

As noted in previous chapters, many partner-abusive clients have personality dysfunction and other problems that can impede treatment progress. Young and colleagues (2003) developed schema therapy, an extension of cognitive therapy, to treat personality problems and cases who do not respond well to traditional CBT. These authors have noted that patients with significant personality problems often violate basic assumptions of CBT, including:

1. *The alliance assumption* that the client can form a collaborative working relationship with the therapist.
2. *The target goal assumption* that presenting problems can be readily identified.
3. *The compliance assumption* that the client will complete treatment tasks such as homework assignments.
4. *The cognitive accessibility assumption* that the client can access and articulate relevant thoughts and feelings with only limited assistance and training.
5. *The cognitive flexibility assumption* that the client can alter problematic thinking through traditional cognitive restructuring procedures.

The basic assumption of schema therapy is that some individuals' dysfunctional thought processes are too deeply ingrained in their sense of self to be altered by standard cognitive intervention strategies outlined in the previous chapter. The goal of schema therapy is to address these underlying core themes, called "early maladaptive schemas." These schemas are defined as "self-defeating emotional and cognitive patterns that begin early in our development and repeat throughout life" (Young et al., 2003, p. 7) and as "a set of memories, emotions, bodily sensations, and cognitions that revolve around a childhood theme, such as abandonment, abuse, neglect, or rejection" (p. 28). From this perspective, behavioral problems such as partner abuse are thought to be "driven by" early maladaptive schemas.

According to Young and colleagues (2003), maladaptive schemas result from unmet emotional needs, most notably the needs for safety and security, autonomy and competence, freedom and self-expression, spontaneity and play, and self-control. Several key types of early experience are thought to produce maladaptive schemas, including the "toxic frustration" of these needs (p. 10), traumatization and victimization, and overindulgence or overinvolvement by caregivers.

When early maladaptive schemas are present, behavioral problems can result in several ways. In surrender reactions to the schema, the individual acts out the core assumptions about the self. For example, individuals with a victimization schema may put themselves in situations where revictimization is likely, for example by selecting a relationship partner with a history of violent or abusive behavior. In avoidance reactions, individuals structure their lives and activities so as to avoid situations that may activate painful schemas, for example by refusing to become involved in close relationships altogether as a way to avoid the possibility of victimization. Finally, in overcompensation, individuals engage in exaggerated efforts to negate or disprove the schema. For example, individuals with a victimization schema become abusive and controlling to counteract feelings of helplessness and vulnerability. Ironically, overcompensation often leads to rein-forcement of the problematic schema. For example, someone with an abandonment schema may act in a controlling way to limit the partner's freedom and autonomy. The partner eventually reacts against this restric-tive engulfment and leaves the relationship, providing a further abandon-ment experience.

## TRAUMA PROCESSING THERAPY
## FOR PARTNER-VIOLENT CLIENTS

### Basic Formulation and Procedures

For some abusive clients, CBT needs to focus on early maladaptive schemas, particularly as they are enacted within close intimate relation-ships. The treatment outlined here focuses primarily on traumatic victim-ization as a key foundation for the development of abusive behavior prob-lems. As a result of the emphasis on interpersonal effects of trauma exposure, and consistent with the cognitive–behavioral focus of the current treatment, techniques derived from cognitive processing therapy (CPT; Resick & Schnicke, 1993; Resick & Calhoun, 2001) were selected as the primary treatment strategy for addressing trauma in partner-abusive cli-ents. CPT is based on an information-processing theory of PTSD and was originally developed for work with rape victims. CPT maintains that PTSD symptoms arise from problems in integrating traumatic experiences and memories into existing belief structures. As a result, the traumatized indi-vidual distorts aspects of the trauma to fit with prior beliefs ("assimila-tion") and/or radically alters prior beliefs to accommodate the trauma ("overaccommodation"). An example of assimilation is self-blame for not having prevented the trauma, which preserves one's belief that bad events are predictable and controllable. An example of overaccommodation is a shift to the rigid belief that the world is unsafe and no one can be trusted. By integrating social learning and trauma perspectives, CPT provides a foundation for understanding and addressing the cognitive and emotional effects of childhood trauma exposure on partner-abusive clients. These experiences have often shaped deep-seated beliefs about safety, trust, and the "proper" conduct of intimate relationships.

The fundamental goal of CPT is to facilitate emotional processing of traumatic memories in order to restore greater balance to the cognitive–affective system (Resick & Schnicke, 1993). This balance implies accep-tance and awareness of the trauma and integration into existing belief structures. In addition to general education about the effects of trauma, CPT can be characterized as having two basic components—exposure and cognitive restructuring. The exposure component involves revisiting one's recollections of a specific traumatic event or events. This is accomplished by having the client write in detail about a traumatic experience. (Clients who have significant difficulty with writing can audiorecord a trauma narrative.) The written recollection is read aloud to the therapist, who listens supportively and reviews it carefully for missing details, signs of avoidance, inconsistencies, incoherence, emotionally charged elements, and irrational thoughts. While maintaining a supportive and affirming stance, the therapist gently directs the client's attention towards gaps and "stuck points" in the trauma narrative, encouraging the client to explore these areas and to redraft the narrative as necessary to facilitate emotional processing. Emotional processing of the trauma is thus facilitated through retelling of the traumatic event with elaboration of details and reactions that have been avoided and suppressed.

A large body of research has examined the effects of writing about traumas across a variety of psychological and physical health outcomes (Pennebaker, Mehl, & Niederhoffer, 2003). These studies have routinely found that, relative to matched controls who write about superficial topics, individuals asked to write for 15–20 minutes per day over a four-day period about a prior traumatic or emotionally upsetting experience report fewer physician visits in the three months postwriting, a variety of improvements in immunological and hormonal functioning, improvements in academic outcomes (among college students), and more rapid job acquisition (among those recently terminated from employment) (Lepore & Smyth, 2002).

Why should we expect writing about emotional and traumatic memories to affect psychological health? According to Pennebaker and colleagues (2003), such positive outcomes appear to be mediated by an increasing number of positive emotion words across writing days, a moderate amount of negative emotion words, and an increasing number of "cognitive" words that indicate a focus on insight and causation. Together, these findings suggest that such linguistic shifts signify attempts at active coping wherein the individual translates amorphous and painful traumatic images into language, with its conceptually rich and interconnected set of images, emotions, and linguistic processes. This translation from the abstract to the linguistic may realign the associations and meanings that surround the traumatic event into a less psychologically damaging entity. Given the social foundations of language, it is also likely that disclosure, and, more important, word usage, has important interpersonal functions, perhaps allowing the traumatized individual to become more socially integrated within his or her social networks and benefit from available social supports (Pennebaker & Graybeal, 2001; Pennebaker et al., 2003).

Given the similarities between the cognitive-processing approach and what is known from basic research on trauma disclosure, a number of potential advantages are likely to emerge in clinical applications of CPT with abusive men. Unlike prolonged exposure therapy (Foa et al., 1999), which promotes emotional processing exclusively through repetitive re-counting of traumatic memories, CPT emphasizes cognitive restructuring of beliefs and assumptions that are linked to the traumatic exposure. Distortions about the trauma itself, as well as distorted beliefs about its effects and implications, are uncovered and explored in order to facilitate emotional processing and promote cognitive–affective balance with respect to the trauma and its effects. The cognitive work can also include structured exploration of common trauma themes that are presented by the therapist (i.e., not necessarily emergent from the client's narratives).

For many partner-abusive clients, childhood trauma influenced core assumptions about self and others that continue to exert strong influences on their own relationship functioning. For example, many have a powerful tendency to assume the partner has harmful intentions, interpreting relationship conflict as victimization. In turn, these thoughts and emotions are used to justify retaliation through abusive and controlling behaviors. This process can be so overlearned and automatic that an objective observer might view the abuse as a pre-emptive strike, even though the abuser sees it as retaliation.

Further examples can be seen among clients who witnessed interadult violence in the home, which is perhaps the most common traumatic childhood experience of partner-violent clients. Intense fear, anger, and guilt were common reactions to the abuse exposure. Child witnesses to the abuse of their mothers often feel a strong pull to protect her, along with strong feelings of helplessness, anger toward the perpetrator, and guilt at not being able to stop the abuse. If the abuser was the child's father or father figure, split loyalties are also common. The client may have wished to protect the mother while also identifying with the abusive father's exertion of power. If the abuser was a boyfriend or otherwise less affiliated male partner of the mother (many clients witnessed a string of abusive boyfriends), intense anger and disgust are often present, and the client may blame the mother for causing or putting up with the abuse. Some clients believe that women want or need to be controlled and abused. Some witnessed their mothers being abusive in repeated relationship contexts and came to believe that all women want to control and abuse men. Such beliefs can be deeply embedded in core relationship schemas, often exerting powerful influences on automatic thoughts and reactions to situations while remaining at the outer edges of conscious awareness.

## Trauma-Related Anger Cognitions

Anger is one of the most common emotional reactions to traumatic exposure, and is a prominent clinical feature of combat veterans with PTSD (Chemtob, Hamada, Roitblat, & Muraoka, 1994; Lasko, Orr, & Pittman,

1994; Novaco & Chemtob, 1992) and crime victims with PTSD (Riggs, Dancu, Gershuny, & Greenberg, 1992). Partner-abusive individuals with traumatic histories often report that they feel out of control and overwhelmed by irritable and angry feelings in their relationships. In childhood, many abusive clients experienced intense anger, helplessness, and frustration at not being protected from witnessing or experiencing abuse. Some continue to seethe with rage at the injustice wrought by an abusive parent. Many such individuals vowed that they would not become abusers, which can add to their shame, embarrassment, and externalization of responsibility for their own abusive behavior. Some abusive clients reveal their childhood scars very directly through their abusive actions, saying or doing the exact same things that they witnessed or experienced as children. Some rationalize and justify the actions of an abusive caregiver, seeing these actions as legitimate forms of discipline or necessary responses to relationship difficulties.

Although a wide array of cognitive consequences may result from traumatic exposure, several themes are prominent among partner-violent clients, reflecting development of belief structures to accommodate the abuse exposure. Surprisingly, the belief in a just world, specifically the notion that people get what they deserve, is a common rationalization for violence and may reflect assimilation of their own traumatic exposures as justifiable, which serves to preserve the bond with an abusive caregiver. If a partner or child acts in a fashion deemed unacceptable, then this individual deserves to be "taught a lesson" and "gets what is coming to them." Closely linked to this rationalization is the notion that aggression is morally correct and effective (i.e., that it will teach others a lesson, set things straight, and restore a sense of balance and order to a situation that feels chaotic or out of control). Another common anger theme is that others want to hurt me. This belief is expressed as hypersensitivity to perceived slights and a pervasive sense of being disrespected, belittled, and hurt. A related assumption is that "I'm the victim here," in which all personal transgressions are rapidly shifted to focus on the failings and shortcomings of the partner. On the basis of these core assumptions, namely that others are out to hurt one, aggression is a correct or necessary response to such situations, and people get what they deserve, individuals can justify all kinds of selfish, controlling, and abusive actions.

## Trauma-Related Guilt Cognitions

In addition to deeply held assumptions that produce rage and rationalize abuse, guilt-related themes are also common reactions to trauma. Kubany (1998) identified four common cognitive features of trauma-related guilt. In "hindsight bias," traumatized individuals believe that they should have known the trauma would happen, such as by seeing the signs that it was about to occur. For example, a client reported that he should have known that his father was going to beat his mother severely on one particular occasion when his mother was injured and sent to the hospital because he had earlier seen his father stumbling out of the corner bar. The fact that his father often came home drunk and did not physically assault his mother on most such occasions and the fact that there was little or nothing the young-ster could have done to prevent the abuse were ignored in recalling the event. In "justification distortion," individuals second-guess their behavior during the trauma and conclude that it was not justified. For example, one client reported the belief that he shouldn't have run upstairs to hide, but should have faced up to his abusive father, despite being deathly afraid and only half his size. In "responsibility distortion", the individual accepts more blame than can be logically justified. For example, a client whose mother was exposed to repeated violence at the hand of several different boyfriends concluded that these things would not have happened if he had taken better care of his mother, despite the fact that he was only 8 to 11 years old and his mother had a serious mental illness. Finally, in "wrongdoing distor-tion," traumatized individuals conclude that they somehow acted against their values or beliefs at the time of the trauma, when there is no clear evi-dence to support this claim. For example, an individual who finally grew large enough to block his father from attacking his mother felt guilty for having done so. Although his father attacked and threw the first blows, and even though the client prevented his mother from being assaulted, he still believed that it was wrong for him to have hit and restrained his father.

## Core Assumptions about the Self in Relationships

A pervasive sense of shame and humiliation, irrational anger, and a dialecti-cal tension between acceptance and rejection of self-definition as a victim form a core set of emotional and cognitive features for many abusive clients with traumatic childhoods. Based on their conditioning history, intimacy and closeness are fraught with danger. For many, relationships present powerful approach/avoidance conflicts. Their behavior toward the partner defies logic, for example in repetitively separating and reuniting, abusing and making up, or cheating on the partner while experiencing strong dependency in the relationship. Themes of rejection and abandonment are applied to both self and partner, each of whom can be seen at times as worthless, undeserving, and worthy of denigration. A desperate need for validation, love, and acceptance may also pervade this complex relation-ship style.

This confusing array of strategies for regulating intimacy and closeness in relationships, which may involve avoidance, preoccupation, fearfulness, and coercive control, is consistent with a disorganized style of attachment. Disorganized attachment is a very common reaction to adverse family environments and childhood maltreatment experiences (Carlson, Cicchetti, Barnett, & Braunwald, 1989; Cassidy & Mohr, 2001), including abuse of the mother by a male partner (Zeahnah et al., 1999). In addition, disorganized attachment is a strong predictor of aggressive behavior in children (Lyons-Ruth, 1996). Initial research indicates that disorganized attachment is common in samples of partner-violent men (Holtzworth-Munroe, Stuart, & Hutchinson, 1997). These findings further support the need to address traumatic childhood experiences in an attempt to resolve attachment insecurities, enhance affect regulation, and promote trusting and secure bonds as an antidote to partner abuse.

# / 11 /

# *Relapse Prevention*

Relapse prevention is both the overarching goal of treatment for violent behavior and a discrete set of clinical ideas and strategies that is typically used in the latter phase of treatment. This chapter presents some core ideas about relapse and long-term behavior change, factors that may increase risk for relapse in abusive clients, and some relapse prevention strategies, including booster sessions at the end of treatment. The emphasis is on stimulating a self-directed change process throughout treatment, anticipating situations and factors that could precipitate a return to assaultive behavior, and facilitating the client's ability to continue the work of treatment after sessions with the therapist have ended.

## DEFINING AND CONCEPTUALIZING RELAPSE IN PARTNER ABUSE TREATMENT

### Basic Definition

Relapse can be defined normatively (in general terms that apply to everyone) or idiographically (in specific terms that apply to an individual client). For clinical purposes, we use both types of definitions. Normatively, relapse can be defined as any physical assault, sexual assault, or threats of assault toward an intimate partner after a period of assault cessation and personal change. These behaviors are socially valid indicators of abuse, being both illegal and potentially injurious. Thus, there is little room for debate regarding the notion that such acts are problematic signs of relapse, worthy of continued or renewed clinical attention.

Idiographically, the relapse process can be defined as a pattern or sequence of behaviors that signals a return to abuse for a specific individual. Clients and their partners often recognize a process of escalating tensions and negative interactions involving specific behaviors that provide cause for significant concern before assault occurs. These may involve withdrawal from engagement in relationship discussions, a condescending attitude, the use of particular words in reference to the partner, name calling, raising of the voice, ultimatums, and specific looks, gestures, or postures.

The relapse process for an individual can be explored by asking questions such as "What types of thoughts and actions on your part would indicate that you are sliding back toward abusive and controlling behavior?" or "How would you recognize that you are at risk for returning to abuse?" It is very important to get detailed information and descriptions of relevant thoughts and behaviors to help in devising relapse prevention strategies. Prior self-monitoring records can also be consulted for insight into the early warning signs of conflict escalation and potential relapse. If possible, the client and/or clinician should also ask the partner for information to assist in identifying the warning signs of potential relapse.

It is important to note that by adopting the term "relapse" from the field of addiction (e.g., Marlatt & Gordon, 1985), we are not implying that partner abuse is an addictive behavior. Rather, the analogy reflects the fact that partner abuse, like addictive behavior, is in part a problem of self-control that involves both elements of conscious choice and powerful emotional and reinforcement factors that may be *experienced* as beyond the person's control. Careful examination of the relapse process highlights the need for constructive coping strategies early in the process of conflict escalation, raising opportunities for exercising greater self-control. In addition, the notion of relapse reflects the distinction between initial behavior change and maintenance of change over time. Current conceptual models indicate that intentional behavior change does not typically follow a perfectly linear progression through the stages of change, but often involves a spiral of temporary return to problem behavior followed by renewed efforts to change. Recognition and awareness of this fact may be helpful in stimulating continued change efforts in the face of temporary setbacks.

## Relapse versus Recidivism

Recidivism refers to any repeat incident of problem behavior during a defined interval. For our purposes this interval is usually a specified follow-up period after treatment, for example the year after treatment completion. The problem behavior is often defined as any act of physical partner assault, but criminal recidivism can also be used or some combination of problematic behaviors. Relapse is a special case of recidivism in which behavior change has occurred during the intervening period between initial problem presentation and recidivism. Relapse implies a return to a problematic pattern of behavior after a respite during which meaningful change occurred. If no behavior change occurred, the pattern of problem behavior is continuous, and relapse is not logically possible. For our purposes, we will use the term "relapse" to mean a return to problematic behavior after a period of successful behavior change. The terms "treatment failure" or "nonresponse" will be used in cases where treatment did not stimulate initial behavior change and the problematic behavior continues.

This distinction is more than semantic. It carries important clinical implications. In treatment nonresponse, if a sufficiently extensive course of treatment was competently administered, it is unlikely that more of the same treatment will bring about the desired change. Typically, nonresponse to treatment implies the need for a different form of intervention, a different formulation of the problem, a different change agent, or treatment for adjunctive conditions that are impeding change. There may also be individuals who, for various reasons, are simply not amenable to change through treatment at a particular point in time. Relapse to problem behavior, in contrast, implies that treatment was effective in stimulating initial change, but not sufficient to maintain the change over time. Therefore, more of the same treatment, or slight adaptations of previously helpful strategies, may be successful in such cases. For example, additional treatment in the form of booster sessions may be helpful in preventing relapse or reorienting the change process after relapse. Alternative treatment strategies may also be needed to address factors that impede the maintenance of change over time.

## Understanding the Relapse Process

The most extensive examination of the relapse process was provided in the area of addictions by Marlatt & Gordon (1985), who distinguished between a "lapse," or temporary "slip-up" in the change process, and a "relapse," or more complete return to the pattern of problem behavior. Thus, the relapse model examines two key influence processes, those that increase the likelihood of an initial slip or lapse and those that facilitate the transition from initial lapse to full-blown relapse. In clinical work with abusive clients, lapses are typically defined as the early warning signs of problem behavior. Most clients can articulate the type of things that they do early in the relapse process that can be used to signal a need for active coping. For many clients, behaviors such as raising one's voice, being unwilling to let go of an argument or disagreement, having jealous thoughts, withdrawing from the partner in anger or disgust, or other similar reactions and behaviors initiate a pattern of abusive escalation. Although clients often report surprise when their behavior escalates to physical aggression, claiming that it happens so fast they can't see it coming, careful exploration often reveals that there is a more lengthy process over the course of hours, days, or even weeks, during which time the "pot is being stirred" and hostilities are simmering before the eventual eruption.

## Factors That Increase Risk for Relapse

Following the logic of relapse prevention therapies from the addictions, it is important to examine a range of factors, both within and outside of the relationship, that may increase the risk of relapse. These include significant life stress, lifestyle imbalance, changes as a function of relationship or family development, the use and abuse of substances, affairs and other forms of betrayal (current or past), and unresolved relationship conflicts. Background life stress is a common contributing factor to relapse after a period of successful behavior change. Being temporarily or permanently out of work, having financial difficulties, serious illness or the death of close relatives, having other people move into the house (e.g., relatives), or the emergence or escalation of conduct problems in children are examples of stressful circumstances that may contribute to relationship tension, irritability, conflict escalation, and relapse to abuse. While some of these things cannot be predicted, others can be anticipated and addressed in treatment, for example seasonal changes in employment, financial problems, and decisions about people moving into and out of the home. Often, the therapist can help the client to think differently about life stress, to use effective problem-solving strategies, or to communicate more effectively with the partner to address relevant concerns.

Lifestyle imbalance is frequently connected with life stress and relationship difficulties and is an often overlooked area in the treatment of partner abuse. Abusive clients often fall into one of two extreme patterns with respect to work/leisure balance—either working very long hours (often at several jobs) or having limited attachment to traditional employment. Some have exploited male privilege in establishing patterns of recreation without taking the needs of the partner or family into consideration, for example by spending a great deal of time out of the home with friends or engaged in leisure pursuits without participating in child care. Others have the reverse pattern, constantly working or engaging in household projects or chores with little or no time to relax. The balance of work, home/family responsibilities, and leisure activities presents a significant challenge for many abusive clients and is often a powerful source of underlying resentment and conflict in their relationships.

Changes as a function of relationship or family development provide an important area of concern for treatment in general and relapse prevention in particular. Escalation to abuse may be likely during periods of transition, which are often stressful and challenging. Young adult clients frequently struggle with the transition to adult domestic arrangements around the time of cohabitation (i.e., "settling down)." They may continue to "party" or "run the streets" while their partner is at home taking care of a newborn child or managing household duties. Themes of resentment and "being controlled" are common for young men facing the transition to adult lifestyle responsibilities and often reflect dichotomous (black-and-white) thinking and lifestyle imbalances that can be addressed in treatment. Another challenging transition involves pregnancy and childbirth. Although pregnancy doesn't appear to increase the risk for partner violence, the rates of violence exposure are quite high among pregnant women (Castro, Peek-Asa, & Ruiz, 2003; Martin, Mackie, Kupper, Buescher, & Moracco, 2001; McFarlane, Parker, & Soeken, 1995). As with the transition to adult relationship arrangements, the introduction of a child dramatically alters the responsibilities and duties for the parents and changes the nature of the interadult relationship. Separations and divorce are the other main period of change and development when many abusive clients are ordered to, or seek out, treatment. Occasionally, abusive clients present for treatment during other periods of family transition, for example after a disability has altered work and family activities, around the time of forced or elected retirement, or after changes in family composition (e.g., when an elderly parent has moved into the house or when grandchildren require extensive caregiving from the client and/or partner).

The use and abuse of alcohol is perhaps the strongest known predictor of postcounseling violence recidivism among partner-abusive men (Fals-Stewart, 2003; Gondolf, 2002). Other drug use, most notably stimulants such as amphetamines or cocaine, also appears to present considerable risk in this regard. A number of important warning signs should indicate the need to address alcohol or drug use as part of abuser treatment and relapse prevention. These include any previous incidents of physical assault while under the influence of drugs or alcohol, unhealthy drinking patterns such as binge drinking (having five or more drinks on one occasion) or high average consumption levels (greater than about two drinks per day on average), alcohol- or drug-related legal issues (e.g., arrests for driving under the influence), other negative consequences from substance use (e.g., missed work due to intoxication, hangovers, etc.), signs of tolerance or withdrawal, or relationship arguments or disagreements about alcohol and drug use. Basic information can be provided and discussed on how alcohol and other drugs impair judgment and may contribute risk for engaging in aggressive acts by reducing awareness of inhibitory cues (Steele & Josephs, 1990). A range of harm-reduction strategies to reduce alcohol consumption and risky drinking can also be considered (Marlatt, 1998; Tatarsky, 2002). Encouragement of active involvement in recovery programs such as Alcoholics Anonymous is a very helpful aspect of treatment for abusive clients with more extensive substance-abuse histories.

Relapse is also quite common in response to affairs and other forms of betrayal, current or past. The discovery of an affair presents a difficult challenge for abusive clients to refrain from physical assault. Sometimes, signs of partner infidelity or knowledge of past infidelity can be addressed directly in treatment to help prevent relapse to abuse. Conversely, many abusive clients have themselves been unfaithful, and their partners may have discovered this fact. Ongoing hurt feelings, resentments, and deep mistrust often surround both abuse and infidelity, presenting a considerable challenge to the abusive client's process of change and recovery. These issues usually require extensive work during treatment, and an ongoing need to address the partner's concerns over past betrayals is an important element in preventing relapse for many such cases.

Finally, relationship conflicts that remain unresolved or are consistently avoided present a considerable barrier to long-term treatment success and a risk for relapse to abuse. Out of a legitimate fear of conflict escalation, many abusive clients present for treatment with one or more relationship conflict areas that are off-limits. This can be a healthy recognition early in treatment and a useful strategy for preventing abuse. However, as treatment progresses, these "don't go there" areas of potential conflict can, for some cases, provide a looming risk for relapse, as they will almost inevitably resurface at some point in the future. Helping clients to identify what these issues are, why they are so volatile, and how they may begin to address them is an important step in relapse prevention. For many clients, anything having to do with the negative effects of their prior abuse on the partner or others is a key "hot button" topic that they consistently avoid or suppress. Obviously, these issues must be addressed during treatment if there is to be any hope of healing and recovery from the effects of past abuse.

## PROMOTING MAINTENANCE OF CHANGE
## AND PREVENTING RELAPSE

### Basic Strategies

From the very beginning, treatment should be conducted with an eye to termination, meaning that the therapist should be cognizant of the fact that the client must eventually "go it alone." Some cognitive therapists use the notion that the client must "become his or her own therapist" in order for treatment to be successful. Clients often describe the experience of "hearing the therapist's voice" or thinking about what the therapist would say or recommend when facing a difficult situation. The following passage from a booster treatment session illustrates client initiative in setting the agenda for personal change.

> "I was thinking a couple of days ago, 'OK, so what do I have to talk to [therapist's name] about? Let's see now . . . so what has my daughter done recently . . . what has my wife done?' And then I thought, 'No, no, no. What have you [I] done? How about focusing on that?

Many of the treatment process recommendations presented earlier in this book were designed to facilitate client involvement in the change process. The development of a fully collaborative therapeutic alliance, the use of motivational enhancement strategies, providing a menu of change options, setting each session agenda collaboratively with the client, engaging the client in designing homework assignments, and periodically reviewing progress are some examples of interventions that are geared toward helping the client develop the skills needed to establish and maintain personal change.

As treatment progresses, an increasing share of the responsibility for determining the goals and strategies for change should fall upon the client's shoulders. Therapists need to facilitate this process by keeping their own helping impulses in check at times in order to allow the client to generate his or her own answers, ideas, and response options. For example, in cognitive restructuring, therapists often have to resist offering clients alternative thoughts in order to allow clients time to generate their own. In addition, as treatment progresses it is important to increase the intensity of role plays and *in vivo* challenges to determine whether the client is prepared for real-life situations. These challenges assess which aspects of treatment have been successfully incorporated into the client's behavior change and where further work is necessary.

Toward the end of a routine course of treatment, ideally the client should be establishing the working agenda for each session and the agenda for continued change efforts between sessions. The therapist should regularly note that the client will need to do this work after treatment is finished, should reinforce the client's efforts and successes in self-directed change, and should help the client make self-attributions for successful change. The therapist should communicate the idea that treatment stimulates an initial change process that the client can continue on his or her own. The therapist should explore the client's efficacy expectations in this regard, as some clients will presume that they cannot make it on their own or can only maintain change with the therapist's perpetual assistance. These assumptions often include cognitive distortions that can be addressed in treatment. It is important also to remember that low self-efficacy for the client to maintain the change process may reflect inadequate preparation, so this type of discussion can be used to reshape treatment goals to promote the client's development of the skills needed for continued self-directed change.

## Booster Sessions

Many clients prefer to taper off of treatment toward the end, rather than ending more abruptly. We typically recommend at least four biweekly sessions after a course of weekly treatment, thus extending the treatment for two additional months with more time for clients to maintain the work on their own between sessions. For some clients, monthly sessions for several months after that provide a helpful opportunity to facilitate self-directed change and relapse prevention. Clients often report that the mere fact of continuing in treatment provides them with impetus to continue their change efforts.

The structure of these booster sessions is somewhat different from previous treatment sessions. Typically, the client is asked to set the session agenda with limited input from the therapist. The therapist may provide suggestions and guidance regarding previously covered areas of treatment to help the client continue the change process. For example, a client may bring up a recent disagreement with his or her spouse, discussing ways in which he or she handled it well and areas for continued improvement. The therapist may direct the client to communication skills such as active listening, reviewing barriers to the use of these skills in real-life situations and ways in which the client can continue to develop listening skills that will be useful in similar disagreement situations in the future.

When new treatment strategies are introduced into booster sessions, they usually reflect areas of concern that were not sufficiently identified or addressed during the core treatment phase. For example, an increase in alcohol consumption in response to recent stressors may become apparent, stimulating the therapist to introduce harm-reduction and coping strategies relevant to alcohol. Depressive symptoms may arise in response to relationship separation, and the therapist may redirect the client's use of cognitive restructuring methods toward depressive thoughts.

In addition, new areas of relationship concern sometimes arise at this phase of treatment. For example, as relationship conflict decreases, a lack of positive shared activities or difficulties with intimacy and sex may become apparent. Sometimes concerns regarding the partner's behavior increase, for example recognition of a budding drug or alcohol problem or increased awareness of traumatic stress reactions. The client may experience guilt in having contributed to these problems and uncertainty in how to approach the partner without resorting to controlling behavior. Occasionally, the partner continues to engage in frequent or intense aggressive behaviors. When such relationship problems are not successfully addressed through individual work, the client may wish to consider conjoint couples' therapy as part of the relapse prevention process. We typically encourage this only after the client has stopped all physical assault and threats for a significant period of time and has made substantial changes in communication and relationship behaviors and only if the client and partner are clearly planning to stay together. The client's attributions of blame and responsibility for ongoing relationship difficulties may need to be carefully addressed before a successful transition to couples' therapy can occur. The therapist may also help the client figure out how to broach the subject of couples' therapy with the partner in a constructive, inviting, and nonblaming fashion.

# References

Abelson, R. P., Kinder, D. R., Peters, M. D. & Fiske, S. T. (1982). Affective and semantic components in political person perception. *Journal of Personality and Social Psychology, 42*(4), 619–630.

Adams, D. (1988). Treatment models of men who batter: A profeminist analysis. In K. Yllo & M. Bograd (Eds.), *Feminist perspectives on wife abuse* (pp. 176–199). Newbury Park, CA: Sage.

Adams, D. & Cayouette, S. (2002). Emerge—A group education model for abusers. In E. Aldarondo & F. Mederos (Eds.), *Programs for men who batter: Intervention and prevention strategies in a diverse society* (pp. 4.1–4.32). Kingston, NJ: Civic Research Institute.

Adams, D., & McCormick, A. (1982). Men unlearning violence: A group approach. In M. Roy (Ed.), *The abusive partner: An analysis of domestic battering* (pp. 170–197). New York: Van Nostrand Reinhold.

Alberti, R., & Emmons, M. (1970). *Your perfect right: A guide to assertive living.* Atascadero, CA: Impact.

Alberti, R., & Emmons, M. (2001). *Your perfect right: Assertiveness and equality in your life and relationships* (8th ed.). Atascadero, CA: Impact.

Alexander, P. C., & Morris, E. (in press). Stages of change in batterers and their response to treatment. *Violence and Victims.*

American Psychiatric Association. (1994). *Diagnostic and statistical manual of mental disorders* (4th ed.). Washington, DC: Author.

American Psychological Association. (1996). *Violence and the family: Report of the American Psychological Association Presidential Task Force on Violence and the Family.* Washington, DC: Author.

Anglin, K., & Holtzworth-Munroe, A. (1997). Comparing the responses of maritally violent and nonviolent spouses to problematic marital and nonmarital situations: Are the skill deficits of physically aggressive husbands and wives global? *Journal of Family Psychology, 11*, 301–313.

Archer, J. (2000). Sex differences in aggression between heterosexual partners: A meta-analytic review. *Psychological Bulletin, 126,* 651–680.

Astin, M. C., Ogland-Hand, S. M., Coleman, E. M., & Foy, D. W. (1995). Posttraumatic stress disorder and childhood abuse in battered women: Comparisons with maritally distressed women. *Journal of Consulting and Clinical Psychology, 63,* 308–312.

Austin, J. B., & Dankwort, J. (1999). Standards for batterer programs: A review and analysis. *Journal of Interpersonal Violence, 14,* 152–168.

Babcock, J. C., Green, C. E., & Robie, C. (2004). Does batterers' treatment work? A meta-analytic review of domestic violence treatment. *Clinical Psychology Review, 23,* 1023–1053.

Babcock, J. C., Jacobson, N. S., & Gottman, J. M. (2000). Attachment, emotional regulation, and the function of marital violence: Differences between secure, preoccupied, and dismissing violent and nonviolent husbands. *Journal of Family Violence, 15,* 391–409.

Babcock, J. C., & LaTaillade, J. (2000). Evaluating interventions for men who batter. In J. Vincent and E. Jouriles (Eds.), *Domestic violence: Guidelines for research-informed practice* (pp. 37–77). Philadelphia: Jessica Kingsley.

Babcock, J. C., Waltz, J., Jacobson, N. S., & Gottman, J.M. (1993). Power and violence: The relation between communication patterns, power discrepancies, and domestic violence. *Journal of Consulting and Clinical Psychology, 61,* 40–50.

Babor, T. F., De la Fuente, J. R., Saunders, J., & Grant, M. (1992). *AUDIT: The alcohol use disorders identification test: Guidelines for use in primary health care.* Geneva, Switzerland: World Health Organization.

Bandura, A. (1986). *Social foundation of thought and action: A social and cognitive theory.* Englewood Cliffs, NJ: Prentice-Hall.

Barbour, K. A., Eckhardt, C. I., Davison, G. C., & Kassinove, H. (1998). The experience and expression of anger in maritally violent and nonviolent men. *Behavior Therapy, 29,* 173–191.

Bargh, J. A. (1997). The automaticity of everyday life. In R. S. Wyer, Jr. (Ed.), *Advances in social cognition: Vol. 10. The automaticity of everyday life* (pp. 1–61). Mahwah, NJ: Erlbaum.

Bargh, J. A., Chen. M., & Burrows, L. (1996). Automaticity of social behavior: Direct effects of trait construct and stereotype activation on action. *Journal of Personality and Social Psychology, 71,* 230–244.

Barling, J., O'Leary, K. D., Jouriles, E. N., Vivian, D., & MacEwen, K. E. (1987). Factor similarity of the conflict tactics scales across samples, spouses, and sites: Issues and implications. *Journal of Family Violence, 2,* 37–54.

Barnett, O. W., & Hamberger, L. K. (1992). The assessment of maritally violent men on the California Psychological Inventory. *Violence and Victims, 7,* 15–28.

Barnett, O. W., Martinez, T. E., & Bluestein, B. W. (1995). Jealousy and romantic attachment in maritally violent and nonviolent men. *Journal of Interpersonal Violence, 10*(4), 473–486.

Baucom, D. H., & Epstein, N. (1990). *Cognitive-behavioral marital therapy.* New York: Brunner/Mazel.

Baucom, D. H., Epstein, N., Daiuto, A. D., Carels, R. A., Rankin, L. A., & Burnett, C. K. (1996). Cognitions in marriage: The relationship between standards and attributions. *Journal of Family Psychology, 10,* 209–222.

Beasley R., & Stoltenberg, C. D. (1992). Personality characteristics of male spouse abusers. *Professional Psychology: Research and Practice, 23,* 310–317.

Beck, A. T. (1976). *Cognitive therapy and the emotional disorders.* New York: International Universities Press.

Beck, A. T. (1999). *Prisoners of hate: The cognitive basis of anger, hostility, and violence.* New York: HarperCollins.

Beck, A. T., Freeman A., Davis, D. D., & Associates (2004). *Cognitive therapy of personality disorders* (2nd ed.). New York: Guilford Press.

Beck, A. T., Rush, A. J., Shaw, B. F., & Emery, G. (1979). *Cognitive therapy of depression.* New York: Guilford Press.

Beck, A. T., & Weishaar, M. (1989). Cognitive therapy. In A. Freeman, K. M. Simon, L. E. Beutler, & H. Arkowitz (Eds.), *Comprehensive handbook of cognitive therapy* (pp. 21–36). New York: Plenum.

Beere, C. A. (1990). *Gender roles: A handbook of tests and measures.* New York: Greenwood Press.

Begun, A. L., Murphy, C. M., Bolt, D., Weinstein, B., Strodthoff, T., Short, L., & Shelley, G. (2003). Characteristics of the Safe at Home instrument for assessing readiness to change intimate partner violence. *Research on Social Work Practice, 13,* 80–107.

Bellack, A., & Hersen, M. (1998). *Behavioral assessment: A practical handbook* (4th ed.). Boston: Allyn & Bacon.

Bennett, L. W., Tolman, R. M., Rogalski, C. J., & Srinivasaraghavan, J. (1994). Domestic abuse by male alcohol and drug addicts. *Violence and Victims, 9,* 359–368.

Benson, P. L., & Vincent, S. (1980). Development and validation of the Sexist Attitudes Toward Women Scale. *Psychology of Women Quarterly, 5,* 276–291.

Berkowitz, L. (1993).Towards a general theory of anger and emotional aggression: Implications of the cognitive neoassociationistic perspective for the analysis of anger and other emotions. In R. S. Wyer, Robert, & T. K. Srull (Eds.), *Advances in social cognition: Vol. 6 Perspectives on anger and emotion* (pp. 1–46). Hillsdale, NJ: Erlbaum.

Berns, S. B., Jacobson, N. S., & Gottman, J. M. (1999). Demand-withdraw interaction in couples with a violent husband. *Journal of Consulting & Clinical Psychology, 67*(5), 666–674.

Bethke, T. M., & DeJoy, D. M. (1993). An experimental study of factors influencing the acceptability of dating violence. *Journal of Interpersonal Violence, 8,* 36–51.

Bloom, L. Z., Coburn, K. L., & Pearlman, J. C. (1975). *The new assertive woman.* New York: Dell.

Bograd, M. (1984). Family systems approaches to wife battering: A feminist critique. *American Journal of Orthopsychiatry, 54,* 558–568.

Bograd, M., & Mederos, F. (1999). Battering and couples therapy: Universal screening and selection of treatment modality. *Journal of Marital and Family Therapy, 25,* 291–312.

Bohn, M. J., Babor, T. F., & Kranzler, H. R. (1995). The Alcohol Use Disorders Identification Test (AUDIT): Validation of a screening instrument for use in medical settings. *Journal of Studies on Alcohol, 56,* 423–432.

Bordin, E. S. (1979). The generalizability of the psychoanalytic concept of the working alliance. *Psychotherapy: Theory, Research, and Practice, 16,* 252–260.

Bowers, T. G., & Clum, G. A. (1988). Relative contribution of specific and non-specific treatment effects: Meta-analysis of placebo-controlled behavior therapy research. *Psychological Bulletin, 103,* 315–323.

Boyle, D. J., & Vivian, D. (1996). Generalized and spouse-specific anger/hostility and men's violence against intimates. *Violence and Victims, 11,* 293–317.

Bradbury, T. N., & Fincham, F. D. (1990). Attributions in marriage: Review and critique. *Psychological Bulletin, 107,* 3–33.

Brannen, S. J., & Rubin, A. (1996). Comparing the effectiveness of gender-specific and couples groups in a court-mandated spouse abuse treatment program. *Research on Social Work Practice, 6,* 405–424.

Brehm, S. S., & Brehm, J. W. (1981). *Psychological reactance: A theory of freedom and control.* New York: Academic Press.

Brisson, N. J. (1983). Battering husbands: A survey of abusive men. *Victimology, 6,* 338–344.

Brown, P. D., & O'Leary, K. D. (2000). Therapeutic alliance: Predicting continuance and success in group treatment for spouse abuse. *Journal of Consulting and Clinical Psychology, 68,* 340–345.

Browne, K. O., Saunders, D. G., & Staecker, K. M. (1997). Process-psychodynamic groups for men who batter: A brief treatment model. *Families in Society: The Journal of Contemporary Human Services, 78,* 265–271.

Burke, L. K., & Follingstad, D. R. (1999). Violence in lesbian and gay relationships: Theory, prevalence, and correlational factors. *Clinical Psychology Review, 19,* 487–512.

Burman, B., Margolin, G., & John, R. S. (1993). America's angriest home videos: Behavioral contingencies observed in home reenactments of marital conflict. *Journal of Consulting and Clinical Psychology, 61,* 28–39.

Burt, M. R. (1980). Cultural myths and supports for rape. *Journal of Personality and Social Psychology, 38,* 217–230.

Bushman, B. J., & Anderson, C. A. (2001). Is it time to pull the plug on the hostile versus instrumental aggression dichotomy? *Psychological Review, 108,* 273–279.

Buss, A. H. (1961). *The psychology of aggression.* Oxford, UK: Wiley.

Buss, A. H., & Durkee, A. (1957). An inventory for assessing different kinds of hostility. *Journal of Consulting Psychology, 21,* 343–349.

Buss, A. H., & Perry, M. (1992). The Aggression Questionnaire. *Journal of Personality and Social Psychology, 63,* 452–459.

Butcher, J. N., Graham, J. R., Williams, C. L., & Ben-Porath, Y. S. (1989). *Development and validation of the MMPI-2 content scales.* Minneapolis: University of Minnesota Press.

Buzawa, E. S., & Buzawa, C.G. (1996). *Do arrests and restraining orders work?* Thousand Oaks, CA: Sage.

Byrne, C. A., & Arias, I. (1997). Marital satisfaction and marital violence: Moderating effects of attributional processes. *Journal of Family Psychology, 11,* 188–195.

Caine, T. M., Foulds, G. A., & Hope, K. (1967). *Manual of the Hostility and Direction of Hostility Questionnaire (HDHQ).* London: University of London Press.

Campbell, J. C. (1986). Nursing assessment of risk of homicide with battered women. *Advances in Nursing Science, 8,* 36–51.

Campbell, J. C. (1995). Prediction of homicide of and by battered women. In J. Campbell (Ed.), *Assessing dangerousness: Violence by sexual offenders, batterers, and child abusers* (pp. 96–113). Thousand Oaks, CA: Sage.

Cantos, A. L., Neidig, P. H., & O'Leary, K. D. (1993). Men and women's attributions of blame for domestic violence. *Journal of Family Violence, 8,* 289–302.

Cantos, A. L., Neidig, P. H., & O'Leary, K. D. (1994). Injuries of women and men in a treatment program for domestic violence. *Journal of Family Violence, 9,* 113–124.

Capaldi, D. M., & Clark, S. (1998). Prospective family predictors of aggression toward female partners for at-risk young men. *Developmental Psychology, 34,* 1175–1188.

Carlson, V., Cicchetti, D., Barnett, D., & Braunwald, K. (1989). Disorganized/disoriented attachment relationships in maltreated infants. *Developmental Psychology, 25,* 525–531.

Cascardi, M., Langhinrichsen, J., & Vivian, D. (1992). Marital aggression: Impact, injury, and health correlates for husbands and wives. *Archives of Internal Medicine, 152,* 1178–1184.

Cassidy, J., & Mohr, J. J. (2001). Unsolvable fear, trauma, and psychopathology: Theory, research, and clinical considerations related to disorganized attachment across the life span. *Clinical Psychology: Science and Practice, 8,* 275–298.

Castro, R., Peek-Asa, C., & Ruiz, A. (2003). Violence against women in Mexico: A study of abuse before and during pregnancy. *American Journal of Public Health, 93,* 1110–1116.

Chalk, R., & King, P. A. (Eds.). (1998). *Violence in families: Assessing prevention and treatment programs (executive summary).* Washington, DC: National Academy Press.

Chase, K. A., O'Leary, K. D., & Heyman, R. E. (2001). Categorizing partner-violent men within the reactive-proactive typology model. *Journal of Consulting and Clinical Psychology, 69,* 567–572.

Check, J. V. (1985). *The Hostility Toward Women Scale.* Unpublished doctoral dissertation, University of Manitoba, Winnipeg, Canada.

Chemtob, C. M., Hamada, R. S., Roitblat, H. L., & Muraoka, M. Y. (1994). Anger, impulsivity, and anger control in combat-related posttraumatic stress disorder. *Journal of Consulting and Clinical Psychology, 62,* 827–832.

Chemtob, C. M., Novaco, R. W., Hamada, R. S., & Gross, D. M. (1997). Cognitive-behavioral treatment for severe anger in posttraumatic stress disorder. *Journal of Consulting and Clinical Psychology, 65,* 184–189.

Chermack, S. T., Fuller, B. E., & Blow, F. C. (2000). Predictors of expressed partner and non-partner violence among patients in substance abuse treatment. *Drug and Alcohol Dependence, 58,* 43–54.

Claes, J. A., & Rosenthal, D. M. (1990). Men who batter women: A study in power. *Journal of Family Violence, 5,* 215–224.

Coccaro, E. F., & Kavoussi, R. J. (1997). Fluoxetine and impulsive aggressive behavior in personality-disordered subjects. *Archives of General Psychiatry, 54,* 1081–1088.

Cogan, R., & Porcerelli, J. H. (2003). Psychoanalytic psychotherapy with people in abusive relationships: Treatment outcome. In D. Dutton & D. J. Sonkin (Eds.), *Intimate violence: Contemporary treatment innovations* (pp. 29–46). Binghamton, NY: Haworth Press.

Cohen, R. A., Rosenbaum, A., Kane, R. L., Warnken, W. J., & Benjamin, S. (1999). Neuropsychological correlates of domestic violence. *Violence and Victims, 14,* 397–411.

Cook, D. R., & Franz-Cook, A. (1984). A systemic treatment approach to wife battering. *Journal of Marital and Family Therapy, 10,* 83–93.

Cook, W. W., & Medley, D. M. (1954). Proposed hostility and Pharisaic-virtue scales for the MMPI. *Journal of Applied Psychology, 38,* 414–418.

Cordova, J. V., Jacobson, N. S., Gottman, J. M., Rushe, R., & Cox, G. (1993). Negative reciprocity and communication in couples with a violent husband. *Journal of Abnormal Psychology, 102,* 559–564.

Craske, M. G. & Barlow, D. H. (2001). Panic disorder and agoraphobia. In D. H. Barlow (Ed.), *Clinical handbook of psychological disorders* (3rd ed.), pp. 1–59). New York: Guilford Press.

Cromwell, R. E., & Olson, D. H. (Eds.). (1975). *Power in families.* Oxford, UK: Sage.

Cunradi, C. B., Caetano, R., Clark, C. L., & Schafer, J. (1999). Alcohol-related problems and intimate partner violence among white, black, and Hispanic couples in the U.S. *Alcoholism: Clinical and Experimental Research, 23,* 1492–1501.

Danielson, K. K., Moffitt, T. E., & Caspi, A. (1998). Comorbidity between abuse of an adult and DSM-III-R mental disorders: Evidence from an epidemiological study. *American Journal of Psychiatry, 155,* 131–133.

Davies, P. T., & Cummings, E. M. (1994). Marital conflict and child adjustment: An emotional security hypothesis. *Psychological Bulletin, 116,* 387–411.

Davison, G. C., Robins, C., & Johnson, M. K. (1983). Articulated thoughts during simulated situations: A paradigm for studying cognition in emotion and behavior. *Cognitive Therapy and Research, 7,* 17–40.

Deffenbacher, J. L. (1992). Trait anger: Theory, findings and implications. In C. D. Spielberger & J. N. Butcher (Eds.), *Advances in personality assessment* (Vol. 9, pp. 177–201). Hillsdale, NJ: Erlbaum.

Deffenbacher, J. L. (1994). Anger reduction: Issues, assessment, and intervention strategies. In A. W. Siegman & T. W. Smith (Eds.), *Anger, hostility, and the heart* (pp. 239–269). Hillsdale, NJ: Erlbaum.

Deffenbacher, J. L., Demm, P. M., & Brandon, A. D. (1986). High general anger: Correlates and treatment. *Behaviour Research and Therapy, 24,* 481–489.

Deffenbacher, J. L., Oetting, E. R., Thwaites, G. A., Lynch, R. S., Baker, R. S.,

Thacker, S., & Eiswerth-Cox, D. (1996). State–Trait Anger Theory and the utility of the Trait Anger Scale. *Journal of Counseling Psychology, 43,* 131–148.

Deffenbacher, J. L., & Sabadell, P. M. (1992). Comparing high trait anger individuals with low trait anger individuals. In M. Muller (Ed.), *Anger and aggression in cardiovascular disease.* Bern, Switzerland: Hans Huber AG.

Delsol, C., & Margolin, G. (2004). The role of family-of-origin violence in men's marital violence perpetration. *Clinical Psychology Review, 24,* 99–123.

DeMaris, A., & Jackson, J. K. (1987). Batterers' reports of recidivism after counseling. *Social Casework, 68,* 458–465.

Desnoes, M., & Deffenbacher, J. L. (1995). *Evaluation of state–trait anger theory.* Paper presented at the Rocky Mountain Psychological Association convention, Boulder, CO.

DiClemente, C. C. (1991). Motivational interviewing and the stages of change. In W. R. Miller & S. Rollnick, *Motivational interviewing: Preparing people to change addictive behavior* (pp. 191–202). New York: Guilford Press.

DiGiuseppe, R. (1991a). A Rational-Emotive model of assessment. In M. Bernard (Ed.), *Using rational emotive therapy effectively* (pp. 151–172). New York: Plenum Press.

DiGiuseppe, R. (1991b). Comprehensive cognitive disputing in RET. In M. Bernard (Ed.), *Using rational emotive therapy effectively* (pp. 173–196). New York: Plenum Press.

DiGiuseppe, R., Tafrate, R., & Eckhardt, C. (1994). Critical issues in the treatment of anger. *Cognitive and Behavioral Practice, 1,* 111–132.

Dinwiddie, S. H. (1992). Psychiatric disorders among wife batterers. *Comprehensive Psychiatry, 33,* 411–416.

Dishion, T. J., McCord, J., Poulin, F. (1999). When interventions harm: Peer groups and problem behavior. *American Psychologist, 54,* 755–764.

Dishion, T. J., Spracklen, K. M., Andrews, D. W., & Patterson, G. R. (1996). Deviancy training in male adolescent friendships. *Behavior Therapy, 27,* 373–390.

Dobash, R. E., & Dobash, R. P. (1979). *Violence against wives: A case against the patriarchy.* New York: Free Press.

Dobash, R. E., & Dobash, R. P. (1984). The nature and antecedents of violent events. *British Journal of Criminology, 24*(3), 269–288.

Dodge, K. A. (1991). The structure and function of reactive and proactive aggression. In D. J. Pepler & K. H. Rubin (Eds.), *The development and treatment of childhood aggression* (pp. 201–218). Hillsdale, NJ: Erlbaum.

Douglas, K., & Webster, C. (1999). The HCR-20 violence risk assessment scheme: Concurrent validity in a sample of incarcerated offenders. *Criminal Justice and Behavior, 26,* 3–19.

Dunford, F. W. (2000). The San Diego Navy experiment: An assessment of interventions for men who assault their wives. *Journal of Consulting and Clinical Psychology, 68,* 468–476.

Dutton, D. G. (1986a). The outcome of court-mandated treatment for wife assault: A quasi-experimental evaluation. *Violence and Victims, 1,* 163–175.

Dutton, D. G. (1986b). Wife assaulter's explanations for assault: The neutralization of self-punishment. *Canadian Journal of Behavioural Science, 18,* 381–390.

Dutton, D. G. (1995a). Male abusiveness in intimate relationships. *Clinical Psychology Review, 15*, 567–581.

Dutton, D. G. (1995b). Trauma symptoms and PTSD-like profiles in perpetrators of intimate abuse. *Journal of Traumatic Stress, 8*, 299–316.

Dutton, D. G. (1998). *The abusive personality: Violence and control in intimate relationships.* New York: Guilford Press.

Dutton, D. G., Bonarchuk, M., Kropp, R., Hart, S. D., & Ogloff, J. P. (1997). Client personality disorders affecting wife assault post-treatment recidivism. *Violence and Victims, 12*, 37–50.

Dutton, D. G., Starzomski, A., & Ryan, L. (1996). Antecedents of abusive personality and abusive behavior in wife assaulters. *Journal of Family Violence, 11*(2), 113–132.

Dutton, D. G., & Strachan, C. E. (1987). Motivational needs for power and spouse-specific assertiveness in assaultive and nonassaultive men. *Violence and Victims, 2*, 145–156.

Eckhardt, C. I., Barbour, K. A., & Davison, G. C. (1998). Articulated thoughts of maritally violent and nonviolent men during anger arousal. *Journal of Consulting and Clinical Psychology, 66*, 259–269.

Eckhardt, C. I., Barbour, K. A., & Stuart, G. L. (1997). Anger and hostility in maritally violent men: Conceptual distinctions, measurement issues, and literature review. *Clinical Psychology Review, 17*, 333–358.

Eckhardt, C. I., & Deffenbacher, J. L. (1995). Diagnosis of anger disorders. In H. Kassinove & Howard (Ed.), *Anger disorders: Definition, diagnosis, and treatment* (pp. 27–47). Philadelphia: Taylor & Francis.

Eckhardt, C. I., & Dye, M. L. (2000). The cognitive characteristics of maritally violent men: Theory and evidence. *Cognitive Therapy and Research, 24*, 139–158.

Eckhardt, C. I., Holtzworth-Munroe, A., Norlander, B., Sibley, A., & Cahill, M. (in press). Readiness to change, partner violence subtypes, and treatment outcomes among men in treatment for partner assault. *Violence and Victims.*

Eckhardt, C. I., Jamison, T. R., & Watts, K. (2002). Experience and expression of anger among male perpetrators of dating violence. *Journal of Interpersonal Violence, 17*, 1102–1114.

Eckhardt, C. I., Norlander, B., & Deffenbacher, J. L. (2004). The assessment of anger and hostility: A critical review. *Aggression and Violent Behavior, 9*, 17–43.

Ehrensaft, M. K., Cohen, P., & Brown, J. (2003). Intergenerational transmission of partner violence: A 20-year prospective study. *Journal of Consulting and Clinical Psychology, 71*, 741–753.

Eifert, G. H., Schulte, D., Zvolensky, M. J., Lejuez, C. W., & Lau, A. W. (1997). Manualized behavior therapy: Merits and challenges. *Behavior Therapy, 28*, 499–509.

Elbow, M. (1977). Theoretical considerations of violent marriages. *Social Casework, 58*, 515–526.

Ellis, A. (1962). *Reason and emotion in psychotherapy.* New York: Citadel Press.

Ellis, A. (1994). *Reason and emotion in psychotherapy (2nd ed.).* New York: Citadel Press.

Fals-Stewart, W. (2003). The occurrence of partner physical aggression on days of alcohol consumption: A longitudinal diary study. *Journal of Consulting and Clinical Psychology, 71,* 41–52.

Fals-Stewart, W., Birchler, G. R., & O'Farrell, T. J. (1996). Behavioral couples therapy for male substance-abusing patients: Effects on relationship adjustment and drug-using behavior. *Journal of Consulting and Clinical Psychology, 64,* 959–972.

Fals-Stewart, W., Kashdan, T. B, & O'Farrell, T. J. (2002). Behavioral couples therapy for drug-abusing patients: Effects on partner violence. *Journal of Substance Abuse Treatment, 22,* 87–96.

Fazio, R. H., Sanbonmatsu, D. M., Powell, M. C., & Kardes, F. R. (1986). On the automatic activation of attitudes. *Journal of Personality and Social Psychology, 50,* 229–238.

Feder, L., & Ford, D. (1999, July). *A test of the efficacy of court-mandated counseling for convicted misdemeanor domestic violence offenders: Results from the Broward experiment.* Presented at the Sixth International Family Violence Research Conference, Durham, NH.

Feldbau-Kohn, S., Heyman, R. E., & O'Leary, K. D. (1998). Major depressive disorder and depressive symptomatology as predictors of husband to wife physical aggression. *Violence and Victims, 13,* 347–360.

Feldbau-Kohn, S., Schumacher, J. A., & O'Leary, K. D. (2000). Partner abuse. In V. B. Van Hasselt & M. Hersen (Eds.), *Aggression and violence: An introductory text* (pp. 116–134). Needham Heights, MA: Allyn & Bacon.

Fincham, F. D. (1994). Cognition in marriage. *Applied and Preventive Psychology, 3,* 185–198.

Fincham, F. D., Bradbury, T. N., Arias, I., Byrne, C. A., & Karney, B. R. (1997). Marital violence, marital distress, and attributions. *Journal of Family Psychology, 11,* 367–372.

Fincham, F. D., Bradbury, T. N., & Beach, S. R. (1990). To arrive where we began: A reappraisal of cognition in marriage and in marital therapy. *Journal of Family Psycholog, 4,* 167–184.

First, M. B., Spitzer, R. L., Gibbon, M., & Williams, J. (1996). *Structured Clinical Interview for DSM-IV Axis I Disorders–Patient Edition (SCID-I/P, Version 2.0).* New York: Biometrics Research Department, New York State Psychiatric Institute.

Fiske, S. T., & Taylor, S. E. (1991). *Social cognition* (2nd ed.). New York: McGraw-Hill.

Flournoy, P. S., & Wilson, G. L. (1991). Assessment of MMPI profiles of male batterers. *Violence and Victims, 6,* 309–320.

Foa, E. B. Dancu, C. V., Hembree, E. A., Jaycox, L. H., Meadows, E. A., & Street, G. P. (1999). A comparison of exposure therapy, stress inoculation training, and their combination for reducing posttraumatic stress disorder in female assault victims. *Journal of Consulting and Clinical Psychology, 67,* 194–200.

Foa, E. B., & Franklin, M. E. (2001). Obsessive-compulsive disorder. In D. H. Barlow (Ed.), *Clinical handbook of psychological disorders* (3rd ed., pp. 209–263). New York: Guilford Press.

Follingstad, D. R., Rutledge, L. L., Berg, B. J., Hause, E. S., & Polek, D. S. (1990).

The role of emotional abuse in physically abusive relationships. *Journal of Family Violence, 5,* 107–120.

Frieze, I. H. (1983). Investigating the causes and consequences of marital rape. *Signs, 8,* 532–553.

Fruzzetti, A. E., & Levensky, E. R. (2000). Dialectical behavior therapy for domestic violence: Rationale and procedures. *Cognitive and Behavioral Practice, 7,* 435–447.

Gemar, M. C., Segal, Z. V., Sagrati, S., & Kennedy, S. J. (2001). Mood-induced changes on the implicit association test in recovered depressed patients. *Journal of Abnormal Psychology, 110,* 282–289.

George, D. T. (2003, April). *Domestic violence and the brain.* Talk presented to the Maryland Domestic Abuser Research Collaborative.

George, D. T., Hibbeln, J. R., Ragan, P. W., Umhau, J. C., Phillips, M. J., Doty, L., Hommer, D., & Rawlings, R. R. (2000). Lactate induced rage and panic in a select group of subjects who perpetrate acts of domestic violence. *Biological Psychiatry, 47,* 804–812.

Gidron, Y., Davidson, K., & Ilia, R. (2001). Development and cross-cultural and clinical validation of a brief comprehensive scale for assessing hostility in medical settings. *Journal of Behavioral Medicine, 24,* 1–15.

Gilbert, D. T., & Malone, P. S. (1995) The correspondence bias. *Psychological Bulletin, 117,* 21–38.

Gilbert, D. T., Pelham, B. W., & Krull, D. S. (1988). On cognitive busyness: When person perceivers meet persons perceived. *Journal of Personality and Social Psychology, 54,* 733–739.

Goldfried, M. R., & Davison, G. C. (1994). *Clinical behavior therapy* (2nd ed.). New York: Wiley.

Goldstein, D., & Rosenbaum, A. (1985). An evaluation of the self-esteem of maritally violent men. *Family Relations, 34,* 425–428.

Gondolf, E. (1985). *Men who batter: An integrated approach to stopping wife abuse.* Holmes Beach, FL: Learning Publications.

Gondolf, E. W. (1988). Who are those guys? Toward a behavioral typology of batterers. *Violence and Victims, 3,* 187–203.

Gondolf, E. W. (1997). Patterns of reassault in batterer programs. *Violence and Victims, 12,* 373–387.

Gondolf, E. W. (1999). MCMI results for batterer program participants in four cities: Less "pathological" than expected. *Journal of Family Violence, 14,* 1–17.

Gondolf, E. W. (2002). *Batterer intervention systems: Issues, outcomes, and recommendations.* Thousand Oaks, CA: Sage.

Gondolf, E. W., & Russell, D. (1986). The case against anger control treatment programs for batterers. *Response, 9*(3), 2–5.

Gondolf, E. W., & White, R. J. (2001). Batterer program participants who repeatedly reassault: Psychopathic tendencies and other disorders. *Journal of Interpersonal Violence, 16,* 361–380.

Gottman, J., Notarius, C., Gonso, J., & Markman, H. (1976). *A couple's guide to communication.* Champaign, IL: Research Press.

Gray-Little, B., & Burks, N. (1983). Power and satisfaction in marriage: A review and critique. *Psychological Bulletin, 93*(3), 513–538.

Guidano, V. F., & Liotti, G. (1983). *Cognitive processes and emotional disorders: A structural approach to psychotherapy.* New York: Guilford Press.

Hale, G., Zimostrad, S., Duckworth, J., & Nicholas, D. (1988). Abusive partners: MMPI Profiles of male batterers. *Journal of Mental Health Counseling, 10,* 214–224.

Hamberger, L. K. (1997). Cognitive behavioral treatment of men who batter their partners. *Cognitive and Behavioral Practice, 4,* 147–169.

Hamberger, L. K., & Hastings, J. E. (1990). Recidivism following spouse abuse abatement counseling: Treatment program implications. *Violence and Victims, 5,* 157–170.

Hamberger, L. K., & Hastings, J. E. (1991). Personality correlates of men who batter and nonviolent men: Some continuities and discontinuities. *Journal of Family Violence, 6,* 131–147.

Hamberger, L. K., Lohr, J. M., Bonge, D., & Tolin, D. F. (1996). A large sample empirical typology of male spouse abusers and its relationship to dimensions of abuse. *Violence and Victims, 11,* 277–292.

Hamberger, L. K., & Potente, T. (1994). Counseling heterosexual women arrested for domestic violence: Implications for theory and practice. *Violence and Victims, 9,* 125–138.

Harrell, A. (1991). *Evaluation of court-ordered treatment for domestic violence offenders: Final report.* Washington, DC: The Urban Institute.

Harris, J. A. (1997). A further evaluation of the Aggression Questionnaire: Issues of validity and reliability. *Behaviour Research and Therapy, 35,* 1047–1053.

Hart, S. D., Dutton, D. G., & Newlove, T. (1993). The prevalence of personality disorder among wife assaulters. *Journal of Personality Disorders, 7,* 329–341.

Hastings, J. E., & Hamberger, L. K. (1988). Personality characteristics of spouse abusers: A controlled comparison. *Violence and Victims, 3,* 31–48.

Hayes, A. M., & Strauss, J. L. (1998). Dynamic systems theory as a paradigm for the study of change in psychotherapy: An application to cognitive therapy for depression. *Journal of Consulting and Clinical Psychology, 66,* 939–947.

Healey, K., Smith, C., & O'Sullivan, C. (1998). *Batterer intervention: Program approaches and criminal justice strategies.* Washington, DC: National Institute of Justice.

Heggen, C. H. (1996). Religious beliefs and abuse. In C. C. Kroeger & J. R. Beck (Eds.), *Women, abuse, and the Bible: How scripture can be used to hurt or heal* (pp. 15–27). Grand Rapids, MI: Baker Academic.

Hershorn, M., & Rosenbaum, A. (1991). Over- versus undercontrolled hostility: Application of the construct to the classification of maritally violent men. *Violence and Victims, 6,* 151–158.

Heyman, R. E., & Neidig, P. H. (1997). Physical Aggression Couples Treatment. In W. K. Halford & H. J. Markman (Eds.), *Clinical handbook of marriage and couples interventions* (pp. 589–617). New York: Wiley.

Hollander, E., Tracy, K., Swann, A., Coccaro, E., McElroy, S., Wozniak, P., Sommerville, K., & Nemeroff, C. (2003). Divalproex in the treatment of impulsive aggression: Efficacy in cluster B personality disorders. *Neuropsychopharmacology, 28,* 1186–1197.

Holtzworth-Munroe, A. (1992). Social skills deficits in maritally violent men: Interpreting the data using a social information processing model. *Clinical Psychology Review, 12,* 605–617.

Holtzworth-Munroe, A. (2000). Social information processing skills deficits in maritally violent men: Summary of a research program. In J. P. Vincent & E. N. Jouriles (Eds.), *Domestic violence: Guidelines for research-informed practice* (pp. 13–36). London: Jessica Kingsley.

Holtzworth-Munroe, A., & Anglin, K. (1991). The competency of responses given by maritally violent versus nonviolent men to problematic marital situations. *Violence and Victims, 6,* 257–169.

Holtzworth-Munroe, A., Bates, L., Smutzler, N., & Sandin, E. (1997a). A brief review of the research on husband violence: I. Maritally violent versus nonviolent men. *Aggression and Violent Behavior, 2,* 65–99.

Holtzworth-Munroe, A., & Hutchinson, G. (1993). Attributing negative intent to wife behavior: The attributions of maritally violent versus nonviolent men. *Journal of Abnormal Psychology, 102,* 206–211.

Holtzworth-Munroe, A., & Jacobson, N. S. (1985). Causal attributions of married couples: When do they search for causes? What do they conclude when they do? *Journal of Personality and Social Psychology, 48,* 1398–1412.

Holtzworth-Munroe, A., Jacobson, N. S., Fehrenbach, P. A., & Fruzzetti, A. (1992). Violent married couples' attributions for violent and nonviolent self and partner behaviors. *Behavioral Assessment, 14,* 53–64.

Holtzworth-Munroe, A., Meehan, J. C., Herron, K. (2000a). Testing the Holtzworth-Munroe and Stuart (1994) batterer typology. *Journal of Consulting and Clinical Psychology, 68,* 1000–1019.

Holtzworth-Munroe, A., Rehman, U., & Herron, K. (2000b). General and spouse-specific anger and hostility in subtypes of maritally violent men and nonviolent men. *Behavior Therapy, 31,* 603–630.

Holtzworth-Munroe, A., & Smutzler, N. (1996). Comparing the emotional reactions and behavioral intentions of violent and nonviolent husbands to aggressive, distressed, and other wife behaviors. *Violence and Victims, 11,* 319–339.

Holtzworth-Munroe, A., Smutzler, N., & Stuart, G. L. (1998). Demand and withdraw communication among couples experiencing husband violence. *Journal of Consulting and Clinical Psychology, 66,* 731–743.

Holtzworth-Munroe, A. & Stuart, G. L. (1994a). Typologies of male batterers: Three subtypes and the differences among them. *Psychological Bulletin, 116,* 476–497.

Holtzworth-Munroe, A., & Stuart, G. L. (1994b). The relationship standards and assumptions of maritally violent versus nonviolent husbands. *Cognitive Therapy and Research, 18,* 87–103.

Holtzworth-Monroe, A., Stuart, G. L., & Hutchinson, G. (1997b). Violent versus nonviolent husbands: Differences in attachment patterns, dependency, and jealousy. *Journal of Family Psychology, 11,* 314–331.

Holtzworth-Munroe, A., Stuart, G. L., Sandin, E., Smutzler, N., & McLaughlin, W. (1997c). Comparing the social support behaviors of violent and nonviolent husbands during discussions of wife personal problems. *Personal Relationships, 4,* 395–412.

Hoover, S. A. (2002). *Parenting by men in treatment for domestic abuse.* Unpublished doctoral dissertation, University of Maryland, Baltimore County.

Hornung, C. B., McCullough, C., & Sugimoto, T. (1981). Status relationships in marriage: Risk factors in spouse abuse. *Journal of Marriage and the Family, 43,* 675–692.

Hotaling, G. T., & Sugarman, D. B. (1986). An analysis of risk markers in husband to wife violence: The current state of knowledge. *Violence and Victims, 1,* 101–124.

Huss, M. T., & Langhinrichsen-Roling, J. (2001, November). *The utility of psychopathy and typologies within a battering population.* Paper presented at the annual meeting of the Association for Advancement of Behavior Therapy, New Orleans, LA.

Huston, T. L. (1983). Power. In H. H. Kelley, E. Bersheid, A. Christensen, J. H. Harvey, T. L. Huston, G. Levinger, E. McClintock, L. A. Peplau, & D. R. Peterson, *Close relationships* (pp. 162–219). New York: Freeman and Company.

Jacobson, N. S., Holtzworth-Munroe, A., & Schmaling, K. B. (1989). Marital therapy and spouse involvement in the treatment of depression, agoraphobia, and alcoholism. *Journal of Consulting and Clinical Psychology, 57,* 5–10.

Jacobson, N. S. (1994). Rewards and dangers in researching domestic violence. *Family Process, 33,* 81–85.

Jacobson, N. S., Gottman, J. M., Waltz, J., Rushe, R., Babcock, J., & Holtzworth-Munroe, A. (1994). Affect, verbal content, and psychophysiology in the arguments of couples with a violent husband. *Journal of Consulting and Clinical Psychology, 62,* 982–988.

Jacobson, N. S., & Margolin, G. (1979). *Marital therapy: Strategies based on social learning and behavior exchange principles.* New York: Brunner/Mazel.

Jennings, J. L. (1987). History and issues in the treatment of battering men: A case for unstructured group therapy. *Journal of Family Violence, 2,* 193–214.

Johnson, M. P. (1995). Patriarchal terrorism and common couple violence: Two forms of violence against women. *Journal of Marriage and the Family, 57,* 283–294.

Jones, A. S., & Gondolf, E. W. (2001). Time-varying risk factors for reassault among batterer program participants. *Journal of Family Violence, 16,* 345–359.

Jones, J. P., Thomas-Peter, B. A., & Trout, A. (1999). Normative data for the Novaco Anger Scale from a non-clinical sample and implications for clinical use. *British Journal of Clinical Psychology, 38,* 417–424.

Jouriles, E. N., & O'Leary, K. D. (1985). Interspousal reliability of reports of marital violence. *Journal of Consulting and Clinical Psychology, 53,* 419–421.

Kantor, G. K., & Straus, M. A. (1987). The "drunken bum" theory of wife beating. *Social Problems, 34,* 213–230.

Kassinove, H., & Sukhodolsky, D. G. (1995). Anger disorders: Basic science and practice issues. In H. Kassinove (Ed.), *Anger disorders: Definition, diagnosis, and treatment* (pp. 1–27). Washington, DC: Taylor & Francis.

Kemp, A., Rawlings, E. I., & Green, B. L. (1991). Post-traumatic stress disorder

(PTSD) in battered women: A shelter sample. *Journal of Traumatic Stress, 4,* 137–148.

Kessler, R. C., Molnar, B. E., Feurer, I. D., & Appelbaum, M. (2001). Patterns of mental health predictors of domestic violence in the United States: Results from the National Comorbidity Survey. *International Journal of Law and Psychiatry, 24,* 487–508.

Kistenmacher, B. R, & Weiss, R. L. (in press). Motivational interviewing as a mechanism for change in men who batter: A randomized controlled trial. *Violence and Victims.*

Kropp, P. R., & Hart, S. D. (2000). The Spousal Assault Risk Assessment (SARA) Guide: Reliability and validity in adult make offenders. *Law and Human Behavior, 24,* 101–118.

Kropp, P. R., Hart, S. D., Webster, C. W., & Eaves, D. (1995). *Manual for the Spousal Assault Risk Assessment Guide* (2nd ed). Vancouver, BC: British Columbia Institute Against Family Violence.

Kubany, E. S. (1998). Cognitive therapy for trauma-related guilt. In V. M. Follette, J. I Ruzek, & F. R. Abueg (Eds.), *Cognitive-behavioral therapies for trauma* (pp. 124–161). New York: Guilford Press.

Lambert, M. J., & Bergin, A. E. (1994). The effectiveness of psychotherapy. In A. E. Bergin & S. L. Garfield (Eds.), *Handbook of psychotherapy and behavior change* (4th ed., pp. 143–189). New York: Wiley.

Lasko, N. B., Gurvits, T. V., Kuhne, A. A., Orr, S. P., & Pittman, R. K. (1994). Aggression and its correlates in Vietnam veterans with and without chronic post-traumatic stress disorder. *Comprehensive Psychiatry, 35,* 373–381.

Leonard, K. E. (1993). Drinking patterns and intoxication in marital violence: Review, critique, and future directions for research. In U.S. Department of Health and Human Services, *Alcohol and interpersonal violence: Fostering multidisciplinary perspectives* (Research Monograph 24, NIH Publication No. 93–3496, pp. 253–280).

Leonard, K. E. (2002). Alcohol and substance abuse in marital violence and child maltreatment. In C. Wekerle & A. M. Wall (Eds.), *The violence and addiction equation: Theoretical and clinical issues in substance abuse and relationship violence* (pp. 194–219). New York: Brunner-Routledge.

Lepore, S. J., & Smyth, J. (2002). *The writing cure.* Washington DC: American Psychological Association.

Levesque, D. A., Gelles, R. J., & Velicer, W. F. (2000). Development and validation of a stages of change measure for men in batterer treatment. *Cognitive Therapy and Research, 24,* 175–199.

Levinson, D. (1987). Family violence in cross-cultural perspective. In V. B. Van Hasselt, R. L. Morrison, A. S. Bellack & M. Hersen (Eds.), *Handbook of family violence* (pp. 435–455). New York: Plenum Press.

Linehan, M. M. (1993a). *Cognitive-behavioral treatment of borderline personality disorder.* New York: Guilford Press.

Linehan, M. M. (1993b). *Skills training manual for treating borderline personality disorder.* New York: Guilford Press.

Lipkus, I. M., & Barefoot, J. C. (1994). The assessment of anger and hostility. In A.

W. Siegman & T. W. Smith (Eds.), *Anger, hostility, and the heart* (pp. 43–66). Hillsdale, NJ: Erlbaum.

Lynch, L. A., DeDeyn, J. M., & Murphy, C. M. (2003, November). *A qualitative case analysis of partner violent men who respond poorly to cognitive-behavioral group therapy.* Paper presented at the meeting of the Association for Advancement of Behavior Therapy, Boston.

Lyons-Ruth, K. (1996). Attachment relationships among children with aggressive behavior problems: The role of disorganized early attachment patterns. *Journal of Consulting and Clinical Psychology, 64,* 64–73.

Magdol, L., Moffitt, T. E., Caspi, A., & Silva, P. A. (1998). Developmental antecedents of partner abuse: A prospective-longitudinal study. *Journal of Abnormal Psychology, 107,* 375–389.

Maiuro, R. D., Cahn, T. S., Vitaliano, P. P., Wagner, B. C., & Zegree, J. B. (1988). Anger, hostility, and depression in domestically violent versus generally assaultive men and nonvonviolent control subjects. *Journal of Consulting and Clinical Psychology, 56,* 17–23.

Maiuro, R. D., Hagar, T. S., Lin, H., & Olson, N. (2002). Are current state standards for domestic violence perpetrator treatment adequately informed by research? A question of questions. *Journal of Aggression, Maltreatment and Trauma, 5,* 21–44.

Malik, N. M., & Lindahl, K. M. (1998). Aggression and dominance: The roles of power and culture in domestic violence. *Clinical Psychology: Science and Practice, 5,* 409–423.

Margolin, G., John, R. S., & Gleberman, L. (1988). Affective responses to conflictual discussions in violent and nonviolent couples. *Journal of Consulting and Clinical Psychology, 56,* 24–33.

Marlatt, G. A. (1998). *Harm reduction: Pragmatic strategies for managing high risk behaviors.* New York: Guilford Press.

Marlatt, G. A. & Gordon, J. R. (Eds.). (1985). *Relapse prevention: Maintenance strategies in the treatment of addictive behaviors.* New York: Guilford Press.

Marshall, A. D., & Holtzworth-Munroe, A. (2002). Varying forms of husband sexual aggression: Predictors and subgroup differences. *Journal of Family Psychology, 16,* 286–296.

Marshall, L. L. (1992). Development of the Severity of Violence Against Women Scales. *Journal of Family Violence, 7,* 103–121.

Marshall, L. L. (1994). Physical and psychological abuse. In W. R. Cupach & B. H. Spizberg (Eds.), *The dark side of interpersonal communication* (pp. 281–311). Hillsdale, NJ: Erlbaum.

Martin, D. (1976). *Battered wives.* New York: Pocket Books.

Martin, S. L., Mackie, L., Kupper, L. L., Buescher, P. A., & Moracco, K. E. (2001). Physical abuse of women before, during, and after pregnancy. *JAMA: Journal of the American Medical Association, 285,* 1581–1584.

McDonald, G. W. (1980). Family power: The assessment of a decade of theory and research, 1970–1979. *Journal of Marriage and the Family, 42*(4), 841–854.

McFall, R. M. (1982). A review and reformulation of the concept of social skills. *Behavioral Assessment, 4,* 1–33.

McFarlane, J., Parker, B., & Soeken, K. (1995). Abuse during pregnancy: Frequency, severity, perpetrator, and risk factors of homicide. *Public Health Nursing, 12,* 284–289.

McGinn, L. K., & Young, J. E. (1996). Schema-focused therapy. In P. M. Salkovskis (Ed), *Frontiers of cognitive therapy* (pp. 182–207). New York: Guilford Press.

McKenry, P. C., Julian, T. W., & Gavazzi, S. M. (1995). Toward a biopsychosocial model of domestic violence. *Journal of Marriage & the Family, 57*(2), 307–320.

McMullin, R. E. (1986). *Handbook of cognitive therapy techniques.* New York: Norton.

McMullin, R. E. (2000) *Handbook of cognitive therapy techniques* (2nd ed.). New York: Norton.

Meyer, S. L., Vivian, D., & O'Leary, K. D. (1998). Men's sexual aggression in marriage. *Violence Against Women, 4,* 415–435.

Micklow, P. L. (1988). Domestic abuse: The pariah of the legal system. In V. B. Van Hasselt & R. L. Morrison (Eds.), *Handbook of family violence* (pp. 407–433). New York: Plenum.

Miller, T. Q., Smith, T. W., Turner, C. W., Guijarro, M. L., & Hallet, A. J. (1996). A meta-analytic review of research on hostility and physical health. *Psychological Bulletin, 119,* 322–348.

Miller, W. R. (2000). *Motivational Interviewing Skill Coding (MISC).* Unpublished coding manual, University of New Mexico.

Miller, W. R., & Rollnick, S. (1991). *Motivational interviewing: Preparing people to change addictive behavior.* New York: Guilford Press.

Miller, W. R. & Rollnick, S. (2002). *Motivational interviewing: Preparing people to change addictive behavior* (2nd ed.). New York: Guilford Press.

Miller, W. R., Zweben, A., DiClemente, C. C., & Rychtarik, R. G. (1992). *Motivational Enhancement Therapy Manual: A clinical research guide for therapists treating individuals with alcohol abuse and dependence.* NIAAA Project MATCH Monograph, Vol. 2 (DHHS Pub No 92-1894). Washington, DC: Government Printing Office.

Millon, T. (1994). *Millon Clinical Multiaxial Inventory-III.* National Computer Systems: Minneapolis, MN.

Miranda, J., Persons, J. B., & Byers, C. N. (1990). Endorsement of dysfunctional beliefs depends on current mood state. *Journal of Abnormal Psychology, 99,* 237–241.

Monahan, J., & Steadman, H. J. (1994). *Violence and mental disorder: Developments in risk assessment.* Chicago, IL: University of Chicago Press.

Monahan, J., Steadman, H. J., Silver, E., Appelbaum, P. S., Robbins, P. C., Mulvey, E. P., Roth, L. H., Grisso, T., & Banks, S. (2001). *Rethinking risk assessment: The MacArthur study of mental disorder and violence.* New York: Oxford University Press.

Morrel, T. M., Elliott, J. D., Murphy, C. M., & Taft, C. T. (2003). Cognitive behavioral and supportive group treatments for partner violent men. *Behavior Therapy, 34,* 77–95.

Mosher, D. L., & Sirkin, M. (1984). Measuring a macho personality constellation. *Journal of Research in Personality, 18,* 150–163.

Munley, P. H., Bains, D. S., Bloem, W. D., & Busby, R. M. (1995). Post-traumatic stress disorder and the MMPI-2. *Journal of Traumatic Stress, 8,* 171–178.

Murphy, C. M., & Baxter, V. A. (1997). Motivating batterers to change in the treatment context. *Journal of Interpersonal Violence, 12,* 607–619.

Murphy, C. M., & Cascardi, M. (1999). Psychological abuse in marriage and dating relationships. In R. L. Hampton (Ed.), *Family violence prevention and treatment* (2nd ed., pp. 198–226). Beverly Hills, CA: Sage.

Murphy, C. M., & Hoover, S. A. (1999). Measuring emotional abuse in dating relationships as a multifactorial construct. *Violence and Victims, 14,* 39–53.

Murphy, C. M., Hoover, S. A., & Taft, C. (1999, November). *The multidimensional measure of emotional abuse: Factor structure and subscale validity.* Paper presented at the annual meeting of the Association for Advancement of Behavior Therapy, Toronto, Ontario.

Murphy, C. M., & Meyer, S. L. (1991). Gender, power and violence in marriage. *Behavior Therapist, 14,* 95–100.

Murphy, C. M., Meyer, S. L., & O'Leary, K. D. (1993). Family of origin violence and MCMI-II psychopathology among partner assaultive men. *Violence and Victims, 8,* 165–176.

Murphy, C. M., Meyer, S. L., & O'Leary, K. D. (1994). Dependency characteristics of partner assaultive men. *Journal of Abnormal Psychology, 103,* 729–735.

Murphy, C. M., Morrel, T. M., Elliott, J. D., & Neavins, T. M. (2003). A prognostic indicator scale for the treatment of domestic abuse perpetrators. *Journal of Interpersonal Violence, 18,* 1087–1105.

Murphy, C. M., Musser, P. H., & Maton, K. I. (1998). Coordinated community intervention for domestic abusers: Intervention system involvement and criminal recidivism. *Journal of Family Violence, 13,* 263–284.

Murphy, C. M., & O'Farrell, T. J. (1994). Factors associated with marital aggression in male alcoholics. *Journal of Family Psychology, 8,* 321–335.

Murphy, C. M., & O'Farrell, T. J. (1996). Marital violence among alcoholics. *Current Directions in Psychological Science, 5,* 183–186.

Murphy, C. M., & O'Farrell, T. J. (1997). Couple communication patterns of maritally aggressive and nonaggressive male alcoholics. *Journal of Studies on Alcohol, 58,* 83–90.

Murphy, C. M., O'Farrell, T. J., Fals-Stewart, W., & Feehan, M. (2001). Correlates of intimate partner violence among male alcoholic patients. *Journal of Consulting and Clinical Psychology, 69,* 528–540.

Murphy, C. M. & O'Leary, K. D. (1989). Psychological aggression predicts physical aggression in early marriage. *Journal of Consulting and Clinical Psychology, 57,* 579–582.

Musser, P. H., Semiatin, J. N., Taft, C. T., & Murphy, C. M. (2005). *Motivational interviewing as a pre-group intervention for partner violent men.* Manuscript under review.

Neidig, P. H., & Friedman, D. H. (1984). *Spouse abuse: A treatment program for couples.* Champaign, IL: Research Press.

Neidig, P. H., Friedman, D. H., & Collins, B. S. (1986). Attitudinal characteristics of males who have engaged in spouse abuse. *Journal of Family Violence, 1,* 223–233.

Norlander, B., & Eckhardt, C. I. (2005). Anger, hostility, and male perpetrators of intimate partner violence: A meta-analytic review. *Clinical Psychology Review, 25*, 119–152.

Novaco, R. W. (1975). *Anger control.* Lexington, MA: Heath.

Novaco, R. W. (1994). Anger as a risk factor for violence among the mentally disordered. In J. Monahan & H. J. Steadman (Eds.), *Violence and mental disorder: Developments in risk assessment* (pp. 21–59). Chicago: University of Chicago Press.

Novaco, R. W., & Chemtob, C. M. (1992). Anger and combat-related posttraumatic stress disorder. *Journal of Traumatic Stress, 15*, 123–132.

O'Farrell, T. J. (1993). A behavioral marital therapy couples group program for alcoholics and their wives. In T. J. O'Farrell (Ed.), *Marital and family therapy in alcoholism treatment* (pp. 170–209). New York: Guilford Press.

O'Farrell, T. J., Choquette, K. A., & Cutter, H. S. (1998). Couples relapse prevention sessions after behavioral marital therapy for male alcoholics: Outcomes during the three years after starting treatment. *Journal of Studies on Alcohol, 59*, 357–370.

O'Farrell, T. J., Cutter, H. S., & Choquette, K. A. (1992). Behavioral marital therapy for male alcoholics: Marital and drinking adjustment during the two years after treatment. *Behavior Therapy, 23*, 529–549.

O'Farrell, T. J., Cutter, H. S., & Floyd, F. J. (1985). Evaluating behavioral marital therapy for male alcoholics: Effects on marital adjustment and communication from before to after treatment. *Behavior Therapy, 16*, 147–167.

O'Farrell, T. J., Fals-Stewart, W., Murphy, M., & Murphy, C. M. (2003). Partner violence before and after individually-based alcoholism treatment for male alcoholic patients. *Journal of Consulting and Clinical Psychology, 71*, 92–102.

O'Farrell, T. J., & Murphy, C. M. (1995). Marital violence before and after alcoholism treatment. *Journal of Consulting and Clinical Psychology, 63*, 256–262.

O'Farrell, T. J., & Murphy, C. M. (2002). Behavioral couples therapy for alcoholism and drug abuse: Encountering the problem of domestic violence. In C. Wekerle & A. Wall (Eds.), *The violence and addiction equation: Theoretical and clinical issues in substance abuse and relationship violence* (pp. 293–303). New York: Brunner-Routledge.

O'Farrell, T. J., Van Hutton, V., & Murphy, C. M. (1999). Domestic violence after alcohol treatment: A two-year longitudinal study. *Journal of Studies on Alcohol, 60*, 317–321.

O'Leary, K. D. (1987). *Assessment of marital discord: An integration for research and clinical practice.* Hillsdale, NJ: Erlbaum.

O'Leary, K. D. (1988). Physical aggression between spouses: A social learning theory perspective. In V. B. VanHasselt, R. L. Morrison, A. S. Bellack, & M. Hersen (Eds.), *Handbook of family violence* (pp. 31–55). New York: Plenum Press.

O'Leary, K. D. (1993). Through a psychological lens: Personality traits, personality disorders, and levels of violence. In R. J. Gelles & D. Loseke (Eds.), *Current controversies on family violence* (pp. 7–29). Newbury Park, CA: Sage.

O'Leary, K. D. (1999). Developmental and affective issues in assessing and treating partner aggression. *Clinical Psychology: Science and Practice, 6*(4), 400–414.

O'Leary, K. D., & Beach, S. R. (1990). Marital therapy: A viable treatment for depression and marital discord. *American Journal of Psychiatry, 147*, 183–186.

O'Leary, K. D., & Curley, A. (1986). Assertion and family violence: Correlates of spouse abuse. *Journal of Marital and Family Therapy, 12*, 281–289.

O'Leary, K. D., Heyman, R. E., & Neidig, P. H. (1999). Treatment of wife abuse: A comparison of gender-specific and conjoint approaches. *Behavior Therapy, 30*, 475–505.

O'Leary, K. D., Malone, J., & Tyree, A. (1994). Physical aggression in early marriage: Prerelationship and relationship effects. *Journal of Consulting and Clinical Psychology, 62*, 594–602.

O'Leary, K. D., & Vivian, D. (1990). Physical aggression in marriage. In F. D. Fincham & T. N. Bradbury (Eds.), *The psychology of marriage* (pp. 323–348). New York: Guilford Press.

O'Leary, K. D., Vivian, D., & Malone, J. (1992). Assessment of physical aggression against women in marriage: The need for multimodal assessment. *Behavioral Assessment, 14*, 5–14.

Palmer, S. E., Brown, R. A., & Barrera, M. E. (1992). Group treatment program for abusive husbands: Long-term evaluation. *American Journal of Orthopsychiatry, 62*, 276–283.

Pan, H. S., Neidig, P. H., & O'Leary, K. D. (1994a). Male-female and aggressor-victim differences in the factor structure of the modified Conflict Tactics Scale. *Journal of Interpersonal Violence, 9*, 366–382.

Pan, H. S., Neidig, P. H., & O'Leary, K. D. (1994b). Predicting mild and severe husband-to-wife physical aggression. *Journal of Consulting and Clinical Psychology, 62*, 975–981.

Patterson, G. R. (1982). *Coercive family process.* Eugene, OR: Castalia.

Pence, E., & Paymar M. (1993). *Education Groups for Men Who Batter: The Duluth Model.* New York: Springer.

Pennebaker, J. W., & Graybeal, A. (2001). Patterns of natural language use: Disclosure, personality, and social integration. *Current Directions in Psychological Science, 10*, 90–93.

Pennebaker, J. W., Mehl, M., & Niederhoffer, K. G. (2003). Psychological aspects of natural language use: Our words, our selves. *Annual Review of Psychology, 54*, 547–577.

Persons, J. B. (1989). *Cognitive therapy in practice: A case formulation approach.* New York: Norton.

Persons, J. B., & Tompkins, M. A. (1997). Cognitive-behavioral case formulation. In T. D. Eells (Ed.), *Handbook of psychotherapy case formulation* (pp. 314–339). New York: Guilford Press.

Prochaska, J. O. (1994). Strong and weak principles for progressing from precontemplation to action on the basis of twelve problem behaviors. *Health Psychology, 13*, 47–51.

Prochaska, J. O., & DiClemente, C. C. (1984). *The transtheoretical approach: Crossing the traditional boundaries of therapy.* Homewood, IL: Dow Jones Irwin.

Prochaska, J. O., DiClemente, C. C., & Norcross, J. C. (1992). In search of how people change: Applications to addictive behaviors. *American Psychologist, 47*, 1102–1114.

Quigley, B. M., & Leonard, K. E. (1996). Desistance of husband aggression in the early years of marriage. *Violence and Victims, 11*(4), 355–370.

Rathus, J. H., & Feindler, E. L. (2004). *Assessment of partner violence: A handbook for researchers and practitioners.* Washington, DC: American Psychological Association.

Remington, N., & Murphy, C. (2001, November). *Treatment outcomes of partner violence perpetrators with psychopathic and borderline personality characteristics.* Paper presented at the annual meeting of the Association for Advancement of Behavior Therapy, Philadelphia.

Remington, N., Murphy, C., Scott, E., & Simoneti, S. (1999, November). *Relationship and behavioral characteristics associated with antisocial personality disorder among domestic violence perpetrators.* Paper presented at the annual meeting of the Association for Advancement of Behavior Therapy, Toronto, Ontario.

Resick, P. A., & Calhoun, K. S. (2001). Posttraumatic stress disorder. In D. H. Barlow (Ed.), *Clinical handbook of psychological disorders* (3rd ed., pp. 60–113). New York: Guilford Press.

Resick, P. A., Nishith, P. & Weaver, T. L. (2002). A comparison of cognitive-processing therapy with prolonged exposure and a waiting condition for the treatment of chronic posttraumatic stress disorder in female rape victims. *Journal of Consulting and Clinical Psychology, 70*, 867–879.

Resick, P. A., & Schnicke, M. K. (1993). *Cognitive processing therapy for rape victims: A treatment manual.* Newbury Park, CA: Sage.

Riggs, D. A. (1993). Relationship problems and dating aggression: A potential treatment target. *Journal of Interpersonal Violence, 8*, 18–35.

Riggs, D. A., Dancu, C. V., Gershuny, B. S., & Greenberg, D. (1992). Anger and post-traumatic stress disorder in female crime victims. *Journal of Traumatic Stress, 5*, 613–625.

Riggs, D. A., & O'Leary, K. D. (1996). Aggression between heterosexual dating partners: An examination of a causal model of courtship aggression. *Journal of Interpersonal Violence, 11*, 519–540.

Rodenburg, F. A., & Fantuzzo, J. W. (1993). The measure of wife abuse: Steps toward the development of a comprehensive assessment technique. *Journal of Family Violence, 8*, 203–228.

Rogers, C. R. (1961). *On becoming a person.* Boston: Houghton Mifflin.

Rogge, R. D., & Bradbury, T. N. (1999). Till violence does us part: The differing roles of communication and aggression in predicting adverse marital outcomes. *Journal of Consulting and Clinical Psychology, 67*, 340–351.

Roscoe, B. (1985). Courtship violence: Acceptable forms and situations. *College Student Journal, 19*, 389–393.

Rosenbaum, A., Hoge, S. K., Adelman, S. A., & Warnken, W. J. (1994). Head injury in partner-abusive men. *Journal of Consulting and Clinical Psychology, 62*, 1187–1193.

Rosenbaum, A., & O'Leary, K. D. (1981). Marital violence: Characteristics of abusive couples. *Journal of Consulting and Clinical Psychology, 49,* 63–71.

Ross, L. (1977). The intuitive psychologist and his shortcomings. In L. Berkowitz (Ed.), *Advances in experimental psychology* (Vol. 10, pp. 173–220). San Diego, CA: Academic Press.

Rouse, L. P. (1984). Models, self-esteem, and locus of control as factors contributing to spouse abuse. *Victimology: An International Journal, 9,* 130–141.

Russell, D. E. H. (1982). *Rape in marriage.* New York: Macmillan.

Russell, M. N. (1995). *Confronting abusive beliefs: A group treatment for abusive men.* Thousand Oaks, CA: Sage.

Saunders, D. G. (1988). Wife abuse, husband abuse, or mutual combat? A feminist perspective on the empirical findings. In K. Yllo & M. Bograd (Eds.), *Feminist perspectives on wife abuse* (pp. 90–113). Newbury Park, CA: Sage.

Saunders, D. G. (1992). A typology of men who batter: Three types derived from cluster analysis. *American Journal of Orthopsychiatry, 62,* 11–22.

Saunders, D. G. (1996). Feminist-cognitive-behavioral and process-psychodynamic treatments for men who batter: Interaction of abuser traits and treatment models. *Violence and Victims, 11,* 393–414.

Saunders, D. G., Lynch, A. B., Grayson, M., & Linz, D. (1987). The inventory of beliefs about wife beating: The construction and initial validation of a measure of beliefs and attitudes. *Violence and Victims, 2,* 39–57.

Schafer, J., Caetano, R., & Clark, C. L. (2002) Agreement about violence in U.S. couples. *Journal of Interpersonal Violence, 17,* 457–470.

Schafer, J., Caetano, R., & Cunradi, C. (2004). A path model of risk factors for intimate partner violence among couples in the United States. *Journal of Interpersonal Violence, 19,* 127–142.

Schecter, S. (1982). *Women and male violence: The visions and struggles of the battered women's movement.* Boston: South End Press.

Schmidt, J. D., & Sherman, L. W. (1993). Does arrest deter domestic violence? *American Behavioral Scientist, 36,* 601–609.

Schulte, D., Kunzel, R., Pepping, G., & Schulte-Bahrenberg, T. (1992). Tailor-made versus standardized therapy of phobic patients. *Advances in Behaviour Research and Therapy, 14,* 67–92.

Schumacher, J. A., Feldbau-Kohn, S., Slep, A. M. S., Heyman, R. E. (2001). Risk factors for male-to-female partner physical abuse. *Aggression and Violent Behavior, 6,* 281–352.

Schweinle, W. E., Ickes, W., & Bernstein, I. (2002). Empathic inaccuracy in husband to wife aggression: The overattribution bias. *Personal Relationships, 9,* 141–158.

Scott, K. L., & Wolfe, D. A. (2003). Readiness to change as a predictor of outcome in batterer treatment. *Journal of Consulting and Clinical Psychology, 71,* 879–889.

Scotti, J. R., Evans, I. M., Meyer, L. H., & Walker, P. (1991). A meta-analysis of intervention research with problem behavior: Treatment validity and standards of practice. *American Journal of Mental Retardation, 96,* 233–256.

Shepard, M. F. & Campbell, J. A. (1992). The abusive behavior inventory: A measure of psychological and physical abuse. *Journal of Interpersonal Violence, 7,* 291–305.

Sherman, L. W., & Berk, R. A. (1984). The specific deterrent effects of arrest for domestic assault. *American Sociological Review, 57,* 261–272.

Shields, N. M., & Hanneke, C. R. (1983). Attribution processes in violent relationships: Perceptions of violent husbands and their wives. *Journal of Applied Social Psychology, 13,* 515–527.

Simoneti, S., Scott, E. C., & Murphy, C. M. (2000). Dissociative experiences in partner assaultive men. *Journal of Interpersonal Violence, 15,* 1262–1283.

Smith, C. (1988). *Status discrepancies and husband-to-wife violence.* Paper presented at the Eastern meeting of the Sociological Society.

Smith, T. W. (1994). Concepts and methods in the study of anger, hostility, and health. In A. W. Siegman & T. W. Smith (Eds.), *Anger, hostility, and the heart* (pp. 23–42). Hillsdale, NJ: Erlbaum.

Sonkin, D. J., & Durphy, M. (1997). *Learning to live without violence: A handbook for men.* Volcano, CA: Volcano Press.

Sonkin, D. J., & Dutton, D. (2003). Treating assaultive men from an attachment perspective. In D. Dutton and D. J. Sonkin (Eds.), *Intimate violence: Contemporary treatment innovations* (pp. 105–133). Binghamton, NY: Haworth Press.

Sonkin, D. J., Martin, D., & Walker, L. E. A. (1985). *The male batterer: A treatment approach.* New York: Springer.

Spanier, G. B. (1976). Measuring dyadic adjustment: New scales for assessing the quality of marriage and similar dyads. *Journal of Marriage and the Family, 38,* 15–28.

Spielberger, C. D. (1988). *Manual for the State–Trait Anger Expression Inventory.* Odessa, FL: Psychological Assessment Resources.

Spielberger, C. D. (1999). *State–Trait Anger Expression Inventory-2: Professional Manual.* Odessa, FL: Psychological Assessment Resources.

Spielberger, C. D., Jacobs, G., Russell, J. S., & Crane, R. S. (1983). Assessment of anger: The State–Trait Anger Scale. In J. N. Butcher & C. D. Spielberger (Eds.), *Advances in personality assessment* (Vol. 2, pp. 161–189). Hillside, NJ: Erlbaum.

Stark, E., & Flitcraft, A. (1996). *Women at risk: Domestic violence and women's health.* Thousand Oaks, CA: Sage.

Steele, C. M., & Josephs, R. A. (1990). Alcohol myopia: Its prized and dangerous effects. *American Psychologist, 45,* 921–933.

Stets, J. E., & Pirog-Good, M. A. (1987). Violence in dating relationships. *Social Psychology Quarterly, 50,* 237–246.

Stets, J. E., & Straus, M. A. (1990). Gender differences in reporting marital violence and its medical and psychological consequences. In M. A. Straus and R. J. Gelles (Eds.), *Physical violence in American families* (pp. 151–165). New Brunswick, NJ: Transaction Publishers.

Stith, S. M., Rosen, K. H., & McCollum, E. E. (2002). Developing a manualized couples treatment for domestic violence: Overcoming challenges. *Journal of Marital and Family Therapy, 28,* 21–25.

Stordeur, R. A., & Stille, R. (1989). *Ending men's violence against their partners: One road to peace.* Newbury Park, CA: Sage.

Stosny, S., (1995). *Treating attachment abuse: A compassionate approach.* New York: Springer.

Straus, M. A. (1979). Measuring intrafamily conflict and violence: The Conflict Tactics Scales. *Journal of Marriage and the Family, 41,* 75–88.

Straus, M. A. (1990). The Conflict Tactics Scales and its critics: An evaluation and new data on validity and reliability. In M. A. Straus & R. J. Gelles (Eds.), *Physical violence in American families* (pp. 49–74). New Brunswick, NJ: Transaction Publishers.

Straus, M. A., & Gelles, R. J. (1990). How violent are American families? In M. A. Straus & R. J. Gelles (Eds.), *Physical violence in American families* (pp. 95–112). New Brunswick, NJ: Transaction.

Straus, M. A., Hamby, S. L., Boney-McCoy, S., & Sugarman, D. B. (1996). The revised Conflict Tactics Scales (CTS-2). *Journal of Family Issues, 7,* 283–316.

Sugarman, D. B., & Frankel, S. L. (1996). Patriarchal ideology and wife-assault: A meta-analytic review. *Journal of Family Violence, 11,* 13–40.

Szinovacz, M. E. (1983). Using couple data as a methodological tool: The case of marital violence. *Journal of Marriage and the Family, 45,* 633–644.

Taft, C. T., Murphy, C. M., Elliott, J. D., & Morrel, T. M. (2001). Attendance enhancing procedures in group counseling for domestic abusers. *Journal of Counseling Psychology, 48,* 51–60.

Taft, C. T., Murphy, C. M., King, L. A., DeDeyn, J. M., & Musser, P. H. (in press). Posttraumatic stress disorder symptomatology among partners of men in treatment for relationship abuse. *Journal of Abnormal Psychology.*

Taft, C. T., Murphy, C. M., King, D. W., Musser, P. H., & DeDeyn, J. M. (2003). Process and treatment adherence factors in group cognitive-behavioral therapy for partner violent men. *Journal of Consulting and Clinical Psychology, 71,* 812–820.

Taft, C. T., Murphy, C. M., Musser, P. H., & Remington, N. A. (2004). Personality, interpersonal, and motivational predictors of the working alliance in group cognitive-behavioral therapy for partner violent men. *Journal of Consulting and Clinical Psychology, 72,* 349–354.

Tatarsky, A. (Ed.) (2002). *Harm reduction psychotherapy: A new treatment for drug and alcohol problems.* Northvale, NJ: Jason Aronson.

Thompson, R. H., & Iwata, B. A. (2001). A descriptive analysis of social consequences following problem behavior. *Journal of Applied Behavior Analysis, 34,* 169–178.

Tolman, R. M. (1989). The development of a measure of psychological maltreatment of women by their male partners. *Violence and Victims, 4,* 159–177.

Tolman, R. M., & Bennett, L. W. (1990). A review of quantitative research on men who batter. *Journal of Interpersonal Violence, 5,* 87–118.

Turk, C. L., Heimberg, R. G., & Hope, D. A. (2001). Social anxiety disorder. In D. H. Barlow (Ed.), *Clinical handbook of psychological disorders* (3rd ed., pp. 114–153). New York: Guilford Press.

Waldo, M. (1988). Relationship enhancement counseling groups for wife abusers. *Journal of Mental Health Counseling, 10,* 37–45.

Walen, S. R., DiGiuseppe, R., & Dryden, W. (1992), *A practitioner's guide to Rational-Emotive Therapy.* New York: Oxford University Press.

Walker L. E. (1979). *The battered woman.* New York: Harper and Row.

Walker, L. E. (1984). *The battered woman syndrome.* New York: Springer.

Waltz, J. (2003). Dialectical behavior therapy in the treatment of abusive behavior. In D. Dutton & D. J. Sonkin (Eds.), *Intimate violence: Contemporary treatment innovations* (pp. 75–103). Binghamton, NY: Haworth Press.

Waltz, J., Babcock, J. C., Jacobson, N. S., & Gottman, J. M. (2000). Testing a typology of batterers. *Journal of Consulting and Clinical Psychology, 68,* 658–669.

Watson, D., & Clark, L. A. (1992). Affects separable and inseparable: On the hierarchical arrangement of the negative affects. *Journal of Personality and Social Psychology,* 62(3), 489–505.

Watson, D. L., & Tharp, R. G. (1997). *Self-directed behavior: Self-modification for personal adjustment* (7th ed.). Monterey, CA: Brooks-Cole.

Weiss, R. L. (1980). Strategic behavioral marital therapy: Toward a model for assessment and intervention. In J. P. Vincent (Ed.), *Advances in family intervention, assessment, and theory* (Vol. 1, pp. 229–271). Greenwich, CT: JAI Press.

Weisz, A. N., Tolman, R. M., & Saunders, D. G. (2000). Assessing the risk of severe domestic violence: The importance of survivors' predictions. *Journal of Interpersonal Violence, 15,* 75–90.

Wexler, D. B. (2000). *Domestic violence 2000: An integrated skills program for men: Group leaders manual.* New York: Norton.

White, R. J., & Gondolf, E. W. (2000). Implications of personality profiles for batterer treatment. *Journal of Interpersonal Violence, 15,* 467–486.

Whitfield, C. L., Anda, R. F., Dube, S. R. (2003). Violent childhood experiences and the risk of intimate partner violence in adults: Assessment in a large health maintenance organization. *Journal of Interpersonal Violence, 18,* 166–185.

Williams, T. Y., Boyd, J. C., Cascardi, M. A., & Poythress, N. (1996). Factor structure and convergent validity of the Aggression Questionnaire in an offender population. *Psychological Assessment, 8,* 398–403.

Wilson, G. T. (1996). Manual-based treatments: The clinical application of research findings. *Behaviour Research and Therapy, 34,* 295–314.

Wilson, G. T. (1997). Treatment manuals in clinical practice. *Behaviour Research and Therapy, 35,* 205–210.

Wilson, M., & Daly, M., (1998). Lethal and nonlethal violence against wives and the evolutionary psychology of male sexual proprietariness. In Dobash, R. E. & Dobash, R. P. (Eds.), *Rethinking violence against women* (pp. 199–230). Thousand Oaks, CA: Sage.

Winters, J., Fals-Stewart, W., O'Farrell, T. J., Birchler, G. R., & Kelley, M. L. (2002). Behavioral couples therapy for female substance-abusing patients: Effects on substance use and relationship adjustment. *Journal of Consulting and Clinical Psychology, 70,* 344–355.

Wolfe, D. A., Wekerle, C., Scott, K., Straatman, A., Grasley, C., & Reitzel-Jaffe, D.

(2003). Dating violence prevention with at-risk youth: A controlled outcome evaluation. *Journal of Consulting and Clinical Psychology, 71,* 279–291.

Woodworth, M., & Porter, S. (2002). In cold blood: Characteristics of criminal homicides as a function of psychopathy. *Journal of Abnormal Psychology, 111,* 436–445.

Yalom, I. D. (1995). *The theory and practice of group psychotherapy* (4th ed.). New York: Basic Books.

Yelsma, P. (1996). Affective orientations of perpetrators, victims, and functional spouses. *Journal of Interpersonal Violence, 11,* 141–152.

Yllo, K., & Bograd, M. (Eds.). (1988). *Feminist perspectives on wife abuse.* Newbury Park, CA: Sage.

Young, J. E., Klosko, J. S., & Weishaar, M. E. (2003). *Schema therapy: A practitioner's guide.* New York: Guilford Press.

Zeanah, C. H., Danis, B., Hirshberg, L., Benoit, D., Miller, D. & Heller. S. S. (1999). Disorganized attachment associated with partner violence: A research note. *Infant Mental Health Journal, 20,* 77–86.

# Index